Publishing

in

Rhetoric and Composition

Publishing in Rhetoric and Composition

Edited by
Gary A. Olson
Todd W. Taylor

Foreword by
J. Hillis Miller

State University of New York Press

Published by
State University of New York Press, Albany

Printed in the United States of America
Edited and designed by Gary A. Olson and Todd W. Taylor

For information, address State University of New York
Press, State University Plaza, Albany, N.Y., 12246

Production by Diane Ganeles; marketing by Bernadette LaManna

Library of Congress Cataloging in Publication Data

Publishing in rhetoric and composition / edited by Gary A. Olson and Todd
W. Taylor; foreword by J. Hillis Miller.

      p. cm.—
Includes bibliographical references and index.
      ISBN 0-7914-3395-1 (hardcover: acid-free paper) —
      ISBN 0-7914-3396-X (pbk: acid-free paper)
1. English language—Rhetoric—Study and teaching—United States.
2. English language—Rhetoric—Study and teaching—Authorship.
3. English language—Rhetoric—Study and teaching—Research.
4. English language—Composition and exercises—Authorship.
5. English language—Composition and exercises—Research
6. English language—Textbooks—Authorship. 7. Rhetoric—Authorship.
8. Scholarly Publishing
I. Olson, Gary A., date.   II. Taylor, Todd W.

PE1405.U6P83   1997

808'.042'07—dc20   96-36302
                                                   CIP

10 9 8 7 6 5 4 3

For

Emma and Jill

Contents

Negotiating the Conversation:
Examining Issues in Scholarly Publishing

Acknowledgments

We would like to acknowledge the support and friendship of Sara M. Deats, chair of the Department of English at the University of South Florida, and William T. Ross, both of whom have taken a personal interest in the success of scholarship in rhetoric and composition. Also, we would like to thank Priscilla Ross at SUNY Press for her editorial acumen and unflagging encouragement, Diane Ganeles and Bernadette LaManna for their expert work in producing and marketing this book, and the anonymous manuscript reviewers for their constructive suggestions.

Foreword

J. Hillis Miller

This distinguished collection is the best book I know on how to publish scholarship in rhetoric and composition—and why one should. The contributors provide helpful, detailed, and expert advice on how to write and publish articles, reviews, books, and textbooks in this field. No similar book that I have encountered exists for this or other areas of the humanities. (Certainly, no one told me anything at all about how to publish in literary studies when I was getting started in that field.) The collection will also have great value for those outside rhetoric and composition, since much of the advice and information is easily transferable. *Publishing in Rhetoric and Composition*, however, is far more than a "How To" book. It also marks a distinct stage in the professionalization of a discipline that is certain to become increasingly more important in the coming years. Moreover, this collection of essays by leading specialists in the field provides a remarkably comprehensive survey of what is going on in this field at the moment. I congratulate Gary Olson and Todd Taylor for their enterprise in putting this timely book together.

My thoughts concerning publishing scholarship have long been haunted by a character in David Lodge's *Small World*: Rodney Wainwright, who teaches in the University of North Queensland, in Cooktown, Queensland, Australia, up near the Great Barrier Reef. Wainwright knows he will never get ahead in his profession, never have a chance to escape the Great Barrier Reef, if he does not publish. All through the novel the reader sees him intermittently at work on a paper for a conference in Jerusalem on "The Future of Criticism." He is stuck in the middle of a sentence that begins, "Clearly. . . ." Clearly what? He cannot for the life of him get beyond that "clearly." Had he been able to read *Publishing in Rhetoric and Composition*, all his problems might have been solved. The great barrier of his colossal writer's block would have been broken by the practical advice he would have found in this book. He might have figured out, among other things, that the future of criticism is a non-question, that he needed to change his direction entirely, perhaps by taking up rhetoric and composition rather than literary criticism. *Publishing in Rhetoric and Composition* has exorcised the ghost of Rodney Wainwright from my mind.

This exorcism has happened, however, only at the cost of another haunting. Now I am haunted by the three figures in Jasper Neel's exuberantly brilliant fable in "Getting Booked: Commodity, Confinement, Conundrum," one of the essays in this book. These figures are McGarrett, Baldwin, and Woolf, named for Steve McGarrett (the hero of "Hawaii Five-O"), for James Baldwin, and for Virginia Woolf. McGarrett, Baldwin, and Woolf are Neel's names for his three paradigmatic examples of how to get ahead by publishing: the professional, the romantic, and the innovator. These quasi-mythological characters will now trouble my dreams as Rodney Wainwright had troubled them until now. This is true even though Neel's three scholars are all in different ways successful and do not suffer from writer's block. What is most disquieting about Neel's fable is the way it recognizes the fortuitous aspect of success in an academic field when it is in the process of rapid change and is becoming thoroughly professionalized. I am especially haunted by Neel's character named Baldwin. Baldwin goes through graduate school and the stages to tenure in a dream: "He never intended to become an English major, he got started teaching writing as an M.A. candidate who entered graduate school largely because no attractive alternative presented itself, and he finally settled on rhet/comp as a specialization because it seemed the most humane, least ideological work he could find." After writing a dissertation that is a "mess"—a large, loose, baggy monster—he lands a job: "He is not quite sure how he got where he is, he finds both the politics and the professionalism of his new department disgusting, and he knows he must get a book published within five years." Baldwin's book is written in a continuation of his dream state, just as, in an analogy Neel makes explicit, Coleridge's "Kubla Khan" almost got itself written. Baldwin writes this way "not because he is persuaded by romantic theory but because he has no clear notion of how to proceed other than to sit at the keyboard hoping for the best." Success comes by sheer accident: "But, as fate would have it, luck smiles." (This could almost as well read, "As luck would have it, fate smiles.") "Somehow, through an agonizing process as mysterious as dreams themselves, a wonderful book emerges." Baldwin wins prizes for his book, serves on editorial boards, and rapidly achieves tenure, a high salary, the directorship of the writing program, and so on. What is most disquieting about this fabulous story is that it seems so plausible. Its final irony is that the effect of Baldwin's success is to grant him "sufficient privilege and financial security to imprison him." Jasper Neel's version of "publishing in rhetoric and composition" is very different from the narrative suggested by the rest of the book, with its guiding metaphor of publishing in these fields as "joining the scholarly conversation." What Neel stresses is the contingency and, to a degree, the senselessness of success in publishing in a professionalized field: "But, as fate would have it, luck smiles."

Now, I would not say that the present-day flourishing of rhetoric and composition has been a matter of sheer luck or fate. Hundreds of gifted men and women have worked for over twenty-five years to professionalize this field, to give it respectability and prominence within the university. Whatever John Guillory may say about the dangers of prematurely professionalizing graduate students, professionalization, as anyone who has looked into the way the United States academic system works, is the way to power, money, and influence.[1] Professionalization means making your field a research discipline, with lots of journals. There were three in rhetoric and composition in 1971. By 1993 there were over one hundred, not to mention more than twenty Internet discussion groups. I am sure that number has now, three years later, increased still further. Making your field a research discipline means giving it a limited focus—ideally, in the humanities, one with a historical side, and one also with an empirically verifiable aspect. Hence the rise of "rhetoric" as a term paired with composition, as in the title of this book, and hence the concomitant focus on local pedagogical research: "How do students best learn to write in this particular university or college?" All this professionalization has been brilliantly accomplished by those in this new discipline. Just as other humanistic disciplines such as English literature professionalized themselves by imitating previously established academic disciplines like law, medicine, or engineering, so too has rhetoric and composition professionalized itself by imitating already existing disciplines in the humanities and social sciences.

Let me illustrate this by telling two stories of my own. When I began working at Yale in 1972, the composition program was rudimentary. The received opinion was that Yale did not need expository writing because the gifted and elite students who entered Yale must already be good writers. When I became chair a few years later, the Director of Undergraduate Studies, Paula Johnson, spent a lot of time patiently and courteously trying to persuade me that this received opinion was false, that many Yale undergraduates had deep problems with writing. By 1986 Yale had an ambitious and expensive across-the-board writing program. The untenured faculty member who ran the writing program during my last years at Yale, Linda Peterson, has since then received tenure and has been appointed chair of the English Department.

Second story: The institution where I now teach, the University of California at Irvine, had, when I arrived in 1986, a large writing program staffed entirely by lecturers, graduate students, and "freeway flyers," teachers from the region who also taught at neighboring community colleges and the like, flying by freeway from one school to another in a car full of composition papers to grade. Though more and more students at Irvine are Asian-Americans (now about fifty percent), a substantial percentage for whom English is a second language, the then dean of humanities thought ESL was a marginal program, the need for which would soon disappear. ESL was administered by a lecturer on a succession of one-year appointments. Now, in 1996, ESL is much more solidly institutionalized. The Department of English has three tenured or tenure-track positions in rhetoric or composition. We more and more think of this field as a central part of the English

Department's research and teaching mission, while the literature side of the department has been considerably reduced by California's "budget crisis."

A number of outside forces have combined to make possible the success of rhetoric and composition as a professionalized discipline. All the effort in the world during the same period, for example, would not have sufficed to return Greek and Latin to the centrality in the university they once had, nor will strenuous and well-meaning efforts suffice to restore the old-fashioned programs in English literature (from Beowulf to Virginia Woolf), now in their twilight, to the viability and centrality they until recently had. Just what are the new forces that have conspired to make rhetoric and composition flourish while literature departments are being "downsized" practically everywhere? The changes are overdetermined and are accelerating. Many factors have worked together to bring about the rise of rhetoric and composition and the decline of literary studies: the end of the cold war; the weakening of nations states' power and integrity; the globalization of economics and information systems; the information revolution brought about by the computer and the Internet; the rapid shift in funding for colleges and universities from federal and state sources to transnational corporations; the consequent redefinition of the university's mission from cold war research and indoctrination in a single set of national values to "preparing a skilled workforce for competition in the global marketplace," as Richard C. Atkinson, University of California President, recently put it; the growing and widespread recognition that the United States is a multicultural and multilingual nation, a nation that has never had a single unified culture in the way European countries have or think they have (or think they had); the massive flight from literary study to cultural studies as younger scholars, recognizing that literature has less and less importance in United States culture, want to be where the action is: in film, television, mass culture and mass media, women's studies, ethnic studies, fields within which literary study still exists but plays an increasingly subordinate role; the increasing hostility of the general public, generated by carefully orchestrated journalistic disinformation, to "theory" and to the new developments in cultural studies, women's studies, and the like.[2]

Since the late nineteenth century, the United States university has increasingly had as its reason for being the training of what John Guillory calls the "New Class"—that is, the professional-managerial class of scientists, technicians, bureaucrats, engineers, politicians, lawyers, and the like. This class today cares less and less about literary education. They are in fact more and more suspicious of it. Imagine what it would do to Bill Clinton's political fortunes, or Bob Dole's, if either began quoting Emily Dickinson, Walt Whitman, or Wallace Stevens, much less Alexander Pope, William Wordsworth, or Emily Brontë. The "New Class," however, understands very well the need to write clearly and correctly. Effective writing is necessary in order to remain competitive in the new global economy. The managerial class is willing to give strong support to writing. (A rich oilman set up the writing program at Yale.) Most university administrators probably secretly, or not so secretly, believe the main value of the humanities is to teach "communication skills."

At the same time, it is becoming more and more difficult to gain financial support for literary study. As the transformations I have sketched from federal and state support to transnational corporation support of the university accelerate in coming years, rhetoric and composition will likely continue to flourish, while the "Future of Criticism," poor Rodney Wainwright's non-subject, will, I fear, become dimmer and dimmer. This will give composition programs an increasing responsibility to teach reading along with writing. I hope they will discharge this obligation well. I hope also that they will have compassion for literary programs as such programs are downsized further. I am bound to say, however, that those of us in literature did not always have such compassion for rhetoric and composition when they were marginalized in our colleges and universities.

Notes

[1] John Guillory, "Pre-professionalism: What Graduate Students Want." ADE Meeting. Iowa City. 15 Jun. 1995 (a talk Christina Murphy refers to in her essay opening this collection).

[2] The best book I know on these changes is Bill Readings', *The University in Ruins*. Cambridge: Harvard UP, 1996.

Introduction

Publishing in Rhetoric and Composition is a collection of essays about the politics and practices of generating scholarship in rhetoric and composition and literacy studies. It contains sixteen chapters by prominent compositionists addressing a range of timely and important issues.

The book is divided into three parts. **Part 1**, Joining the Scholarly Conversation: Publishing Articles and Chapters, presents the viewpoints of several journal editors on publishing composition scholarship, including such topics as breaking into print, writing about teaching, developing an appropriate style, and introducing the "personal" into academic writing. **Part 2**, Shaping the Conversation: Publishing Monographs and Textbooks, discusses book-length scholarly projects, from transforming a dissertation into a book to producing monographs and edited collections; it also explores the production of composition textbooks, from creating a prospectus to publishing rhetorics and readers. **Part 3**, Negotiating the Conversation: Examining Issues in Scholarly Publishing, contains six chapters analyzing such topics as the politics of how composition research is valued in departments of English, recent developments in electronic publishing, the work habits of successful academic writers, and the complications of mentoring graduate students in a publish-or-perish profession.

Despite the fact that there are over 11,000 members of the Conference on College Composition and Communication and that there are several thousand more instructors of composition throughout the nation who are not members of CCCC, only a relatively small number of these compositionists regularly produce scholarly books and articles. Part of the reason why many professionals do not attempt to author their own scholarship or fail to get their scholarship published is a lack of familiarity with the politics, conventions, and procedures of publishing scholarship. *Publishing in Rhetoric and Composition* affords insight into these issues so that more professionals can successfully enter the ongoing scholarly conversations.

The types of credentials necessary to secure an entry-level position in the field have changed drastically over the last ten years so that new Ph.D.'s must typically have published scholarship prior to entering the job market, and full-time faculty are being asked to publish at unprecedented levels in order to advance toward tenure and promotion. This text will benefit both constituencies, as well as accomplished scholars who serve as mentors to other faculty. However, this book is more than a "how-to" manual for those who wish to join the field's scholarly conversations through publication in that it includes commentary from major figures in rhetoric and composition who, in examining, defining, and problematizing the nature of what we do as teachers and scholars, are producing a kind of "meta-study" of the field. Thus, it could be seen as a kind of adjunct to Stephen North's *The Making of Knowledge in Composition* and might be used in graduate classes as a companion to that text.

Many of the contributors to *Publishing in Rhetoric and Composition* are eminent scholars in the field. For example, Jasper Neel, who in this collection writes about the politics and production of scholarly monographs, is one of only two scholars in rhetoric and composition ever to have won national awards for two separate scholarly monographs. Janice Lauer, who writes about questions of mentoring, directs one of the field's most successful graduate programs. James Murphy, Professor Emeritus and founder of the International Society for the History of Rhetoric, discusses producing scholarship in the history of rhetoric. Linda Flower, the field's acknowledged leader in empirical research, addresses the complexities of observation-based research. Lynn Bloom, Distinguished Aetna Chair of Writing at the University of Connecticut and a long-time advocate of using belletristic essays in composition classes, describes the ins and outs of publishing essay anthologies. Cynthia Selfe, chair of CCCC, book series editor, and editor of numerous collections of essays, describes how the essay collection can be a valuable contribution to scholarship.

Many of the contributors are current or past editors of the discipline's most prestigious scholarly journals: Richard Gebhardt and Joseph Harris, *College Composition and Communication*; Gary Olson and Thomas Kent, *Journal of Advanced Composition*; Theresa Enos, *Rhetoric Review*; Christina Murphy, *Composition Studies* and *English in Texas*; Jasper Neel, *ADE Bulletin*; Gail Hawisher and Cynthia Selfe, *Computers and Composition*; James Murphy, *Rhetorica*. Collectively, these editors have their finger on the pulse of composition's most current scholarship and offer invaluable insight into the production and publication of original research. In addition, the collection also contains a chapter by Robert Boice, the nation's foremost authority on the psychology of academics' scholarly work habits, as well as a foreword by J. Hillis Miller, past president of the Modern Language Association and one of the world's most eminent literary critics.

We hope this collection helps demystify the processes of producing scholarship and encourages more compositionists to join the many scholarly conversations that over the last three decades have made rhetoric and composition one of the most intellectually stimulating disciplines in the academy.

Gary A. Olson
Todd Taylor

Joining the Scholarly Conversation:

Publishing Articles and Chapters

Breaking the Print Barrier:
Entering the Professional Conversation

CHRISTINA MURPHY

In 1951, Robert S. Hunting published an essay in *College Composition and Communication* in which he offered advice to graduate students and new professionals on ways to advance their academic careers in view of a highly competitive job market: give only "the minimum required time to teaching freshman composition" and concentrate, instead, upon research and publication (3). For all the emphasis Hunting places upon publishing, though, he offers no suggestions to beginning scholars on how they should approach getting their manuscripts into print—a significant oversight in an "academic marketplace" based upon the principle of "publish or perish" (Purdy 816). In this regard, Hunting's essay is rather typical; novice professionals seeking advice on shaping the trajectories of their academic careers will find numerous articles describing the importance of publishing to survival and advancement in the academy but few that offer practical wisdom on how to achieve this essential goal.

Hunting's essay also notes the divided loyalties the novice professional feels as both a teacher and a researcher, a dichotomy of objectives and philosophies that dates back to the influence of the German system of higher education on American institutions in the late eighteenth and early nineteenth centuries (Connors; Baugh). Here the goal was one of knowledge production within the academy and within the broader parameters of intellectual inquiry; essentially, academicians were judged on their ability to apply critical methodologies and to convey the insights so developed by publishing their ideas in scholarly journals. One both taught and researched, but, in this value-laden dichotomy, the greater merit lay with the researcher who contributed new knowledge to his or her discipline. As a consequence, publication quickly became "the most tangible and negotiable evidence of scholarship" (Archer 450), and scholarship became the most measurable evidence of professional merit. As Dwight H. Purdy contends, the first commandment of the academy is "Thou shalt publish" (816).

The Emphasis on Scholarship

The implications of this emphasis have been a source of debate, with numerous theorists pointing out the advantages and perils of relying upon publication as the most significant indicator of academic success. The debate has become particularly significant in light of increased demands for pre-professionalism placed upon graduate students within the last decade. This topic formed the basis for an intense discussion that occurred on the Internet's PURTOPOI list this past spring as graduate students commented on the pressures they felt to produce scholarship *as* professionals while they were studying to *become* professionals. It also was the subject of a presentation by John Guillory, "Pre-professionalism: What Graduate Students Want," at the 1995 ADE meeting in Iowa City. Guillory contends that a dire job market has created a situation in which graduate students are required to publish before they have developed adequate scholarly knowledge and experience. His talk points to the fact that market-driven forces now require graduate students to present credentials for entry into the profession that a few years ago would have qualified many of them for tenure at numerous colleges and universities. (For more on this subject, see Maureen Hourigan's chapter in this book).

Other theorists, while acknowledging the difficulties of the job market and the high levels of accomplishment expected of beginning professionals, find merit in a system that emphasizes both aspects of the teacher/researcher dichotomy. For these theorists, the two activities are interrelated in that an individual is likely to be a more effective teacher if he or she stays cognizant of issues in the field and remains a steady contributor to its knowledge base. Peter Nagourney claims that the "practical and real intellectual requirements of academic publishing" provide the "intellectual stimulation" necessary for effective teaching (821). In a similar vein, James F. Fullington asserts that "there are few teachers worth their salt who are not regularly engaged in some kind of creative scholarly activity" and that "it is so obvious that the teacher must be a scholar that to neglect his scholarly training is absurd" (260).

Fullington's impassioned statement raises the question of what kind of "training for scholarly investigation" graduate students receive before they enter the profession and the concomitant question of what training they need. As Dwight H. Purdy writes,

> I emerged from graduate school knowing no more than a stone about academic publishing [since] the problems of publishing had [never] been discussed in any of my graduate courses. My fall from innocence was consequently, probably typically, rude. How amazed I was to discover that a decent idea does not an article make, that style counts for something with editors. Today my amazement embarrasses me, and I am ashamed of my innocence. But every recent Ph.D. I have asked says that the facts of academic life were not revealed in graduate school.... Just as senior scholars notoriously fail to teach their students to teach, they fail to teach them survival in a publish or perish world. (820)

Invariably, the institutionalized response to these issues has been a course on bibliographical methods offered and often required in many graduate programs. Here graduate students learn the rudiments of academic research, but the process of how one moves from a knowledge of the academic conventions of research to a finished, publishable essay often remains unclear. The truth is that "professional academic writing is as separate an arena of expertise as any other field, although rarely is it taught as part of, or in conjunction with, most advanced degrees" (Matkin and Riggar 4). Similarly, extensive reading on a subject or an extensive search of the scholarship can create for many aspiring scholars a sense that everything has been done, that every topic has been covered, that there is nothing new to contribute. This anxious realization often develops into a major stumbling block that keeps many individuals from writing: they feel overwhelmed by the scholarship that has come before them and are reduced to self-imposed silence (Murray 147). This situation can be particularly difficult for those who are teaching writing courses in which they are advising their own students on how to overcome "writer's block" while at the same time dealing with the identical predicament themselves. The confusion that attends this circumstance can lead to self-reproach and feelings of hypocrisy. Ultimately, too, it can lead to inertia.

Breaking into Print: Attitude and Opportunities

What, then, is the novice professional to do in seeking to break the print barrier and contribute to the scholarship of his or her field? Interestingly, the classroom itself and the student-teacher relationship may offer some insights. Donald M. Murray and Chris Crowe claim that the most important role a writing teacher performs for a student is to model the writing process and to exemplify the intellectual and personal rewards that arise from approaching writing as a means of discovery. As Murray puts it, "Publishing promises a lifetime of exploration and learning, active membership in a scholarly community, and the opportunity for composition teachers to practice what we preach" (146).

Furthermore, the anxieties students feel when required to write for a class often provide insight into the experiences of novice professionals, too. Both situations involve being judged—or what Andrew F. Macdonald calls the experience of "rhetorical superiority" in which writers seek to win favor from individuals who are in the position to accept or reject their work (13-15). Acceptance is exhilarating; rejection is disappointing and at times devastating to one's ego. Murray claims that "our attitudes usually predict and limit our accomplishments" (146), and certainly a fear of failure can keep many talented individuals from even attempting to write for publication. As Jo Bennett states,

> Some writers are unwilling to share their work with others, perhaps from a lack of confidence, or underestimation of the work's merit, or an ignorance of the publishing process. That reticence or ignorance perpetuates the myth that only the well-known are published or have anything to say. Even the most successful and prolific author began with one lonely manuscript submitted to one journal. (31)

Often the problem can be traced to the fact that novice academics are unaware of the "invisible" steps involved in writing for publication. They see only the published work of other scholars and overlook the many crucial steps involved in creating the finished product:

> For example, who sees the hours devoted to conceptualizing an idea, researching references, writing notes, outlining topics, writing first drafts, rewriting and editing, submitting the manuscript, waiting for acceptance (or rejection), rewriting for clarification and final editorial approval, and reading and correcting galley proofs prior to publication? This is not glamorous stuff, but it is, nevertheless, essential for those who write for publication. (Matkin and Riggar 7).

Murray's advice when dealing with a fear of failure is to "lower your standards" (151). He claims that advice from the poet William Stafford has gotten him through many a difficult period of self-doubt and inactivity:

> I believe that the so-called "writing block" is a product of some kind of disproportion between your standards and your performance.... One should lower his standards until there is no felt threshold to go over in writing. It's *easy* to write. You just shouldn't have standards that inhibit you from writing.
> I can imagine a person beginning to feel that he's not able to write up to that standard he imagines the world has set for him. But to me that is surrealistic. The only standard I can rationally have is the standard I'm meeting right now.... You should be more willing to forgive yourself. It really doesn't make any difference if you are good or bad today. The assessment of the product is something that happens after you've done it. (152)

Like Robert Boice in another chapter of this book, Murray believes that what discourages people from writing is that they do not write on a regular basis. Skills deteriorate if one uses them infrequently and intensify with repeated honing and application. Murray encourages scholars to write every day, to make time for writing, and to be selfish and focused about the time set aside. A planning notebook is an essential tool because in it one can write down thoughts, questions, and speculations and begin to perceive important patterns that suggest further exploration. He admits to following the counsel of Horace, Pliny, Trollope, and Updike: *nulla dies sine linea*—never a day without a line, which for Murray means "the daily habit of talking to myself in writing, playing with ideas, letting a piece of writing grow and ripen until it is ready to be written" (148). He emphasizes the importance of "doing it now" and not waiting for a period in which there will be time:

> The academic schedule encourages the illusion that you can get your writing done on the day free from teaching, during the semester with a lower teaching load, between semesters, next summer, or on sabbatical. Nonsense. When those times come you can't suddenly take up an alien craft. The productive scholar is in the habit of writing, at least notes, at least lists, at least fragmentary drafts, at least something that keeps the topic alive and growing so that writing will come that is ready to be written. (148)

Murray emphasizes the individual writer's efforts to obtain his or her professional goals. Many academicians, though, first enter into print through collaborative efforts with mentors and colleagues. Often, novice professionals find collaboration to be one of the most effective ways to get published, especially when they coauthor or coedit projects with experienced scholars in the field. These projects generally have a high probability of being published because of the scholar's professional stature and knowledge of the journals and publishers in the field. Many an established scholar in rhetoric and composition has inaugurated or advanced his or her career by working as a graduate student with a dissertation director or other mentor to learn the craft of scholarship and publication. Seeking out such relationships is the prerogative of anyone seriously committed to academic publishing, and it certainly finds a rich climate of opportunity today when collaborative writing and publishing have found such a strong niche within the academy—as Andrea Lunsford and Lisa Ede point out in *Singular Texts/Plural Authors*. Collaborative efforts often emerge, too, from writing groups that graduate students and academics establish to provide feedback on ideas and works in progress and to offer collegial support through the difficult process of seeing a project through from start to finish. Writing groups provide an accessible and informed audience as well as the opportunity for the members to function as writers, listeners, and critics (Van Ryder).

Whether one is writing alone, as a collaborator, or as a member of a writing group, knowledge of the discipline and its various publication requirements is still the most essential element for success. While the pressure to publish has never been higher, it is also true that opportunities to publish have never been greater. In 1971, NCTE sponsored three academic journals that published articles on rhetoric and composition. Since that time, there has been a virtual explosion in opportunities for scholars to publish in this field. The most recent *CCCC Bibliography of Composition and Rhetoric* (1993) lists well over one hundred journals as publishing sources and twenty-three Internet discussion groups that provide opportunities for specialists in rhetoric and composition to seek information on scholarship, try out ideas, and receive feedback from others with similar interests. The Appendix of this book contains a partial listing of such scholarly forums.

As the opportunities have increased, so has the importance of knowing the requirements of the various journals and the audiences they serve. Much of this information is available in the *MLA Directory of Periodicals: A Guide to Journals and Serials in Languages and Literatures*, which offers information on the journals listed in the *MLA International Bibliography*. The directory is updated biennially and provides descriptions of each journal's focus, requirements for submissions, and editorial guidelines. The MLA directory also offers information on how long a journal typically takes to respond to a manuscript with an acceptance or rejection, as well as indicating the percentage of submissions accepted for publication. This information is important in selecting a journal for submission since journals that are backlogged and that take a year or more to respond, and even longer to publish, and those that publish only a small percentage of manuscripts received, are probably not the most appropriate journals for the beginning scholar to try first.

No matter what journal one chooses, though, editors consistently stress how important it is for the writer to know the journal's audience and scholarly focus. In a survey of fifty journal editors, Kenneth T. Henson found that nearly all agreed that "the most frequent mistake writers make is failing to acquaint themselves with the journal and its readers" (637). Editors recommend that authors examine the journal before submitting an essay to make sure that the article fits the editorial emphases that represent the journal's particular "style" or "signature" within a discipline. Essays based on quantitative research, for example, are unlikely to find a home in journals that rely heavily upon personal essays and more informal modes of argumentation and that tend to shy away from statistical research. This holds true no matter how well the quantitative essay is written. Conversely, journals that focus upon empirical research will most likely have little interest in essays based upon narrative examples and personal reflection. Thus, even though the name of a journal might seem to fit an author's focus, the actual content of the journal may not. To avoid wasting the editor's time (and one's own as well), it is best to study a journal's conceptual approach before submitting a work. One can subscribe to a journal, examine it in the library, or request a copy through interlibrary loan. Editors will often supply a sample copy of a journal upon request—either for free, or for a small fee. Such efforts help an author become familiar with the tenor of a journal and its scholarly focus, thereby expediting the publication process and assuring a higher degree of success (Henson; Sewell and Linck).

Knowing the journal saves time and disappointment in another way, too. Often editors are reluctant to publish an essay on a topic they have just covered in detail. For example, if a journal has recently devoted an entire issue to the debate over social constructionism, the editor might not want to publish yet another essay on that topic for a while. One might innocently submit such an essay, unaware that the journal has just published a special issue on that topic. Even though the essay may be quite good, it is unlikely that it will be accepted under such circumstances. Had the novice investigated more fully, he or she most likely would have submitted to another journal and had a greater chance for success.

Beginning professionals seeking to publish often ask, "What can *I* publish?"—a question that carries with it the suggestion that a novice has little to say of great value to others more advanced in the discipline. Such a point of view, though, overlooks the richness of each individual's environment and scholarly interests. Ideas can arise from one's teaching, especially as one sees the efficacy of, or comes to question the value of, certain methods or approaches applied in the classroom. The students one interacts with are also a rich source of narrative ideas and material that can complement the scholarly focuses or arguments one is developing. Further, graduate courses can also provide insight into areas that need further investigation or into supplemental materials—such as bibliographies, textbooks, collections and anthologies, and so forth—that professionals in the field require for their own teaching and scholarship. One's own reading often suggests gaps in the scholarly knowledge on a particular subject and ways that a subject can be brought into greater focus by sustained research and investigation.

Book Reviews and Interviews

One of the most important ways novice professionals can break the print barrier is by publishing book reviews. Many of the journals in rhetoric and composition, as well as in ancillary fields, publish reviews of scholarly monographs and books of general interest to their readers. Journal editors may assign book reviews—that is, the editors will contact a person and ask if he or she would be willing to write a review for the journal—or they may be open to suggestions from potential reviewers. The process is simple. Once a person becomes familiar with the types of books a journal reviews, he or she can contact the editor and propose reviewing a book for the journal. Many editors are grateful for such offers and eagerly accept. The process can lead to a continuing relationship between the editor and reviewer in which the editor will in the future assign books for review or remain open to suggestions about other books the reviewer is interested in critiquing.

Book reviews generally provide the reader with a sense of what new knowledge or perspectives the author is providing, how well the author expresses what he or she has to say, how effective the organization of the book is, and whether, ultimately, the book is worth the reader's time and money. Some book reviews are quite short—no more than an announcement of a new book and a brief summary of its contents. Other reviews are extensive and seek to place the book in the intellectual context of its research and primary focus. The reviewer seeks to address such issues as whether the book has anything new to say or is plowing familiar ground. Obviously, a critique of this sort requires that the reviewer be familiar with related works in the field. While this might seem a formidable task, most scholars will not find it too difficult since knowledge of the major texts in a field is the core of most people's scholarly interests and also of their graduate training. Assessing style is important, too, because an unreadable book with a repetitious or convoluted style is of little interest, even if some of its ideas are of value. The reviewer must give the reader a sense of the book's content—in essence, a summary and assessment of the major ideas the book's author develops within the course of his or her investigation. The reviewer must decide how well the author succeeds in bringing the book's major ideas together cohesively into an insightful and engaging presentation of academic inquiry or argumentation.

A mistake some novice reviewers make is being reluctant to give negative reviews to books that deserve them. This reluctance is a major failing in terms of the reviewer's obligation to the reader. The reader trusts the reviewer to assess the book fairly and not to recommend a book that has significant limitations and problems. To gloss over such problems out of a sense of intimidation or insecurity is to falter in one's responsibility to the community of scholars. To review is to assess; that is the essence of the reviewer's duties. The sad truth is that some books, even those published by prestigious presses, are poorly conceived and written; publication is no guarantee of quality. Consequently, distinguishing books of quality is one of the most important responsibilities of a book reviewer.

Occasionally, journal editors in rhetoric and composition are eager to receive interviews with important figures in the field. Interviews are an especially engaging means for readers to gain timely insights into the ideas and personalities that define the field and its various scholarly conversations. Editors may have compiled a list of people they would like to interview and are pleased when authors volunteer to conduct these interviews. Authors interested in proposing interviews for publication should first contact the person they wish to interview and secure their agreement to participate before communicating with the journal editor. Often, major scholarly figures teach at an author's university or at a nearby institution, or authors can meet these figures at national or regional conferences and propose the idea of an interview. Most people who have attained a measure of stature in a field appreciate the opportunity to discuss their views and to offer personal insights into their work and lives, and so a novice author should not hesitate to propose an interview and suggest a journal that might be interested in publishing it. Most interviews are taped and then later transcribed; however, an interview can be conducted via correspondence or e-mail. Once permission for the interview has been obtained, the author should contact the editor of a journal that has featured interviews in the past and ask if the editor would be interested in considering the interview for publication. The odds are high that the editor will be interested and will offer suggestions for concepts he or she would like to see included in the interview.

Scholarly Articles
While book reviews and interviews can be the first step toward professional self-actualization for some writers, scholarly articles generally serve the same function for others. The advice novice professionals receive on selecting publication venues for their scholarship tends to vary. Murray, for example, urges writers to "start at the top" by submitting to the best journal in one's field. As he states, "Maybe the best journals will not publish my stuff, but at least they've had their chance" (147). Matkin and Riggar advocate a similar point, claiming that "acceptance of a single paper by a well-reputed, widely circulated journal may be worth ten papers published in lesser-known journals" (62). Not all editors and published scholars agree, though. Many advocate a steady progression that begins with local outlets—especially

regional journals—and culminates with national journals of high repute (Bennett; Sewell and Linck). The assumption is that few novices write at such an accomplished level early in their careers as to compete effectively with established scholars with international reputations and a host of publications to their credit. Steady work as an apprentice allows the novice the opportunity to develop and hone writing skills through practice and a gradual accumulation of insight into the publishing process.

While there is merit to both approaches, and certainly many scholars have prospered either by starting at the top or by working their way up from the bottom, it cannot be denied that one's chances for publication are higher in lesser-known journals. Part of the reason is the volume of submissions that major journals receive annually. Sometimes the number can be in the thousands, and each of these manuscripts must be sent out to several readers as part of the review process. Depending upon the number of manuscripts each reviewer receives, the reviewer might take up to six months to respond. Similarly, the editor may take several months to complete the review process and make a decision. It is not uncommon for an author to wait a year or more to learn of a manuscript's fate; nor is it uncommon for the author to wait a year or two longer to see the manuscript in print. With lesser-known journals and with regional journals, the volume of submissions is usually less, and so editors can more easily expedite the decision and publication processes. Authors generally receive comments about their essays and see their work in print in a far shorter period of time. Often, regional journals reach a larger audience than many well-known national journals, and so an author can establish a professional presence within a region and become widely known in that area.

Whichever approach an author chooses, the fundamentals of submission remain the same. Generally, unless a publication specifies otherwise in its editorial policies and guidelines, journals do not accept multiple submissions. The reasons for this policy are evident. Editors and editorial reviewers spend substantial time in responding to manuscripts and selecting particular ones for publication. If after all this effort has been invested the author then withdraws the manuscript from publication because it has been accepted by another journal, the editor has wasted valuable time and has been put at a disadvantage in terms of developing a particular issue of the journal. Professional courtesy requires that authors submit their manuscripts to one journal at a time.

One would think that any author submitting a manuscript for publication would have checked all sources carefully and produced a highly readable print copy. Often this is not the case. Citations are missing or incomplete, typos are frequent, and the print quality of the manuscript itself is so poor that it is difficult to read. Consequently, every author should double-check a manuscript for errors and should submit a clear and readable copy. Editors do not want to waste time hunting down sources for the author or contacting the author to look up missing information. Anything that saves the editor time will dispose the editor favorably toward the author's work; conversely, anything that aggravates the editor can create a negative feeling toward the work itself.

Cover letters can be an important asset when submitting an article to a journal. The cover letter can be a mere formality, but generally those that go into detail about the issues the essay addresses can help the editor assess the essay's relevance to the journal and determine which reviewers to send the article to. The cover letter should make clear the purposes the article seeks to achieve and the implications of the author's ideas. Further, it should indicate why the essay's subject would be of interest to the journal's readership. A short biographical sketch of the author is also helpful in indicating the author's achievements, research interests, and background and training. Including a computer word count of the essay can be useful to the editor in calculating how much space the essay will consume in the journal. Despite what such guidebooks as *Writer's Market* might suggest, authors should not list the rights, such as First North American Serial Rights, under which they will agree to publish a manuscript. In the academic world, publication rights almost always belong to the journal, and the editor will indicate to the author the terms of publication. If these are not acceptable, the author can withdraw the manuscript or attempt to renegotiate the rights. Authors who include this information appear both amateurish and uninformed about scholarly publication and risk rejection if the terms they state are not consistent with a journal's policies.

Patience and Perseverance

Many authors feel that the most difficult aspect of the publication process is generating ideas, conducting the research, and writing and editing the essay; an even larger number of authors believes that the most difficult part is dealing with rejection. Unless one is extremely lucky, or gifted, or both, rejection is an inevitable part of the publication process. In fact, Dorothy H. Eichorn and Gary R. VandenBos speculate that "the vast majority of authors with forty to fifty journal publications have had that many (and generally more) rejections" (1315). They found that ninety-eight percent of the published authors they surveyed had the first manuscript they submitted for publication rejected. However, the acceptance rate for revised manuscripts rose to between twenty and forty percent, which means that the editorial review process can yield positive results along with the pain of rejection.

Frequently, a rejected manuscript is accompanied by readers' comments and suggestions for improvement and revision. Numerous authors find such commentary invaluable since it provides insight into how the manuscript affected an informed reader within the field. Readers' comments can be viewed as a type of tutorial relevant to the author's style, content, reasoning strategies, scholarship, and knowledge of a field. Since reviewers are usually prominent figures in the field, their cogent insights can serve as a type of mentoring that complements a novice professional's graduate training or an established scholar's proficiency. Reviewers' comments and suggestions for revision often improve the writer's work and open new avenues for publication. For example, a study of over two thousand Ph.D.s in sociology found that those who started writing early in their careers seemed to produce the most and to continue writing the longest; in part, the feedback they received in the review process aided their determination to continue and also facilitated their success (Clemente). Henson confirms this phenomenon, observing that almost three-fourths of the articles that are revised in accordance with readers' suggestions eventually are published.

Clearly, then, revision is extremely important. B.B. Reitt provides a detailed checklist of the major characteristics editors and reviewers look for, and authors can apply, in determining the quality of a manuscript submitted for publication: (1) is the manuscript complete? (2) is it authoritative? (3) is it expert? (4) is it singular? and (5) is it finished? A manuscript is complete if its goals and objectives are clearly stated and the purpose of the article is achieved. These aims, in turn, involve a logical presentation of the ramifications of the author's perspective and the significance of the author's conclusions. A manuscript is authoritative if its information is documented and current and its references are relevant to the topic. Reitt emphasizes the importance of a proportional mix of the author's and others' ideas—an important point in that many essays are rejected because they rely too heavily upon others' ideas and consequently have no conceptual framework or "voice" of their own. In this regard, Henson claims that "the most deadly error a writer can make is trying to impress readers through the use of the inflated writing style and ornamental trappings of scholarship." He suggests that "authors should use direct and conversational language and should spice up their manuscripts with concrete examples wherever possible"; ultimately, they should "avoid jargon and write with their readers in mind" (637). In an expert manuscript, the author uses an appropriate methodology upon which to base his or her conclusions, and the reasons for choosing this methodology are sound. A manuscript is singular if it presents new ideas or provides new information to confirm existing knowledge. No editor or reader will find engaging or valuable an essay that rehashes old information and adds nothing new to the existing body of knowledge in a discipline. Finally, a manuscript is finished if its references have been checked and conform to the journal's documentation style (such as MLA, APA, or Chicago), if it follows the journal's guidelines, if it avoids sexist language, and if the manuscript has been carefully and thoroughly proofread.

Nearly all commentators on the "competitive arena of publishing" recognize the difficulties involved in the process and the perseverance it requires (Matkin and Riggar ix). As Murray indicates, writing for publication requires practice; one gets better with time and through sustained effort.

Further, as Matkin and Riggar point out, publication involves a continuum of "discovery-production" in which the novice academic must be patient in pursuing "a developmental process that involves acquiring knowledge and learning" (6). Ultimately, they claim, "practice, patience, and starting with short manuscripts will, with persistence, eventually lead to longer more complex works" (7).

While it is certainly true that "publish or perish" pressures push many a novice into the "competitive arena of publishing," it is also true that this one motivation alone will not keep the novice there for long. The rigorous requirements of academic publishing also demand a level of personal commitment—what Jerome G. Manis calls the "psychic factors" that constitute a person's dedication to achievement and self-actualization (272). Certainly, with all the pressures upon academics to publish one can become cynical about the reasons for this pressure and the possible commodification of knowledge for one's survival and advancement in the academy. Nevertheless, as Donald H. Reiman indicates,

> There may be, after all, a direct correlation between productive research and effective teaching, and abuses of the publish-or-perish system may well be merely abuses, those inevitable serpents in any well-ordered garden, rather than tragic flaws in the system itself. (10)

Murray claims that "writing is also an extension of teaching and a stimulation to teaching. . . . We need to be practitioners of our discipline if we are to stay alive and if we are to bring new ideas to our teaching" (153). Perhaps his best advice to aspiring scholars is to "respect your own judgment," "write to discover what you have to say," and "if it isn't fun, don't do it" (147-51). Ultimately, as Murray writes, "the true rewards are internal—the satisfaction of asking your own questions and finding your own answers" (153). Manis, too, claims that the single greatest factor that motivates scholars to research and publish their ideas is "intellectual curiosity," a desire to know more about and to resolve the issue at hand (272). Perhaps the broadest implications of one's personal commitment to publishing as an academic scholar are suggested by Sewell and Linck, who served for five years as editors of a regional journal out of "zealousness for our profession":

> We English teachers have clung tenaciously to our conviction that we were an absolute necessity. As we were the touchstone without which there could be no education, then there was no reason for preparing a defense. The days of complacency are gone. We are in danger of becoming the obsolete necessity. For our own profit, *it's time to write that article to inform John Q. and Jonette Public of our good works.* (34)

If Sewell and Linck are right, an academic's most significant reason for breaking the print barrier might be to demonstrate the value of intellectual inquiry and the merits of scholarship to a public that supports and sustains the academic's work as an educator. In this regard, "publish or perish" might really mean "publish and inform."

Works Cited

Archer, Jerome W. "Professional Career of the College English Teacher: Present Practices and Some Desirable Principles." *College English* 23 (1961-62): 445-69.

Baugh, Albert C. "Graduate Work in English." *English Journal* 18.1 (1929): 135-46.

Bennett, Jo. "Getting Your Manuscript into Print." *English Journal* 69.7 (1980): 31-34.

Clemente, Frank. "Early Career Determinants of Research Productivity." *American Journal of Sociology* 79 (1973): 409-19.

Connors, Robert J. "Rhetoric in the Modern University: The Creation of an Underclass." *The Politics of Writing Instruction: Postsecondary*. Ed. Richard Bullock and John Trimbur. Portsmouth, NH: Boynton, 1991. 55-84.

Crowe, Chris. "Why Write for Publication?" Dahl 74-80.

Dahl, Karin L., ed. *Teacher as Writer: Entering the Professional Conversation*. Urbana: NCTE, 1992.

Eichorn, Dorothy H., and Gary R. VandenBos. "Dissemination of Scientific and Professional Knowledge." *American Psychologist* 40 (1985): 1309-316.

Fullington, James F. "Training for Teaching or Research." *College English* 10 (1948): 259-65.

Guillory, John. "Pre-professionalism: What Graduate Students Want." ADE Meeting. Iowa City. 15 Jun. 1995.

Hawisher, Gail E., and Cynthia L. Selfe, eds. *CCCC Bibliography of Composition and Rhetoric 1993*. Carbondale: Southern Illinois UP, 1993.

Henson, Kenneth T. "Writing for Professional Publication: Ways to Increase Your Success." *Phi Delta Kappan* 65 (1984): 635-37.

Hunting, Robert S. "A Training Course for Teachers of Freshman Composition." *College Composition and Communication* 2 (1951): 3-6.

Lunsford, Andrea, and Lisa Ede. *Singular Texts/Plural Authors: Perspectives on Collaborative Writing*. Carbondale: Southern Illinois UP, 1990.

Macdonald, Andrew F. "Peer Tutoring and the Problem of Rhetorical Superiority." *Freshman English News* 7.3 (1979): 13-15.

Manis, Jerome G. "Some Academic Influences Upon Publication Productivity." *Social Forces* 29 (1950): 267-72.

Matkin, Ralph E., and T.F. Riggar. *Persist and Publish: Helpful Hints for Academic Writing and Publishing*. Niwot: UP of Colorado, 1991.

Murray, Donald M. "One Writer's Secrets." *College Composition and Communication* 37 (1986): 146-53.

Nagourney, Peter. "Conceptual Scholarship." *College English* 40 (1979): 821-26.

Purdy, Dwight H. "The Destructive Element: Academic Publishing." *College English* 40 (1979): 816-20.

Reiman, Donald H. "Research Revisited: Scholarship and the Fine Art of Teaching." *College English* 23 (1961): 10-14.

Reitt, B.B. "An Academic Author's Checklist." *Scholarly Publishing* 16 (1984): 65-72.

Sewell, Ernestine D., and Charles E. Linck, Jr. "We Have Found your Article Perspicacious in Many Respects; However. . ." *English Journal* 73.4 (1984): 33-34.

Van Ryder, Betty. "Writing Groups: A Personal Source of Support." Dahl 34-43.

Publishing Scholarship in Rhetoric and Composition: Joining the Conversation

> The simple truth is this: the world of publishing, for the overwhelming majority of faculty members, is a strange and foreign land, complete with an unfamiliar language all its own and impenetrable rites of passage at every turn. Ralph Newbert

"These are not easy times in which to get published. The rejection rates from journals are high, sometimes as high as ten to one, and many smaller journals are folding because of financial problems, thus reducing the size of the field," writes Stephen Judy in the introduction to *Publishing in English Education* (ii). Judy's words are even more appropriate today—a decade and a half later. Scholarly publication has virtually become an industry, and, like any marketplace flooded with products (in this case, the plethora of scholarly articles generated through institution-mandated pressure to publish), the competition is fierce. Survival within this competitive, almost cut-throat, environment demands that we adopt a kind of *entrepreneurial spirit*—an attitude often foreign to most of us in the humanities. You may think me somewhat crass to sully academic scholarship by describing it as an enterprise driven by capitalistic impulses, and I *could* spend a great deal of time discussing how the system of scholarly writing and publishing has been corrupted by institutional forces that have misunderstood the nature of scholarship and its relative "value" within the marketplace of academe. However, I'd like to begin not with how the world of scholarly publication *should* be but with how it *is*.

The fact that scholarly writing is no longer the same leisurely, gentlemanly activity that it had been when academia was populated predominantly by white, affluent males and when institutions of higher learning were not the corporate entities they are today does not mean that scholarship itself has lost its significance. Yes, scholarship still is a noble, humanly significant activity—or at least our own scholarship can be if we maintain the right attitude. Yet, we can't ignore the fact that times *have* changed, that scholarship *is* a kind of business activity, and that published works are the currency with which we purchase tenure, promotion, salary increases, and the respect of colleagues.[1] Understanding these socioeconomic dynamics should not "spoil" the activity of scholarly writing for us; rather, it should help equip us to undertake meaningful scholarship with open eyes. Toward that end, I'd like to discuss the process of writing the scholarly article. Drawing on my experience as a published author and as editor and associate editor of various scholarly journals, I will provide several observations about the nature of scholarship, the kinds of things editors frequently look for in scholarly articles, and strategies for dealing with editors.

Joining the Conversation

Becoming a successful, publishing scholar is largely a matter of understanding how academic publishing works and adopting the right attitude. Many scholars who are not in the habit of publishing frequently are intimidated by the process, feeling that it is the reserve of only distinguished, high-powered scholars. Such an attitude prevents many potential scholars from even attempting to produce substantive scholarship. Turning this attitude around is the first step toward becoming a productive scholar. Richard C. Gebhardt, former editor of *College Composition and Communication* and other composition journals, argues that the first and most important habit of any working academic must be to think of yourself as a publishing scholar: "If you cultivate for yourself the role of a publishing scholar-teacher for whom research and critical theory and classroom performance all are important, you probably will stumble over article ideas fairly often" (31). Comparing your own work with that of the most seasoned luminaries in the field is perhaps the most serious mistake any beginning scholar can make, in that it can help prevent you from seeing yourself as a scholar. As Robert Boice points out in another chapter of this book, there is no need to let the system defeat you, as it does some academics.

Understanding the nature of scholarship is half the battle. I find it especially useful to think of scholarship as a series of ongoing conversations. In any given field, scholars will be engaged in several major conversations about important disciplinary issues. These discussions transpire in our scholarly journals and books and in our professional conferences. The participants in any main conversation form a "discourse community," and at any given point in time, the discourse community will be focusing on specific issues of interest to scholars in the field.[2] As you might expect, a discourse community's conversations are not always harmonious: there are minority and majority perspectives; issues are debated heatedly; and often it becomes clear that no consensus can be formed about a particular issue. Over time, certain issues are put to rest and new issues are explored. The concerns of any scholarly community will grow and evolve; some ideas will soon seem antiquated in the light of other, newer notions.[3]

There are several advantages to seeing scholarship as an ongoing conversation. First, it allows us to circumvent the age-old notion that scholarship is a matter of coming closer and closer to discovering "truth." Instead, it highlights the dynamic nature of scholarship; it accentuates the fact that scholarship is a *human* endeavor. In addition, this perspective helps us understand some of the dynamics of creating and publishing scholarship and thereby helps to demystify what to some is a recondite and unapproachable activity. For example, just as you would not barge into an ongoing conversation in another room without first stopping and listening to what is being said and determining what has been said, so too would you not barge abruptly into an ongoing conversation in a scholarly journal without first having paid close attention to the discussions published there. For instance, imagine a faculty cocktail party in which various colleagues and their spouses are standing in groups sipping cocktails and engaging in intimate, sometimes passionate discussions. After freshening your cocktail, you approach several people discussing the influence of postmodern theory on composition pedagogy. Obviously, it would be considered rude to jump immediately into the conversation that had been going on before you arrived. Basic etiquette dictates that you join the group, quietly listen to what is being said, and develop a sense of the larger conversation—both its tone and content—before you begin to make a contribution. The same kind of dynamics attend to the scholarly conversation. Before rushing into print about this or that subject, it is imperative that you read what is currently being said about the subject, discover what the positions are and who is taking what position, and, in general, acquire a sense of the larger conversation. Attentiveness to the larger context of scholarship helps you understand which subjects are currently of interest to the discourse community and which are not, thus preventing you from tackling an issue that has long been laid to rest.

Too many academics approach scholarship backwards. They know that they are required to publish, so they search for a subject to write about. They decide to write about a certain subject and then they search for something to say about it. They go back and read what others have written about the subject, searching for some "original" point. Then they try to write an essay from their research. Such a procedure is artificial and reflects a misunderstanding of what true scholarship entails. An active scholar in any field rarely needs to worry about "finding a subject" because that scholar is actively engaged in reading the key journals, studying the new books, attending the major conferences. This person knows intimately what the major scholarly conversations are, who is arguing what points, and where each conversation is leading. Given this scenario, it is difficult to imagine someone *not* having something to say about at least some of the important issues in the field. Too often, editors must reject articles simply because the author quite clearly is unaware of recent developments in the field. Undoubtedly, such authors are not staying abreast with the published work of their colleagues and, instead, are writing in a vacuum, artificially and mechanically "searching" for subjects to write about.

Remember, too, that if scholarship is a series of conversations relevant to a discipline, and journals and publishing houses are the sites of these discussions, then editors are the hosts, if you will, inviting informed conversants into the dialogue. As such, editors are also "gatekeepers," helping to determine what is a legitimate contribution to the dialogue and what is not.[4] That is, editors are far from neutral arbiters; they determine exactly who has admittance to the conversation. "By choosing to publish some works and not to publish others," writes Paul Parsons, editors "play a vital role in the transmission of knowledge within a culture" (7). Consequently, it is essential in writing the scholarly article to remember that you in effect have *two* audiences—the readers of the journal you are targeting, and its editor—and you must prepare your work accordingly. As gatekeeper, the editor has the responsibility to facilitate the conversation by accepting those articles that advance the ongoing discussion and rejecting those that do not.[5] The editor will be especially interested in papers that extend or refine arguments made in recent issues of the journal, or that challenge fundamental assumptions, or that in some way fit the general *context* of the journal's scholarship.

Beginning The Process

I've already suggested that scholarship grows naturally from active participation in the discipline's conversations. Frequent reading of important journals and texts and attending key professional conferences is the intellectual starting point for most scholarship. Given this scenario, there will be little need to "think of a subject to write on," since your active participation already equips you to begin to join the scholarly conversations. One of the most productive starting points of this process is the conference paper. Many germinal articles in various disciplines began as a paper presented at a professional conference and later evolved into a more formal, extended article. Curiously, I am frequently asked if it is "fair" to present a paper at a conference and then to publish a version of it as an article. Not only is it fair, it is the natural course of much scholarship.

As Richard Gebhardt explains in another chapter of this book, the professional convention is the ideal place to test your new ideas, your attempts to join the conversation, since you are likely to receive feedback—both negative and positive—from other participants, helping you refine your ideas later into a workable, publishable article. But please remember that there is a vast difference between a brief conference paper and an extended, fleshed-out journal article. It is a mistake to mail off a transcript of a conference presentation to a journal without taking the time and effort to make it suitable for journal publication. Typically, the first is short, informal, and somewhat general, while the latter is longer, more formal, and meticulously detailed. Nevertheless, it is wise to begin a project first as a presentation and then later to transform it into a substantive, formal article.

In discussing "what to write about" in scholarly writing, Gerald Phillips has categorized fourteen kinds of scholarly articles that academics frequently engage in. He then presents them as "types" of articles (or ways to structure articles). You may find them instructive:

- Editors do not run very many philosophical "think pieces." When they do, the articles are usually authored by veterans in the field. At the beginning of a career, it is wise to concentrate on meticulous scholarship rather than theory building or broad argument.

- A great many articles are confirmations of doubtful ideas. You can help confirm an idea by replicating an experiment or finding a new bit of evidence. You can also contradict an idea by the same means.

- You can apply a novel method of criticism to some writing, a body of ideas or an experiment, or present for criticism something important that has not previously been examined.

- You can add to an understanding of history by filling in details, by describing and interpreting events not previously considered, or by showing that an event was more important than commonly believed.

- Editors are interested in articles that cast doubt on common beliefs and widely accepted theories, but such articles must contain reports of careful experimentation or active examination of phenomena. You can support beliefs and theories by the same means.

- You can offer a new method of data gathering, analysis, or criticism and show how it works or to what it might be applied.

- You can offer a new research design and show how it can advance knowledge.

- You can propose and test a hypothesis.

- You can describe the details of a method of performing, teaching, or doing research and explain its effects.

- You can offer new ways to help understand a complex phenomenon.

- You can compare similar events or ideas to show differences, or different appearing events to show hidden similarities.

- You can evaluate an event or body of knowledge by comparing it to critical standards or with another similar event or body of knowledge.

- You can demonstrate and explain connections between variables or events.

- You can allege that a problem exists and document it. You can propose a plan and argue its practicality. (98-99)

Obviously, despite the type of article you write it is absolutely important that you remain conversant with the current scholarship in the field. First, if you are monitoring the field's conversations and decide to enter a conversation, there is no mystery about where to publish a particular piece: this decision will arise naturally from the type of conversation and where it is occurring. Echoing the advice of many journal editors, Roy O'Donnell recommends that "the decisions determining which audience and which journal to address should be made before the author prepares the manuscript" (74). Janet Binkley provides similar advice. She claims that it is necessary to "pick your outlet before you write," and she contends that "cover letters to a journal editor often suggest that the author finished the manuscript before considering where to send it. If you are well acquainted with a particular journal, such a 'spontaneous' article may grow in a form and with content highly appropriate to that journal" (41-42). Clearly, the best scenario is to be actively working with ideas being published in a particular journal and to compose your article with that periodical in mind.[6]

One of the most productive starting points of this process is the letter of inquiry. Too many people simply mail their articles to a journal unsolicited. While there is nothing wrong with this procedure (and, in fact, it happens more often than not), it makes much more sense to contact the editor before submitting an article to ask whether he or she would be interested in the *kind* of essay you are preparing. Certainly, no editor will accept or reject an article without seeing it; however, inquiring beforehand will enable you to discover whether the editor is interested in the type of research you are conducting and the subject you are addressing. The editor may enthusiastically encourage you to submit your article, or may suggest that what you are working on is not quite appropriate for the journal's publication schedule at this time, thereby saving you many wasted months in the review process. Another advantage of this process is that the letter of inquiry allows you to make personal contact with the editor, helping to personalize your relationship with him or her. In fact, William Van Til, author of over 250 scholarly publications, stresses the importance of sending a query letter, which he refers to as Van Til's First Law:

> "Query, always query." Before you set pencil to pad, or fingers to typewriter, determine the specific publication outlet or outlets in which you would like your writing to appear. Study your proposed outlet as to style, length, content, and even such editorial practices as footnoting. Only then write to the editor. Describe specifically and persuasively what you have in mind. Address the editor by name, rather than as "Dear Editor," thus helping to indicate your familiarity with the periodical. (16-17)

The query letter should be short and succinct, rarely more than one page. It should inform the editor of the thesis and conclusions of your essay, provide a brief rationale as to its contribution to ongoing scholarship, and briefly mention your professional credentials. I can say without hesitation that while unsolicited articles submitted to the journals I have edited are handled expeditiously, it does take a certain amount of time to process them and to initiate the review process; however, I always responded to query letters immediately. It is important to remember that publishing is not a one-way street: article writers begging for publication. Editors are desperately looking for the best articles they can find, and it is therefore in their best interest to respond promptly. The query letter is a way to help entice the editor into paying close attention to your article. In any event, the letter of inquiry will never do any harm, and it may well give you added advantage.[7]

The Scholarly Article
Over the last two decades, the scholarly article has changed drastically. The old-style article in the humanities was a kind of leisurely "journey" through a subject, meandering from point to point, often reserving its thesis for the very end of the article. The modern scholarly article is much different: it usually states its thesis right up front in no uncertain terms; it is succinct and to the point; and it is more a kind of technical writing in your given field than a leisurely and entertaining sojourn. That is, in the present so-called information age, and given the "information explosion" we are all experiencing, academics do not have time to read all the important publications they need to read in their fields. Economy, therefore, is a necessity. The fact that the modern scholarly article is streamlined and to the point is in keeping with our conversation metaphor. If you really do want to make a true contribution to an ongoing conversation, you certainly are not going to risk being interrupted or abandoned before you get to your point; rather, you're going to make your point immediately and then provide the appropriate evidence and examples to support it. The same is true with the contemporary scholarly article.

Editors of scholarly journals agree that one of the most common and frustrating problems with submitted articles is a failure on the part of authors to express their thesis clearly and early in the article. Julie M. Jensen writes,

> I have two hopes for your article: (1) that it states its ideas obviously and precisely and (2) that those ideas are appropriate for our readers. As I glance over what you have written, I wonder what your objective was in submitting the manuscript for publication. What, exactly, did you hope to communicate? ... I can't afford an article that meanders. (2-3)

Jensen's concerns are fairly representative of those of all editors. It is extremely frustrating to be reading page after page of a submitted article and still find yourself questioning, "What *is* this author's point, anyway?" Van Til reiterates, "In writing for your fellow scholars, tell them in your opening precisely and sharply what your article will be about" (70). This is excellent advice for any author of scholarly articles.

Sometimes authors do state their thesis clearly, but they delay stating it by constructing unnecessarily long introductions. For example, Stephen

Judy complains that "a large number of articles submitted to *The English Journal*, both by experienced writers and first-timers," have one common weakness: "the *preambles* were much, much too long. Introductory materials went on for pages" (20). Judy goes on to advise authors to examine their completed essays and to determine whether they truly need the long introductions that they are likely to contain at first. It is understandable why some authors compose lengthy introductions. A good introduction is an essential part of the scholarly paper. It establishes the context within which you are writing and from which you are making your main point, your contribution to the conversation. That is, it establishes the general framework of the ongoing conversation you are about to enter and then situates your own perspective within that framework. Such is the function of a good introduction. However, some writers feel that for one reason or another they must provide an exhaustive review of the literature before progressing on to their own thesis. This, as Judy has mentioned, is not only unnecessary but distracting. Roy O'Donnell writes, "The scope of a journal article, unlike that of a dissertation, does not permit an exhaustive review of related studies. To establish a context, the author should cite selected studies that are pertinent to the problem at hand, avoiding references that are only peripherally related" (76).[8]

Clearly, the most important function of the scholarly article is that it must "say something" about your subject; it must contribute to the conversation. As James Reither has said,

> What counts as a relevant contribution, question, answer, or criticism is determined not only by adherence to a set of discourse conventions, but also by such concerns as whether or not the contribution, question, answer, or criticism has already appeared in "the literature"—whether or not it is to the point, relevant, or timely. A writer addressing dead issues, posing questions already answered, or voicing irrelevant criticisms is judged ignorant and viewed as, at best, an initiate—not yet an insider, not yet a full member of the discipline. (623-24)

Thus, it is essential to specify exactly what the key point of your article is and how it contributes to the discipline's discussions. Van Til writes,

> It's not enough to have a topic; a writer must find a theme. An article must say something. It must contend, demonstrate, attempt to prove. A general reader must learn early what the article is about. If the general reader doesn't, he or she will soon stop being your reader. You and I have both read articles that meandered aimlessly and apparently endlessly. Even when we endured to the end, we couldn't identify the author's thesis. (49)

It is wise to listen to these editors' complaints. Perhaps the single most important thing you can do to increase the receptivity of your scholarly article is to ensure that your introduction is short but establishes the context and that your thesis is clearly stated.

Many editors complain that another major problem with submitted articles is inattention to stylistic issues. Gebhardt believes that "the desire to publish 'important' articles sometimes leads people to look for complex ways to say things.... It makes good rhetorical sense to try to write clear, engaging articles" (31). Gebhardt quips that to write articles "with muddled or pretentious prose deadened by needless passives and confused by tangles of terminology" is not "a very desirable approach" (28). Surely, no one writes this way purposely, but the fact is that too many academic essays exhibit an intolerable unconcern for audience and for the conventions of good prose. In decrying the lack of attention to style in scholarly writing, Phillips urges scholars to spend substantial time revising their articles to eliminate clichés, reduce technical jargon, and correct poor grammar and spelling. He, too, makes the connection between the importance of understanding your audience and a clear and effective style: "Your article should be prepared persuasively with full consideration of the stresses and strains under which the editor operates. Many articles are rejected simply because the reviewers cannot, with reasonable effort, understand what they are about" (103). Reviewers and editors are your first *public* readers. You must first impress them with the importance of your contribution to the conversation; however, if stylistic considerations interfere with their ability to read and understand your article, it may never be published.

Obviously, balance is necessary here, too. Just as it is essential to craft an effective introduction but equally important that it not be a "long preamble," it is necessary that your prose style be appropriate for the specific readers of the field and even of the sub-area you are working in, balancing the technical jargon of your discourse community with a readable prose style. Despite what some commentators recommend, there is certainly nothing wrong with jargon. Jargon is simply the specialized vocabulary of a particular field. As such, it is a convenient shorthand to help members of the discourse community communicate efficiently. Effective use of the vocabulary of your field is one way to demonstrate that you are a full member of your discourse community and that you understand its discourse. This being said, however, it is essential to make sure your prose is as clear and readable as possible. Jargon in and of itself will not make an article unreadable to members of the discourse community; however, it is necessary, *despite* the use of jargon, to make your prose clear and fluid.

The bottom line is that authors often submit their work prematurely, without engaging in the type of extensive revision necessary to turn a good draft into a polished professional article. Rushing into print before subjecting your text to rigorous review is a serious mistake—one you may regret later in your career. Most good writers devote substantial time to the revision process, re-reviewing their work repeatedly and meticulously. It is also wise to ask one or two trusted colleagues to read and comment on your draft. You can never read and revise your draft too many times. Below is a revision checklist that Phillips devised for authors of scholarly articles:

- Make certain you have a clear opening paragraph stating what the article is about, to whom it appeals, and why it is important to them. The opening should also state the divisions in which you will consider the topic so that the reader has guidelines to follow.

- Coordinate your conclusion with your introduction and review the points you have made. It's disturbing to reviewers when the introduction, body, and conclusion of an article do not agree.

- Use subheads in the article, and make certain they correspond to the divisions you made in your first paragraph. Your subheads should comply with the requirements of the particular type of research you are reporting.... A critical study should offer the standards of criticism, a justification for using those standards, and subheads representing each of the components of that brand of criticism. Attention to the scholarly requirements of your research will help you organize your article for maximum clarity and unity of structure.

- Check each paragraph to make sure it fits properly in the structure of the article. Check each paragraph for internal integrity. Do not be afraid to shift paragraphs around until you locate the place where they can do their best work. A careful outline will help you in placement of paragraphs.

- Be sure that the language you use is as simple and direct as possible. Make sure that unfamiliar terms and technical references are properly defined. Do not assume a high level of sophistication among your readers. Do assume a high level of intelligence. In short, your readers will understand your topic, no matter how complicated, if you take care to organize and word it in the clearest possible way.

- Check your footnotes to make sure they are correct and in proper order. Check your text to make sure that everything that requires footnoting is properly identified. If you use direct quotes, check them for accuracy. Don't assume that your editorial reviewer will skip the footnotes. On the contrary, it's common practice for reviewers to check footnotes very carefully, and if you happen to be inaccurate in a reference to a work that the reviewer regards as important, you have lost your persuasive impact. If you have material that requires publisher permission, be sure to include a permission form with your submission.

- Make a final check of your syntax, usage, spelling, and punctuation. Sloppiness in these areas casts doubt on the intelligence and integrity of your work. If you are not skillful at this kind of editing, you can hire an expert to help you. There is nothing wrong with paying for this kind of service. After all, you have to pay your typist. (It is cheaper, however, to learn to do it yourself.) (105)

While Phillips' checklist is rather general, it nonetheless indicates the kinds of considerations an author should pay attention to during the revision process. You'll notice that one of Phillips' suggestion is to use subheads, a procedure relatively new for papers in the humanities, but one gaining more and more acceptance. Dividing your article into sections preceded by descriptive headings greatly increases readability and therefore is a great asset, especially during the review process where reviewers and editors must understand your points accurately and quickly. It is also helpful to you, though, in the revision process because you can review each section and determine whether the section itself stands as a coherent whole.

In short, remember to revise your scholarly article extensively before submitting it to a journal editor. This is an integral and natural part of the writing process, and it will greatly increase your chances of producing an article that will be acceptable for publication.

Dealing with Editors

I mentioned earlier that in scholarly publication you in effect have two readers: the readers of the journal as well as its editor and editorial reviewers. There are many things you can do to ease the work of the editor and reviewers. For example, just as you should know the conversations occurring in the field, you should be familiar with the editorial policy of the journals you are dealing with, especially the one you plan to submit your new article to. W. John Harker writes, "I'm convinced that the most common, and for all concerned the most frustrating, error authors make is not to examine the publisher or publication to whom they submit their work" (121-23). Harker is referring both to authors who submit essays that clearly are not within the scope of those normally published by the particular journal as well as authors who are completely unfamiliar with the style and length requirements imposed by the journal. Always study both the journal's editorial policy and its submission requirements *before writing your essay*. Does the journal accept works in excess of twenty pages? Should you use footnotes or endnotes? Should you prepare your manuscript according to the *Chicago Manual of Style* or MLA's documentation system? How many copies of your manuscript does the journal require? What other stipulations does it make?

Put yourself in the editor's place: how would you feel if you received a submission that clearly indicated an unfamiliarity with your journal and its policies? An author who submits an article prepared using the wrong documentation style and who sends three instead of the required four copies is not going to ingratiate him or herself with the editor. The same can be said for submission letters not personalized for the particular journal you are corresponding with (Dear Editor: ...) and dog-eared manuscripts obviously returned recently from another journal. While such indiscretions are not likely to cause an editor to reject an article outright, they are nonetheless bothersome and they unnecessarily create a negative impression. Remembering your audience will help you avoid such *faux pas*.

In submitting an article for publication, you want everything working to your benefit. You don't even want subconscious negative impressions to interfere with the positive reception of your work. In corresponding with the editor, keep you letter short; there is no need for a lengthy persuasive rationale for accepting your article. In fact, your letter of transmittal should be brief, simply requesting that the editor consider your article for publication. Unless there is some kind of unusual circumstance that needs to be noted, all you need is a brief mention of the article's thesis so as to assist the editor in selecting the most appropriate reviewers for your piece. The article should stand on its own merit. The letter of transmittal should be personalized as much as possible, addressing the editor by name; form letters will not be received well. Make sure that you have followed exactly the journal's style specifications, especially concerning the number of copies to be submitted and in what form. In addition, the copies of your manuscript should be high-quality photocopies or machine copies.

The review process varies from journal to journal and can take anywhere from two months to one year. It is wise to check the journal's official policy on review time so that you are not surprised later at the length of time it takes to be informed of a publication decision. Many journals in rhetoric and composition now require you to send your article on computer disk upon acceptance. These journals are likely to distribute a pamphlet called something like "Preparing Your Electronic Manuscript." This pamphlet will describe the procedures for preparing your manuscript on disk to make the editorial process easy for those who must make your article ready for typesetting. Failure to follow these specifications closely may delay the processing of your article.

Often an editor will ask you to revise and resubmit your article. While this usually is not a promise to publish, it nonetheless is a good sign: it shows that your article is close to the kind of contribution that the journal is interested in and that there is potential for transforming it into an acceptable essay. Of course, your article will need to be sent back through the review process as if it were a new submission. Thus, you should not simply pencil in changes on your manuscript. You will want to completely rework and perhaps even rethink your article, printing fresh copies and composing a new cover letter. Nevertheless, it is generally a good idea to work with an editor to revise your work into acceptable form. Harold Wechsler, former editor of *Thought & Action* and past NEA director of higher education publications, writes, "It is often wise to revise and resubmit. Knowing the history of the article, the editor and referees usually act quickly. Little time is lost if the article is ultimately rejected. An editor looks upon a 'revise and submit' carefully—because of the time and effort already invested by all parties" (16). This is good advice from someone who knows well how the system works.[9]

Finally, we all need to develop a healthy attitude toward rejection. Because of the highly-competitive atmosphere mentioned earlier, many journals have high rejection rates, as high as ninety and ninety-five percent for some. Rejection is not necessarily an indication that your work is inferior, and it's certainly no reason for not trying. Many editors return reviewers' reports along with a rejection; these are extremely useful in helping you see how some readers are perceiving your work and what measures can be taken to make it more acceptable for other members of your discourse community. Because these are real readers reading your work specifically to evaluate it, their comments *can* be quite instructive. While it is true that reviewers, like any readers, can misinterpret or misunderstand your work, it is likely that their suggestions will be valuable indicators of how other readers will receive your work; thus, you can use these reports to assist you in extensive revision before submitting your article to another journal. Despite the advice of some, it is perhaps unwise to stuff your newly rejected article into an envelope and send it to another journal without engaging in careful revision given the reviewers' reports. Harker urges authors to

> avoid developing a repertoire of previously rejected and unrevised manuscripts that they shunt from one publisher or journal to another in hopes of acceptance. I have come to believe that there is a growing number of manuscripts working their way through innumerable editorial offices without benefit of the revisions they need to be converted from unpublishable pieces to ones that editors can use. Cynical disregard for editorial advice almost always ensures rejection. (124)

Even if a reviewer has misunderstood your work, it is advisable to take that reviewer's perceptions seriously and to try to adjust your work accordingly, since other readers could very well come away with the same wrong impressions.

Despite the competitive atmosphere, there are many scholarly journals available in rhetoric and composition. Obviously, there is a hierarchy of journals in any field. The major national journals in rhetoric and composition will, of course, be the most exclusive; but there are many fine regional scholarly journals that are worth your attention.

A Final Note
While Judy may be correct that "these are not easy times in which to get published," it is not too difficult to become a productive, publishing scholar: it entails adopting the proper attitude and becoming familiar both with the scholarly conversations in the field and with the kinds of logistics I've been addressing. Scholarly writing is likely to be most intimidating when you approach it in the artificial way many scholars do. If, however, you remain active in the conversations of rhetoric and composition, faithfully reading the key journals and scholarly texts, you will find that your scholarship grows quite naturally, even prolifically, and is no longer what Newbert has called "a strange and foreign land."

Notes

[1]Gerald Phillips writes, "A distinguished speech communication scholar once commented that an article published in a major journal early in a career could be worth about $25,000 in pay and benefits.... In hard cash, the average scholarly publication could be worth about $200 a year for every year you work" (95).

[2]By "conversation" I don't necessarily mean a direct exchange among scholars on the exact same point, although this does happen. I am referring more generally to discussions of similar topics, whether or not the discussants refer specifically to each other's works.

[3]The conversation metaphor is certainly not original with me; in fact, it has almost become a cliché in discussing scholarly writing. It is an adaptation of Kenneth Burke's notion of history as an ongoing parlor conversation. See Raymond and Olson. I should add, though, that several compositionists have recently problematized notions of "community" and "conversation," pointing out that such terms often conceal productive "conflict." These scholars make a good point, but thinking of scholarship as a conversation nevertheless helps us understand many of its dynamics.

[4]For interesting discussions of the gatekeeping function of editors and publishers, see Coser and Chapter 1 of Parsons.

[5]I realize that the word *gatekeeper* carries with it a slightly negative connotation and that some readers will equate it with *censor*. However, as Parsons points out, "Censorship is the deletion of objectionable material, a process quite different from selection. If publishers did not have the right of selection, they would, in effect, become clerks, publishing everything that entered the gate" (15).

[6]While it is essential to keep up with the scholarship as soon as it is published, it is also important to remember that there is substantial lag time between acceptance and publication of any article, not to mention the time between getting an idea for an article and arriving at a finished product ready for submission. Gebhardt says that published articles provide a "sort of rearview mirror on new trends in the profession" (26), in that by the time an article is published it represents perhaps year-old thinking (or longer)—another reason for staying as current as possible in your field.

[7]Van Til writes that an editor of a scholarly journal with a circulation of over 130,000 reported that "for every query, he receives twenty-five unsolicited manuscripts not preceded by a query" (18). Van Til goes on to suggest that those sending a query letter will get more prompt attention than those who do not. While practices vary from journal to journal, Van Til generally is correct.

[8]Editors of university presses agree that one of the major reasons so many doctoral dissertations are unpublishable as scholarly monographs is that many contain chapter-long literature reviews. Like a good scholarly article, a monograph must establish a context but should not subject readers to a long and tortuous preamble. See Parsons, especially 110-19.

[9]Wechsler's article is part of a special issue of *Thought & Action* on scholarly publishing. It includes an interesting piece by Benjaminson on publishing scholarly books.

Works Cited

Benjaminson, Peter. "Publishing Without Perishing." *Thought & Action* 6.2 (1990) 27-119.

Binkley, Janet R. "Reading an Open Field." Judy 40-52.

Coser, Lewis A. "Publishers as Gatekeepers of Ideas." *Perspectives on Publishing*. Ed. Philip G. Altbach and Sheila McVey. Lexington, MA: Lexington Books, 1976.

Gebhardt, Richard C. "Writing Articles about College English Teaching." Judy 24-39.

Harker, W. John. "Publishing in Canada." Judy 112-26.

Jensen, Julie M. "Publishing in the Elementary Language Arts." Judy 1-13.

Judy, Stephen N., ed. *Publishing in English Education*. Portsmouth, NH: Boynton, 1982.

Newbert, Ralph. "An Overview." *Thought & Action* 6.2 (1990): 3-4.

O'Donnell, Roy C. "Writing about Educational Research." Judy 73-81.

Parsons, Paul. *Getting Published: The Acquisition Process at University Presses*. Knoxville: U of Tennessee P, 1989.

Phillips, Gerald, M. "Publishing in Speech Communication." Judy 95-111.

Raymond, James C. "Imag(in)ing Scholarship." *Editor's Notes* 6.2 (1987): 3-7.

Reither, James A. "Writing and Knowing: Toward Redefining the Writing Process." *College English* 47 (1985): 620-28.

Olson, Gary A. "The Politics of Empowerment: Admitting Emerging Scholars to the Conversation." *Editor's Notes* 8.1 (1989): 20-22.

Van Til, William. *Writing for Professional Publication*. Boston: Allyn, 1981.

Wechsler, Harold S. "Publishing a Journal Article." *Thought & Action* 6.2 (1990): 5-26.

Scholarship and Teaching: Motives and Strategies for Writing Articles in Composition Studies

Richard C. Gebhardt

This decade is a fortunate time for composition studies faculty interested in writing articles related to their work with students. I say this partly because many periodicals, with a wide range of editorial policies, now publish such articles[1] and partly because a tradition of "teacher-research" has evolved in composition studies.[2] And I say it for other reasons, too.

Since the Carnegie Foundation for the Advancement of Teaching published Ernest Boyer's *Scholarship Reconsidered* in 1990, American higher education has echoed with discussion about broadening the concept of academic research to include scholarship of *integration*, of *application*, and of *teaching*, in addition to scholarship of *discovery*. For instance, a committee of the American Association of University Professors has proposed that "scholarship can ... mean work done to further the application or synthesis of knowledge, and new directions in pedagogy clearly fall on both sides of the line between what we see as teaching and what can be classified as scholarship" (AAUP 47). And the National Project on Institutional Priorities and Faculty Rewards—involving a dozen professional associations, including CCCC and MLA—has described "scholarly" work in a way that includes many teaching-related publications:

> An activity will be recognized as [scholarly or professional] in most disciplines if it requires a high level of discipline-related experience; breaks new ground or is innovative; can be replicated or elaborated; can be documented; and has impact on, or significance for, communities, those affected directly by the effort, or the discipline itself.
> (Diamond B2)

In spite of my opening paragraphs, I'm no cockeyed optimist. Across the American academy, it's still true, as Maryellen Weimer wrote in 1993, that "disciplinary journals on pedagogy" often are viewed as "weak siblings of the favored and prestigious research journals" and that many faculty report that "writing about pedagogy isn't regarded as legitimate scholarship" (44). But this is less true in composition studies—represented in Weimer's study by three prestigious journals, *College Composition and Communication*, *College*

English, and *Research in the Teaching of English*—than in many other fields. It probably still is true, as Paul Lacey wrote in a 1990 article about the evaluation of faculty scholarship, that "writing about teaching and a number of other activities that keep teachers intellectually alive and effective in the classroom . . . are excluded by definition" in many tenure and promotion reviews (95). Again, though, this seems less the case for faculty in composition studies than in some fields, for even before *Scholarship Reconsidered* came out an MLA committee had prepared guidelines indicating that the writing of textbooks and the leading of workshops are appropriate evidence of scholarship in composition studies ("Report"). And the MLA's Association of Departments of English more recently issued a "Statement of Good Practice" which ended with this sentence: "Scholarship on teaching—its methods, assessment procedures, and ways to improve it—should be valued on a par with traditional forms of scholarship" ("ADE" 45).

Teaching has occupied an important place in rhetoric and composition for a long time. In fact, much of the scholarship and publication of our field connects, directly or implicitly, to teaching or to students or to student writing. For example, Lil Brannon describes composition studies as "concerned with answering the following questions: (1) What is the nature of the composing process? (2) How does one develop from an inexperienced to a mature writer? (3) How can schools, particularly teachers of writing, assist the development of writers?" (6). James Kinneavy believes that "[m]ost of the interest in the contemporary study of rhetoric in departments of English has come about because of the 'literacy crisis,' . . . in our schools and universities," and that, for many scholars, the "business of teaching students to write well" is the "aspect of rhetoric that . . . is the major professional commitment" (213-14). And Erika Lindemann and Gary Tate feel that "[t]he major concern of most composition specialists is teaching writing well" (v).

Motives

Motivation for writing is a complex subject, and this may be especially true of professional writing by college and university professors. Of course, faculty members have the basic human drive—a healthy *pull*—to communicate: "we *do* have things we want to tell people," Peter Elbow once wrote; we'd like our readers to "love what we write, but in the last analysis, it's enough if we can feel them reading" (210, 212). Of course, many faculty members also have the drive—often it's a *push*—to write for tenure, promotion, and merit pay.[3] Between these motivational extremes of *push* and *pull* are other reasons to write articles related to your work as a teacher of writing.

To begin with, all of the things we tell students about writing as a way of learning—how writing helps clarify complex material, develop connections between ideas, and encourage generalizations and original insights—apply to faculty members, too. So working on a teaching-related article can address the faculty member's *need to learn*—for instance, by helping writers keep up with developments in composition studies; identify trends and forge connections among the varied and expanding bibliography of our field; bring these insights to bear on their teaching; and clarify the meaning and usefulness of published scholarship by viewing it in the context of their courses and students.

Consider a recent scholarly article about teaching: Janis Haswell and Richard Haswell's "Gendership and the Miswriting of Students." It's clear from the authors' diverse Works Cited list and their use of the books and articles listed there that this writing project required wide reading and that it promoted reflective integration of materials from many sources. The classroom (broadly speaking) was one of those sources, since students, how they write, and how their writing is read by others are at the center of the authors' attention. Haswell and Haswell came to a clearer and deeper understanding of the complex issues involved in "the way peer critique and teacher critique are affected by the writer's sex" because they studied and wrote about their own students (225). It seems just as clear that their efforts to write about their research (research based on background sources, as well as research involving writers and readers) helped Haswell and Haswell become more sophisticated teachers of writing.

Of course, "Gendership and the Miswriting of Students" is not a journal entry that the authors wrote privately to explore their subject or to improve their teaching. Rather, the article (1) reports on their study and what they learned from it; (2) presents ideas individual teachers might use to improve their work with student writers; (3) advocates that the field of composition studies "make gendership part of our agenda" in order to "return a part of the writer, a vital part which standard professional practices of critique have excluded"; and (4) argues implicitly that the authors' insights are accurate and their recommendations useful (250). So the article illustrates the way that writing about teaching reflects the faculty member's *desire to influence* the profession—for instance, by

- Summarizing and synthesizing scholarship so readers understand a complex subject more clearly—the "scholarship of integration" (see Boyer 18-21)

- Bringing composition scholarship to bear on the daily work of writing teachers in order to improve teaching through what Arthur Applebee once called a "healthy exploration of what particular research results mean in the complex context of classrooms that differ in student populations, in goals, and in conditions of instruction" (222)

- Explaining an instructional strategy found to be effective in addressing a common teaching challenge—the "how-to" article, of course, and possibly "scholarship of application" (see Boyer 21-23)

- Questioning traditional approaches or proposing new directions for the profession

These four intentions, often working together in various combinations, motivate most authors of articles about teaching writing, and I think you will find it useful to keep them in mind as you develop your own articles. But keep in mind, too, that such audience-oriented intentions—clarifying complex research *for others*, and the like—do not work in isolation. While writing for publication, you will be *learning* (partly from articles others wrote), even as you develop your insights and try to make them useful for readers—including authors who may, in turn, build on your work in their publications.

Writing, John Gage believes, "brings one face to face" with the human responsibilities "to clarify and structure one's ideas" and "to continue to inquire and argue, *toward* the truth, as we are able to discover it through the shared means of discourse, even while knowing that the whole truth will always be beyond our means" (732-33). The fact that you are reading this essay shows that you are interested in assuming those responsibilities. And I hope you'll find the following suggestions helpful as you join our field's continuing conversations by writing articles about composition and its teaching.

Strategies

I wish I could assure your smooth entry into that conversation by giving you ten tips for publishing articles about the teaching of writing. I can't, of course, since professional publication is no more a matter of formulas or rules than is any other kind of writing. But in the next few pages, I will try to sketch a few attitudes and work habits that have been useful for me and other writers I know.

Work at Being a Teacher-Scholar

Your internal job-description—the image you have of yourself as a faculty member—has a lot to say about your work as a writer. Meeting classes, conferencing with students (face to face or electronically), and commenting on papers can absorb so much enthusiasm, energy, and time that none are left over for scholarship or for writing—and, of course, the details and pressures of writing program administration can do the same thing. On the other hand, esoteric scholarly projects (made possible, perhaps, by "releases" from teaching) can dominate attention and time so that little of either is left for teaching and students, let alone for writing about teaching or students. But if you work at being a publishing teacher-scholar (or *scholar*-teacher, if you prefer) for whom both composition scholarship and good teaching are important, you may discover article ideas fairly often as you organize courses, read scholarly articles, prepare syllabi, listen to conference papers, and talk with students about their writing. The key, here, is to stay alert for "contact" points such as the following:

- Your experiences teaching writing classes

- Articles and books you read and papers you hear at professional meetings

- Your own scholarly projects

- Your own practices, frustrations, and successes as a writer

- The writing practices, frustrations, and successes of students in your classes

For instance, while listening to a presentation at the CCCC convention, you may recall an experience from a recent class that serves as a perfect example for the speaker's thesis. Talking with a student one morning, you may find yourself drawing on an *RTE* article you just read to help the student work through a frustrating block with an assignment. Or you may notice—as I have many times over the years—useful contact points in your own experiences as a writer, in your reading of other writers for recreation or research, and in your composition classes.[4] In each of these situations, you are extrapolating "from the research to classroom contexts," an important way for scholarly activity to improve the teaching of writing (Applebee 223). It's serendipitous and quirky extrapolation, to be sure, not careful "exploration of what particular research results mean in the complex context of classrooms" (Applebee 222). But it may prompt you to begin more careful exploration—wider reading on the subject, perhaps, or a classroom-research project—which, in time, results in an article sharing your insights with other teacher-scholars.

Write for Other Teacher-Scholars

"Between the novelist and his most receptive reader," Ralph Ellison once wrote, "there must exist a body of shared assumptions" (68). The same is true of writing articles in our field. A writing project growing out of your concerns and experiences as a scholar-teacher (or *teacher*-scholar) will probably proceed more smoothly if you imagine that your audience is made up of women and men with similar concerns and experiences. In writing this essay, for instance, I have *not* imagined readers who believe that publishing wastes faculty time and drives up the cost of higher education. Nor have I imagined an audience made up of winners of the Richard Braddock Memorial Award, the James Britton Award, the James L. Kinneavy Award, or *TETYC*'s Best Article of the Year Award. Instead, I have written for those who want to publish articles that may compete for such awards in the future.

Some years ago, Carol Berkenkotter found that audience works as a touchstone against which writers test their rhetorical, organizational, and stylistic decisions *while* they draft, and Duane Roen and R.J. Wiley found that audience considerations had greater impact during later *revision* of drafts. Whichever way audience awareness influences your writing (maybe both ways), it's a good idea to let your sense of audience work for you—by testing the rhetorical, organizational, and stylistic decisions you make while you write against an imagined audience likely to be interested in reading about the teaching of writing.

Such an audience is not limited to university and college faculty in composition studies; indeed, composition studies can be viewed as a K-16 enterprise (as it is, for instance, in the membership policies of the Indiana Teachers of Writing). Many students in September's first-year college writing courses were May's high school seniors. College and university composition specialists often teach courses taken by undergraduates preparing to be high school and elementary teachers. And composition specialists frequently work with school teachers in regional writing projects, staff development programs, and collaborative efforts in literacy development and classroom research. If you want to address this broader audience, you may find a larger "market" than you imagined for articles about the teaching of writing. For instance, *English Journal*, NCTE's secondary-level journal, has a circulation of sixty-four thousand, five times that of *CCC*, and NCTE's elementary school journal *Language Arts* has twenty-five thousand subscribers. And all across the country, the journals of NCTE's state affiliates—*Arizona English Bulletin*, *The English Record* (New York), *Illinois English Bulletin*, *Virginia English Bulletin*, and many others—are interested in solid and practical submissions about composition and its teaching.

Write Conference Papers

Every year, the program chairs of numerous professional conferences are eager to review proposals dealing with the teaching of writing from the perspective of research, or theory, or what to do in class on Monday. Some conferences are well-known meetings of national organizations (CCCC, NCTE, Rhetoric Society of America, Writing Centers Association, College English Association, College Language Association, and the like). Some are national meetings sponsored by university departments (among them, the Wyoming and Penn State summer conferences). Some conferences are regional (the two-year college regionals, for instance, or regional writing center association meetings), and others (like the spring or fall meetings of the many NCTE affiliates) occur at the local or state levels. Most of these conferences solicit proposals because they *need* papers—particularly those that fit conference themes—and most of them have a fairly generous acceptance rate compared to journals. (Even the CCCC annual meeting, one of the most competitive conferences in all of English studies, has an acceptance rate of approximately forty percent—much different from the five to ten percent acceptance rate of *CCC*.) So it is a good strategy to skim the meeting calendars published in *PMLA* and *The Chronicle of Higher Education* and to pay attention to flyers, e-mail notices, and journal announcements, looking for conferences or special themes that mesh with article ideas you've had (even the vague ones you've filed away until later).

Finding such a conference can stimulate you to start working toward its submission deadline. And the brevity of reading texts for conference presentations (a twenty-minute paper shouldn't exceed eight double-spaced pages) means that you probably can finish this sort of writing project even if your schedule is crowded with teaching and family commitments. In addition, this sort of project can help strengthen your writing in several ways. To begin with, it helps you anticipate the needs of an audience that can't pause to reread confusing sentences or sort through tangled logic. It requires you to write clearly, with active verbs, compact sentences, explicit transitions, and short quotations (you may want to use overheads or handouts for long quotes and examples). If my experience as a writer and editor is any indication, published articles developed from conference papers may have greater clarity, impact, and flair than essays written with only an audience of readers in mind. In addition, delivering a conference paper can also help your writing. Your audience's body language and expressions will let you gauge the clarity and persuasiveness of your paper. Encouraging nods or puzzled looks may trigger ad lib deletions, expansions, or restatements that you remember and use in later revision. Also, the comments people make about your talk—during a formal question-and-answer period or in a hall or over coffee later—may prove helpful if you decide to revise it for publication.

Bringing you to the point that you have a draft you can consider revising is yet another benefit of writing conference papers. Eight pages setting forth a few generalizations or suggestions based on background reading and/or classroom observations bring you a long way past the "beginning" of an article. Your conference paper may, with only some finetuning, be almost ready for submission to a journal. Or it may be a good start toward a longer article, or it may be the basis of an informed query letter about your project's fit with an editor's plans. At the very least, the conference paper, your work preparing it, and your audience's responses to it give you a good perspective from which to consider future publishing possibilities.

Develop a Good Journal Sense

Probably the advice most frequently given by editors—and disregarded by unsuccessful writers—is that authors need to understand the editorial policies of journals and to submit only manuscripts that fit these policies. This advice is particularly important if you are interested in writing articles about the teaching of writing. Among the journals in our field, editorial policies range widely concerning such issues as the following:

- The proportion of "theory and research" to "application" in submissions

- The proportion of background material (needed for non-specialist readers) to original work in submissions

- Whether pedagogy should be treated explicitly or left for well-informed readers to infer from the research or theory presented in the article

- Whether the journal deals chiefly with college-level matters or a broader sense of composition studies

- Whether "how-to" or "teaching-tip" submissions are welcome

- Whether there should be many or few sources, how formally they should be cited, and in what citation form

Given the large and growing number of composition journals, it's not easy to sort through such editorial policy issues to find those that *may* be interested in the article you're preparing to write.

For purposes of illustration, let's assume that you have been so intrigued by Haswell and Haswell's "Gendership and the Miswriting of Students" that you decide to use one of your writing classes to test the authors' insights and to develop specific teaching strategies. It's now the end of the semester, and you think you have the experience—recorded in a log you kept and illustrated by files of teaching materials, student papers, and the like—to develop an article that other teachers will find valuable (and that the personnel committee in your department will consider a solid addition to your professional record). At this point, even as you are beginning to write, you'll want to spend some time consulting published guides to journals in composition studies.[5]

Flipping through such a guide, you will probably sense that *Research on the Teaching of English*—which publishes "original research on the relationships between language teaching and language learning"—isn't as promising a target-journal for your project as *The Writing Instructor*, with its emphasis on "the interaction of theory and practice in the composition classroom," or the *Journal of Teaching Writing*, which focuses "on the relationship of writing theory and practice" and has a "teacher/researcher emphasis" (Anson and Maylath 180, 186, 172). If you are working in the context of a developmental course, the *Journal of Basic Writing* may seem a natural place to submit your project, but your project may also fit *Teaching English in the Two-Year College*, which expresses an interest in "articles and reviews on trends in teaching composition, especially in freshman and sophomore courses," even if your article does not provide explicit "tips for two-year college instructors" (Anson and Maylath 182-83). Similarly, unless you teach in Minnesota or Texas, the journals of the NCTE affiliates in those states might not come to mind, even though at *Minnesota English Journal* the "primary focus is on college and secondary school rhetoric, composition research, and pedagogy," and even though *English in Texas* puts much "emphasis on theory and the translation of that theory into practice in writing" (Anson and Maylath 176, 166).

The shorthand information in guides to periodicals can help you discover potential target-journals you never knew existed, and these guides can also help you begin to sense how different editors may respond to the article you are trying to write. Such guides, though, may not provide the information you need about such concerns as

- Upcoming theme-issues that might give an advantage to your submission (if it fits a theme) or subject it to even stiffer competition for limited pages (if it doesn't)

- *De facto* themes in recent issues and apparent editorial preferences that might enhance or decrease a journal's interest in your project

- Recent articles to which you might try to link your article in order to increase its fit with the journal

- Current requirements for length, format, citation style, and submission procedures

To obtain this information (and to form such impressions), you will need to consult statements of editorial policy printed in the journals' mastheads, study the author guides that many journals publish periodically or make available through the mail, and *read* the journals to which you want to submit articles.

Naturally, you will need to keep refreshing your journal sense, once you develop it, so that this special kind of audience awareness can be of help as you draft and especially as you revise articles about the teaching of writing. To a large extent, this will happen naturally as you read in preparation for your courses and for future articles. And if you become an active scholar, you are almost certain to have a special source of such updating: the letters of rejection and the editorial suggestions for revision you receive.

Work within Your Personal and Professional Context

You might be tempted to give journal editors undue credit for the frustrations you feel when you receive a letter of rejection or one inviting substantial revision. But much frustration can be reduced before the fact if you try to work within your own personal and professional context. I have in mind, here, factors such as your areas of special expertise and enthusiasm; your teaching load and your administrative and service commitments; your desire to publish; your institution's expectations about faculty research and publication; and your family responsibilities.

These factors (especially the eight-course load I maintained during my first sixteen years as a faculty member) are reflected in my own vita. It contains mainly articles and conference papers, since longer projects never seemed to fit the minimal blocks of time I had for research and writing. And those articles usually dealt with teaching because I considered teaching the heart of our field and because my faculty and administrative duties centered on teaching, curriculum, faculty development and evaluation, and related matters. If I had not felt a strong personal interest in writing, my vita would be much shorter today; if I had needed to teach overload and summer classes every year, it would be shorter still. If my college had given faculty five-course teaching assignments and expected a book in every tenure dossier, my vita would look very different, too. Most importantly, my interest in writing—not to mention my publication record—would have been greatly diminished if I had not found frequent points of contact between my classes and students and the articles and books I was reading.[6]

I have used myself to illustrate some of the ways personal and professional context can influence faculty careers. But the important point for you to consider is the personal and professional context within which *you* work and out of which you will write. What attracted you to composition studies? What are your chief interests within the field? Do you think of yourself as a teacher-scholar or a scholar-teacher—and why? Do you really *want* to write, or do you think publishing is just a requirement of the job? How much (or how little) publishing does your institution expect of faculty? What kind of research and publication does your school require? Can you reserve most weekends and several afternoons and evenings each week for research and writing? Can you devote summers to scholarly projects?

The answers to such questions have much to say about the careers, and feelings of personal satisfaction, of all faculty members. An assistant professor, for instance, may genuinely want to publish (about postcolonial literature, classical rhetoric, portfolio assessment, or whatever) but have so little time—after classes, grading, committee work, summer teaching, child care—that finishing "big" projects is impossible. Regardless of the person's specialty, the issue is much the same: Should I let myself become bitter and frustrated because my book is stalled, or should I shift to article publication? Questions about your personal and professional context, however, take on special significance if you see yourself as a teacher-scholar and you want to publish articles about the teaching of writing. You may genuinely like teaching and want to publish useful how-to articles, for instance, but you may be on the faculty of—or about to sign a contract with—a department that considers only "scholarly" publication for merit pay, tenure, and promotion. If so, you would probably find yourself considering some special issues:

> Can I strengthen the scholarly or research background of my how-to articles so they will count in my personnel reviews? Should I shift to an overtly "scholarly" publishing agenda for now and save how-to ideas for the future? Should I work with department colleagues and committees to help clarify the reciprocal roles of "teaching" and "scholarship" in composition studies? Can I find ways to encourage department discussion about broadening the definition of "scholarship"?

Such discussions are now widespread in American higher education, and some institutions have begun to honor the scholarship of integration and the scholarship of application, rather than expecting all faculty to pursue the scholarship of discovery. Teacher-scholars in composition studies can further this trend through the substance and usefulness of their articles about writing and its teaching.

Notes

[1] In an article in *CCC* Chris Anson and Bruce Maylath present an annotated list of more than one hundred periodicals that publish articles about writing and its teaching. Among the publications open to scholarship related to the teaching of writing are (a) broadly-focused

journals like *College Composition and Communication, College English, Journal of Advanced Composition, Rhetoric Review, Research in the Teaching of English, and Written Communication*; (b) more narrowly-focused journals like *Computers and Composition, Journal of Basic Writing, Language and Learning across the Disciplines, Technical Communication Quarterly, WPA: Writing Program Administration*, and *Writing Center Journal*; (c) compact-article publications like *Composition Chronicle, CEA Forum, Focuses, Teaching English in the Two-Year College, Writing Lab Newsletter, Writing Instructor*, and journals of various NCTE state affiliates; and (d) tradition-bucking publications like *Dialogue: A Journal for Writing Specialists, Radical Teacher, Writing on the Edge*, and the "Burkean Parlor" section of *Rhetoric Review*.

[2]Four books through which this research tradition has evolved are those by Myers, Goswami and Stillman, Daiker and Morenberg, and Ray.

[3]*Scholarship Reconsidered*, the "ADE Statement of Good Practice," and the National Project on Institutional Priorities and Faculty Rewards are but three signs that higher education is rethinking this push toward faculty publication. I explore this development in "Evolving Approaches."

[4]In "Introspection and Observation," I suggest how one's "own writing processes and activities and those of [one's] students" can increase the teacher-scholar's understanding of composition scholarship and improve his or her teaching (39). The article also illustrates how this three-way synergy fostered a number of my own publications.

[5] Since 1986, Chris Anson, sometimes with collaborators, has compiled a series of guides to composition journals, each more complete than the last; I hope he will continue this project. There are several broader guides, new editions of which are published periodically: *Iowa Guide: Scholarly Journals in Mass Communications and Related Fields* (U of Iowa School of Journalism), *MLA Directory of Periodicals*, and *Contributor's Guide to Periodicals in Reading* (International Reading Assoc.).

In the following paragraph, I am using excerpts from editor-provided statements of journal focus that Anson and Maylath include in their 1992 guide to composition journals. By the time this chapter is published, these quotations will be at least four years old, a number of the journals will have new editors, and various editorial policies will have changed. Take the quotes, then, not as sources of information about specific journals, but as illustrations of the fact that reference guides can help you begin to understand the range of editorial concerns in the journals of our field.

[6]For example, "Balancing Theory and Practice in the Training of Writing Teachers," which won the Richard Braddock Award for 1978, grew directly out of a Findlay College class I taught in 1976 for future high school English teachers. In developing the course, I was surprised by how little had been published on the preparation of writing teachers, so when the course went well, I decided to write an article based on the course and its reading list. Over the years that I taught the course, Processes and Teaching of Writing, it continued to be a source of contact points that, as I explain in "Learn, Look Forward, Try Again," led to other articles about composition and its teaching.

Works Cited

AAUP Committee on College and University Teaching, Research, and Publication. "The Work of Faculty: Expectations, Priorities, and Rewards." *Academe* Jan./Feb. 1994: 35-48.

"ADE Statement of Good Practice: Teaching, Evaluation, and Scholarship." *ADE Bulletin* 105 (1993): 43-45.

Anson, Chris M., and Bruce Maylath. "Searching for Journals: A Brief Guide and 100 Sample Species." *Teacher as Writer: Entering the Professional Conversation*. Ed. Karin L. Dahl. Urbana: NCTE, 1992. 150-87.

Applebee, Arthur. "Balancing the Demand for Practical Outcomes." *Research in the Teaching of English* 20 (1986): 221-23.

Berkenkotter, Carol. "Understanding a Writer's Awareness of Audience." *College Composition and Communication* 32 (1981): 388-99.

Boyer, Ernest L. *Scholarship Reconsidered: Priorities of the Professoriate*. Princeton, NJ: Carnegie Foundation for the Advancement of Teaching, 1990.

Brannon, Lil. "Toward a Theory of Composition." *Perspectives on Research and Scholarship in Composition*. Ed. Ben W. McClelland and Timothy R. Donovan. New York: MLA, 1985. 6-25.

Daiker, Donald A., and Max Morenberg, eds. *The Writing Teacher as Researcher: Essays in Theory and Practice of Class-Based Research*. Portsmouth, NH: Boynton, 1990.

Diamond, Robert M. "The Tough Task of Reforming the Faculty-Rewards System." *Chronicle of Higher Education* 11 May 1994: B1-3.

Elbow, Peter. *Writing with Power*. New York: Oxford UP, 1981.

Ellison, Ralph. "Society, Morality, and the Novel." *The Living Novel*. Ed. Granville Hicks. New York: Collier, 1962. 65-97.

Gage, John. "Why Write?" *Rhetoric: Concepts, Definitions, Boundaries*. Ed. William Covino and David Jolliffe. Boston: Allyn, 1995. 715-33.

Gebhardt, Richard C. "Evolving Approaches to Scholarship, Promotion, and Tenure in Composition Studies." *Scholarship and Academic Advancement in Composition Studies*. Ed. Richard C. Gebhardt and Barbara Genelle Smith Gebhardt. Hillsdale, NJ: Erlbaum (forthcoming).

——. "Introspection and Observation for Insight and Instruction in the Processes of Writing." *The Writing Teacher as Researcher*. Daiker and Morenberg 38-51.

——. "Learn, Look Forward, Try Again: Productive Responses to Publishing Rejections." *Teaching English in the Two-Year College* 22 (1995): 61-64.

Goswami, Dixie, and Peter R. Stillman, eds. *Reclaiming the Classroom: Teacher Research as an Agency for Change*. Upper Montclair, NJ: Boynton, 1987.

Haswell, Janis, and Richard H. Haswell. "Gendership and the Miswriting of Students." *College Composition and Communication* 46 (1995): 223-54.

Kinneavy, James L. "Contemporary Rhetoric." *The Present State of Scholarship in Historical and Contemporary Rhetoric*. Rev. ed. Ed. Winifred Bryan Horner. Columbia: U of Missouri P, 1990. 186-246.

Lacey, Paul A. "Encouraging and Evaluating Scholarship for the College Teacher." *Excellent Teaching in a Changing Academy*. Ed. Feroza Jussawalla. San Francisco: Jossey, 1990. 91-100.

Lindemann, Erika, and Gary Tate, eds. *An Introduction to Composition Studies*. New York: Oxford UP, 1991. v-vi.

Myers, Miles. *The Teacher-Researcher: How to Study Writing in the Classroom*. Urbana: NCTE, 1985.

Ray, Ruth E. *The Practice of Theory: Teacher Research in Composition*. Urbana: NCTE, 1993.

Roen, Duane, and R.J. Wiley. "The Effects of Audience Awareness on Drafting and Revising." *Research in the Teaching of English* 22 (1988): 75-88.

"Report of the Commission on Writing and Literature." *Profession 88* New York, MLA, 1988. 70-76.

Weimer, Maryellen. "The Disciplinary Journals on Pedagogy." *Change* Nov./Dec. 1993: 44-51.

Person, Position, Style

JOSEPH HARRIS

It is perhaps not surprising that as composition becomes increasingly disciplined as a field of study anxieties should begin to surface about the roles—writer, teacher, critic, theorist, scholar—that we are offered to play within it. One pleasure of working at the margins of the academy is that what gets done and said there is often less regulated (if only because less prized), and so for decades writers on composition in journals like *CCC* and *College English* have had fair leeway to cultivate a tone more personal than scholarly, more given to advice than criticism, more prone to anecdote than argument. That is no longer quite the case. There are now books and articles to read and cite, canonical figures to contend with, in writing about almost any aspect of composition theory or teaching. We have become more professionalized, more scrupulous, more learned, more self-critical—and thus also more like our colleagues in other disciplines. While this new respectability is of course welcome, it has also been somewhat unsettling for those in composition (and I count myself among them) who have defined their work in some large part *against* the image of the senior professor, the disciplinary specialist, having instead been attracted more to the role of the teacher or writer or intellectual. Or to put it another way, the members of a field long associated (both in the classroom and out) with the writing of personal essays now find themselves answering a demand for research articles.

Signs of this shift and the unease it has provoked are rife: Donald McQuade takes the occasion of his chair's address to the CCCC national meeting to speak of the deaths of his mother and a student; Nancy Sommers tells of her realization in a supermarket parking lot of the need to free herself from the intellectual grip of imposing theorists; Lynn Bloom recounts the details of an attempted rape to lend force to her comments on the position of women in the profession. There is not merely an interplay of the personal and public in such writings, there is a kind of insistence on the personal, on locating what one has to say in the details (whether tragic or banal) of one's life. And beneath this insistence, I think, lurks a worry about the loss of self to profession, of the personal vanishing if it is not asserted. And so, for instance, when in 1988 Jane Tompkins told of her conversion from a performance-based style of teaching to a classroom in which she tries to share authority with students, recycling many of the insights of writing teachers from Britton to Bruffee to Elbow without citation, instead offering up anecdotes about a bad class and a hallway conversation as the origins of her new views on teaching, she was less often criticized for not having done her homework than lauded for the supposed risks she took in telling such a personal story. A few years later Peter Elbow valorized the personal in a similar way when he titled his side of a well-known debate with David Bartholomae, "Being A Writer *vs.* Being An Academic." Elbow complicates this distinction somewhat in his writings, many others do not. And it is an ironic sign of the intensity of feeling that permeates recent talk about the personal that Bartholomae, who as chair of CCCC in 1988 had argued eloquently *against* moves to turn composition studies into a scholarly discipline, is now himself routinely figured as a leading advocate of academic writing. A reason for this confusion, I believe, is that Bartholomae speaks against specialization not in the name of personal writing but of a more free-wheeling style of intellectual inquiry. Such a move is evidently hard for many to read in a field that now expects its practitioners to come out either "for" or "against" the personal in academic work.

"By adding one more confusion, we may add the element that brings clarity" (10). Or so says Saint Burke, and I invoke his guidance here, for I need in the next few pages to follow what may seem diverging lines of thought. I will begin by admitting to some strong misgivings about the recent eagerness of many academics to reveal details from their personal lives in their scholarly writings. But I also feel that such autobiographical moves can sometimes be used to powerful effect, and indeed I want to go on to argue that there are ways in which academic work *should* be personal. To do so I need to distinguish three competing aspects of the personal: the first has to do with content, with the relaying of autobiographical information about the *person* writing; the second with the *position* an author takes toward his or her material; and the third with how a writer creates a sense of voice or presence through his or her prose *style*. What I will try to show is how an overriding concern with the first form of personal writing, with autobiography, has in recent years often deflected interest from what seem to me more pressing questions (at least for critical or academic writers) of position and style.

Person

In a 1985 *College English* essay, "Style as Politics," Pamela Annas describes a course, Writing as Women, in which she tries to show students "not only the importance but the *primacy* of grounding one's conclusions in personal experience" (365; emphasis added). Annas tries to help women students overcome blocks in writing through asking them to experiment with prose whose "arguments [are based] at least as much on lived personal experience as on more conventional sources of information" (369). To illustrate the sort of writing she is after, Annas contrasts the reluctance of the economist Harry Braverman to draw explicitly on his own experiences as a skilled artisan in drafting his masterwork, *Labor and Monopoly Capital,* with the readiness of Robin Lakoff to do so in her brief and spirited book, *Language and Women's Place.* The comparison is telling in ways that Annas perhaps does not intend and is worth considering in some detail.

Annas quotes from the introductions of both books. In the passage she reprints from *Monopoly and Labor Capital,* Braverman begins by speaking of the influence that his years of work as a coppersmith have had on his writing. He then goes on to say:

> But while this occupational . . . background has been useful, I must emphasize that nothing in this book relies on personal experience or reminiscences, and that I have in the formal sense included almost no factual materials for which I could not give a reference which can be checked independently by the reader, as is proper in any scientific work. (qtd. in Annas 363)

In contrast, after reviewing a number of ways of obtaining linguistic data, Robin Lakoff asserts more simply and militantly that

> If we are to have a good sample of data to analyze, this will have to be elicited artificially from someone; I submit that I am as good an artificial source of data as anyone.
> (qtd. in Annas 364)

Annas praises what she calls the "pugnacious" quality of Lakoff's willingness to use her own speech as data, while she regrets that Braverman "capitulates and gives up personal experience" (364). What seems implied is that *Labor and Monopoly Capital* would somehow have been a better book if only Braverman had lightened up a little, told us more about his own on-the-job routines and epiphanies. But such a reading glosses over how Braverman's scrupulous reticence makes sure that his study, which traces the deskilling of the workforce over the last one hundred years by mass industry, cannot be dismissed as the result of a "sentimental attachment to the outworn conditions of now archaic modes of labor" (6); it also discounts the way in which Braverman demonstrates a passionate commitment to his subject through the range of his reading and the clarity and care of his argument. Indeed, what Annas sees as a negative shying away from experience can be viewed instead as an attempt by Braverman to make his work as open to criticism and response as possible, to make sure that his argument rests only on assertions that "can be checked independently by the reader." Her reading thus misses how a writer can use discretion rather than disclosure to forge a personal voice. As Braverman himself remarks in a passage from his introduction that Annas does not quote,

> I had the opportunity of seeing at first hand . . . how the worker, systematically robbed of a craft heritage, is given little or nothing to take its place. Like all craftsmen, even the most inarticulate, I always resented this, and as I reread these pages, I find in them a sense not only of social outrage . . . but also perhaps of personal affront. (6)

Braverman here depicts the personal as something a reader might "sense" in his phrasings rather than have rendered directly in anecdotes. But Annas simply sees Braverman as trapped in an abstract masculine style to which she wants to pose a feminist alternative. In her blunt valuing of Lakoff's use of "intuition, introspection, and her own experience as data," she argues for the autobiographical as less an option than a stylistic *sine qua non* (364).

This linking of personal writing with feminism has since been a popular if troubled move. It's easy enough to see the appeal of the local and particular, of private feeling and domestic detail, as a response to the magisterial *we* invoked by so many previous (male) critics. But one might also argue that the freedom to speak or write in public about one's private life and feelings has until recently been for the most part the perquisite of men: Montaigne, Addison, DeQuincey, Orwell, E.B. White, Lewis Thomas. (Or in composition: Rodriguez, Rose, Villanueva.) To argue that women should also write from personal experience, then, would seem less to call for a new discourse than to claim an older belletristic one—which should in turn raise some questions about the rumored subversive effects of autobiography.

In "Me and My Shadow," for instance, Jane Tompkins writes that she is "tired of the conventions that keep discussion of epistemology, or James Joyce, segregated from meditations on what is happening outside my window or inside my heart" (122-23). Her phrasing here, with its faint echo of the lines beginning Woolf's "Death of a Moth," accurately suggests the tone of her essay. Tompkins writes of how she likes the term *glissade* and how she fears becoming trapped in the "straightjacket" of academic discourse; she makes fun of some bad scholastic prose (and, actually, some not-so-bad prose by Harold Bloom); and she admits to being "hooked by" an essay that promises to theorize "erotic domination" as it "comes to light at the porno newsstands" (128-34). But this cataloging of enthusiasms and anxieties has an ironic effect; rather than revealing a previously hidden or private self, Tompkins ends up offering a portrait of a familiar type: the postmodern literary intellectual, drawn at once to the sexy, the popular, and the theoretical. In trying to break free of one kind of writing (the formal academic article) she uncritically adopts the conventions of another (the informal essay).

This is an important if difficult (because somewhat impolitic) point to make. The advocates of personal academic writing tend to cast it as a revolt against tradition and an embrace of the idiosyncratic. And to the degree that such writing gives us new ideas to think with, I value it too. But most uses of autobiography in scholarly work are in fact quite predictable. They tend to draw on a familiar repertoire of images and events—a view from a window, a conversation with a child, a chance meeting by the coffee machine, an old photograph, a bad class, a remarkable student—and to make a limited set of points: the personal is political, the importance of teaching, the need to live with uncertainty, the need to connect theory to practice, stories are how we make sense of the world. And so, when in "Me and My Shadow" Tompkins writes that she no longer wants to separate in her prose "the voice of a critic" from "the voice of a person who wants to write about her feelings" (122), at one level my response is: Well, who does? But at another level I want to say something like: When I go to my dentist or car mechanic, I don't much care how they feel about their work; I just want them to do a job for me and do it well. Similarly, when I read an academic article, I look for a way of rethinking my work, not for a glimpse into the life of its author.

It is often argued in composition that teachers should do the same sorts of personal writing they frequently assign to students. (Indeed, this is a central tenet of the National Writing Project.) But this confuses two very different discursive situations. If a goal of teaching writing is to suggest something of the complexity of the relationship between language and experience, then it makes good sense to ask students to write autobiographical pieces and to reflect on the problems and successes they have had in representing their actions and feelings with words. The focus in a writing classroom is placed appropriately on the needs of the *author*, in large part because students are paying us to do a job for them: to read their work and teach them how to do it better. But it is the *reader* who has usually paid to attend an academic conference or subscribe to a journal and who thus cannot be expected to indulge his or her fellow professionals in quite the same way. (Much as students cannot be expected to applaud a teacher who seems more interested in his own work than theirs.) And so the briskness, clarity, and self-effacement of classic academic prose can be seen not simply as a surrender to the logic of patriarchy but also as a kind of deference, as a desire not to impose too much on one's readers.

In a recent essay on "The Nervous System," Richard E. Miller notes the "bodily response—the sense of agitation and impatience, the jumping knee, the look at the watch, at the phony chandeliers, at the ground," when a speaker at a conference flouts this customary deference and asks the audience instead to attend to his own feelings or experiences (20). Miller argues that what we see on such occasions is

> the performance of a cultural drama that centers on the form and function of academic work. To present a paper, to write an article, to teach a class is to assume, whether one wants to or not, a role in which one instructs others in how to see and manipulate the world. . . . To be present in any of these contexts and to receive, instead of a demonstration of the speaker's mastery, a request to acknowledge the speaker's presence, an invitation to focus on the minutiae of the speaker's life, a petition to witness a personal declaration of independence, is to be placed (some might say forced) into another role entirely. (20)

I would again argue that there is an economic as well as psychological aspect to this discomfort and anger—that one wants to get what one has paid for. (How Lacan managed to collect for his notorious "short sessions" is beyond me.) Though there is of course an economic imperative to the other side of the argument too. As Miller points out, academics often distance themselves from openly personal discourse as a way of laying claim to a seemingly more neutral form of professional expertise. But still there seems something peculiar about downplaying a sense of "mastery" through calling attention to one's self. Along with the rise of personal critical writing has come a new vogue for interviews with (and sometimes exposés of) leading academics. We need to question how such an interest in the lives and opinions of well-known colleagues is symptomatic of the fascination with celebrity that permeates our culture. In the age of *People, Rikki Lake,* and *Lingua Franca,* the personal does not always seem subversive.

And yet it remains clear that there are points and cases that can only be made through the telling of stories. Mike Rose grounds his criticisms of remedial education by describing how he languished as a boy in the "vocational track" of junior high; Victor Villanueva draws on his frustrations in writing for college as a way of arguing for contrastive cultural rhetorics; Min-Zhan Lu dramatizes her theory of writing as conflict in a story of her girlhood struggles in the classrooms of Maoist China. And in a field like composition, which has long been concerned, in the words of William Coles, with "the actual doing, on how a given theory of rhetoric or approach to the teaching of writing feels as an action," writers will inevitably get tangled up in accounts of teachers and students and classrooms and conversations that are nearly impossible to cite or document in conventional ways (3). The key question is thus not *if* a writer draws on personal experience but *how*. Does the move to autobiography seem a kind of mere indulgence or coloration? Or does the use of the personal clarify the position a writer is taking?

Position

In an interview with Gary Olson, Clifford Geertz speaks of the need for critics and intellectuals to move past producing "books which are written from the moon—the view from nowhere," and to learn instead "how to situate ourselves within the text" as writers. But this is not at all the same, Geertz immediately notes, as writing in a "confessional" mode: "It's not about what I was feeling or something of that sort; it's trying to describe the work I've been doing with myself in the picture" (262). Such a distinction between confessional and *situated* forms of writing is key to understanding how academic work needs to be personal. For Geertz points to how writers can make themselves present in their texts not only through autobiography but also through trying to state what draws them to the subject or issue at hand, to be as clear as possible about the sort of role, if any, that they have played in the events they are discussing, and to define what they see as being at stake for both themselves and others in that discussion.

At times this positioning requires talk about the author. In "Beyond the Personal: Theorizing a Politics of Location in Composition Research," Gesa Kirsch and Joy Ritchie show how the course of interviews are often directed not simply by the questions asked but also *by who the interviewer is*—by the ways in which the gender, race, class, and professional standing of interviewer and subject shape their interactions. The same is clearly true for teaching and learning; writing about a class one has taught is quite different from writing about a class one has observed or has perhaps been a student in. In "Conventions, Conversations, and the Writer," for instance, Carol Berkenkotter, Thomas Huckin, and John Ackerman traced the progress of a student they called "Nate" as he shifted from a highly expressivist M.A. program in composition teaching to a more research-oriented Ph.D. program in rhetoric. After a few beginning hesitancies, Nate is shown as successfully adopting the conventions and attitudes of his new research community, and even as beginning to write "articles for publication with some of his mentor-teachers" (40). The authors base their hopeful analysis of Nate's training with both interviews and close readings of his graduate school writings. What they do not mention, though, is that "Nate" was in fact one of the three authors of this article, while the other two were among his "teacher-mentors." (This fact was revealed several years later in a piece by Berkenkotter.) Knowing this, it seems to me, allows one to read the hopeful story of intellectual growth and assimilation that the authors offer with a kind of informed skepticism. There are strong personal reasons, it turns out, for the authors to want to view Nate's training in a positive light. Learning who "Nate" in fact was doesn't in itself contradict their view, but it does raise questions that they might have dealt with more powerfully and appropriately right from the start. Here then is a case of writers failing to announce their own position in the story they are telling.

More often, though, we get too much of the author and too little of the scene. For instance, in "Resisting the Faith," Nancy Welch offers a harsh criticism of a well-known teacher-training program in composition at what she calls University B, arguing that it offers prospective teachers only a simple choice between conversion to or resistance against a single dogmatic method of teaching writing. This would be a deeply troubling accusation if true, but one that merits some suspicion, since Welch relies entirely on her own memory of classes and conversations during a year at University B to make her argument. At no point in her article does she directly quote the faculty of University B speaking in their own words—even though one might assume that she had copies of their program and course materials, written comments on student essays, and the like. Rather than dealing with such materials, with texts that, to recall once more the words of Harry Braverman, "can be checked independently by the reader," Welch offers only her own impressionistic memories of conversations and encounters she had with teachers and students at University B, weaving these into a story that she concedes "shares more in common with fiction than ethnography" (388).

One can perhaps applaud Welch for admitting to the problematic status of her discourse, as a fiction that is somehow meant to have the force of fact, since so much writing about the classroom is equally anecdotal but much less self-aware. And, certainly, in writing about teaching it can be frustratingly hard to move beyond the level of staffroom gossip—to get past one's own version of what happened and why, to offer a story which does not cast its teller as either hero or sympathetic victim. What one needs, then, is to somehow move beyond personal memory and anecdote, to *textualize* the scene of teaching in ways that allow for competing readings of it. When all we are given is a writer's own account of what went on in a certain class, what that writer has to say about it is not really available *as a position*, as one possible reading of a text among others. But even though teaching is in many ways a curiously private activity (we don't often get to see what goes on behind the closed doors of our colleagues' classrooms and we rarely get to hear directly from their students), the classroom is also a site through which many varied texts circulate: published books and articles, syllabi, assignments, student writings and notes, teacher comments, evaluation forms, and so on. Producing a *situated* account of teaching may thus often turn out to have less to do with offering information about oneself than with creating a nuanced and thick description of the scene of one's work.

And, indeed, writers can sometimes do this work of positioning, of putting themselves in the picture, with little or no recourse to autobiography at all. Cheryl Glenn begins her recent and quite scholarly piece on "sex, lies, and manuscript," for instance, with an anecdote about how, when she received her Ph.D., a friend presented her with a nineteenth-century print showing Aspasia, one of the few known women rhetors in classical Greece, lying beside the Athenian statesman Alcibiades. But Glenn is less interested in relaying the details of this personal story than in pointing to the ways the print pictures Aspasia, whom she goes on to show as a remarkable intellectual in her own right, as a mere handmaiden to the male Alcibiades—and then to use this illustration as a telling instance of how women have been routinely effaced in most views of rhetoric. Glenn thus offers us a way of quite literally changing our perspective on the field, of reconsidering what our history might look like if we were to take into serious account not only Aspasia but the work of other women in rhetoric, both classical and modern. Similarly, in "Importing Composition," Mary Muchiri, Nshindi Mulamba, Greg Myers, and Deoscorous Ndoloi discuss what happens when composition theory is read not by people working in American colleges and universities (which are, of course, almost the only places in the world where something called "composition" is formally taught) but by scholars elsewhere. This sort of literal repositioning or relocation of familiar work results in what seem to me both some surprising elaborations of composition theory and striking insights into its local origins in American classrooms. And the recent arguments among theorists of basic writing teachers over the legacy of Mina Shaughnessy have come about, at least in part, as the result of a similar physical repositioning, as her writings are increasingly read by teachers working in different locales and with different sorts of students—that is, by people who are less trying to continue Shaughnessy's work than to remake or adapt it. But this debate is also the result of an intellectual repositioning, as Shaughnessy's dream of a common language is now subjected to the critique of teachers with a strong grasp of poststructuralist theory.

What all this work shares is a kind of disciplined subjectivity, a willingness to acknowledge one's own position within the profession and culture as a driving force behind (and also a limit on) what one has to argue. It is in this sense that I believe academic writing most needs to be personal. But one also hopes for more than just discipline. In an endnote to their article on "Beyond the Personal," Kirsch and Ritchie somewhat bravely remark that they "recognize the irony of the text we have produced: a relatively univocal, coherent text that argues for multivocal writing. . . . We can imagine more experimental and innovative ways of writing" (27). Well, yes. As teachers of writing, we ought to aim in our own prose for the same kind of clarity, precision, grace, and wit that we urge our students to strive for. The work of academic writers often needs to be complex and allusive, but that is not at all the same as prose that is needlessly dense or plodding. An article on the teaching of writing should itself be well written.

Style
In the end it is the *doing* that counts. I have long been intrigued by how many people working in composition manage to be at once remarkably attuned to nuances of phrasing and structure in the writings of others and remarkably unconcerned with the shape and sound of their own sentences. The impulse to legislate a certain style or register for academic prose—whether formal or personal, succinct or allusive, magisterial or intimate—is an attempt to do away with the problem of writing, with the need for a writer to find or invent for him or herself the particular form that a certain line of thought requires, to forge his or her own voice and style. And so I want to close here not by offering yet more advice about style but simply by urging an attentiveness to academic writing *as writing*. The answer to stale academic prose is not the personal essay but better academic prose—writing that offers the pleasures of craft, surprise, commitment, generosity, while also getting a certain kind of job done. Even though he refused to write of his own experiences, when Harry Braverman reread *Labor and Monopoly Capital* he still found in its pages "a sense of outrage." What similar sense, what intensity, what affect colors our own critical and intellectual work? The question to ask is not what we tell each other of our private lives but what we hear of each other in our turns of thought and phrasing.

Works Cited

Annas, Pamela. "Style as Politics: A Feminist Approach to the Teaching of Writing." *College English* 47 (1985): 360-70.

Bartholomae, David. "Freshman English, Composition, and CCCC." *College Composition and Communication* 40 (1989): 38-50.

Berkenkotter, Carol. "Paradigm Debates, Turf Wars, and the Conduct of Sociocognitive Inquiry in Composition." *College Composition and Communication* 42 (1991): 151-69.

Berkenkotter, Carol, Thomas N. Huckin, and John Ackerman. "Conventions, Conversations, and the Writer: Case Study of a Student in a Rhetoric Ph.D. Program." *Research in the Teaching of English* 22 (1988): 9-44.

Braverman, Harry. *Labor and Monopoly Capital: The Degradation of Work in the Twentieth Century*. New York: Monthly Review, 1974.

Bloom, Lynn Z. "Teaching College English as a Woman." *College English* 54 (1992): 818-25.

Burke, Kenneth. *A Rhetoric of Motives*. 1950. Berkeley: U of California P, 1969.

Coles, William E. *The Plural I*. New York: Holt, 1978.

Elbow, Peter. "Being a Writer vs. Being an Academic." *College Composition and Communication* 46 (1995): 72-83.

Glenn, Cheryl. "Sex, Lies, and Manuscript: Refiguring Aspasia in the History of Rhetoric." *College Composition and Communication* 45 (1994): 180-99.

Kirsch, Gesa E., and Joy S. Ritchie. "Beyond the Personal: Theorizing a Politics of Location in Research in Composition." *College Composition and Communication* 46 (1995): 7-29.

Lu, Min-Zhan. "From Silence to Words: Writing as Struggle." *College English* 49 (1987): 437-48.

McQuade, Donald. "Living In—and On—the Margins." *College Composition and Communication* 43 (1992): 11-22.

Miller, Richard E. "The Nervous System." *College English*, forthcoming 1995.

Muchiri, Mary N., Nshindi G. Mulamba, Greg Myers, and Deoscorous B. Ndoloi. "Importing Composition: Teaching and Researching Academic Writing Beyond North America." *College Composition and Communication* 46 (1995): 175-98.

Olson, Gary A. "The Social Scientist as Author: Clifford Geertz on Ethnography and Social Construction." *JAC* 11 (1991): 245-68.

Rose, Mike. *Lives on the Boundary*. New York: Free, 1989.

Sommers, Nancy. "Between the Drafts." *College Composition and Communication* 43 (1992): 23-31.

Tompkins, Jane. "Me and My Shadow." *New Literary History* 19 (1987): 169-78. Rpt. in *Gender and Theory: Dialogues on Feminist Criticism*. Ed. Linda Kauffman. New York: Blackwell, 1989. 121-39.

———. "Pedagogy of the Distressed." *College English* 52 (1990): 653-60.

Villanueva, Victor. *Bootstraps: From an American Academic of Color*. Urbana: NCTE, 1993.

Welch, Nancy. "Resisting the Faith: Conversion, Resistance, and the Training of Teachers." *College English* 55 (1993): 387-401.

Gender and Publishing Scholarship in Rhetoric and Composition

THERESA ENOS

Because women comprise the majority in rhetoric and composition, the field is often called a "feminized field." Disciplines where women excel—and are acknowledged—are devalued. A field where women are recognized as being highly competent and where they make up the majority generally has lower prestige, is taken less seriously, and is devalued because its work is seen as "women's work." Women's work is characterized by a disproportionate number of women workers (as in the academy's writing programs); it is service oriented (like the teaching of writing in the classrooms of institutions of higher education); it pays less than "men's work" (traditional forms of scholarship); and it is devalued (compared to males, females get fewer promotions and less pay). Thus, males as well as females in a feminized field suffer from salary compression and horizontal rather than upward "promotions."

Indeed, research shows that women are now the majority of tenure-track writing faculty in higher education. If we consider all college writing faculty (eighty percent of our part-time teachers and lecturers are female), we've had a majority of women for some time. And we know that 1987 was the watershed year for female rhetoric and composition hires in tenure-track positions. Of all job candidates holding degrees in rhetoric and composition that year, seventy percent were female. And information taken from the *MLA Job Information List* and a follow-up survey published in the *ADE Bulletin* show that of all candidates hired in rhetoric and composition that year, sixty-six percent were female; we know, therefore, that women are hired in proportion to their representation in the candidate pool. In doctoral programs housed in research universities, males comprise fifty-seven percent of the writing faculty; but, overall, women make up the majority of both faculty and students in rhetoric and composition. (For the survey data and their origin, see Enos, *Faculty*.) What's more, women in 1980 made up sixty-five percent of the participation in the NCTE College Section in contrast to forty-five percent in MLA. And in 1994, sixty-three percent of the CCCC program participants were women.

Like nursing, library science, and some areas of education, then, more women than men work in rhetoric and composition. Unlike these other disciplines, however, impressions from available data suggest that women who teach writing at the college level are under-compensated in terms of status and pay compared to their male counterparts. Some of these questions have been explored recently by Janice Lauer, who offers an alternative perspective to other discussions on the feminization of the field. Lauer's essay is an insightful critique of several "readings" of our history that make claims about the feminization of the field. In both her critique and her own story, she tends to separate teaching and scholarship in rhetoric and composition. In her view *instruction* may be feminized because the majority of writing teachers are women; thus the expressive, student-centered, and nurturing pedagogies can mark feminization. But Lauer argues that in scholarship the field has not been feminized because men publish more than women.

Lauer is correct that in rhetoric and composition men publish more than women; nevertheless, the perception is that teaching writing is women's work. But I believe, as Ernest Boyer argues, that the traditional mindset about higher education that tends to separate teaching from scholarship is what we should be reconsidering. My research over a number of years has shown that men publish more of their work in what we consider our "scholarly" journals, and women publish more of their work in our "pedagogical" journals. The research also points to a recent sharp increase in publication of women's scholarship. Nevertheless, there is still some distinction between how men and women define "intellectual work."

In this chapter, I want to (1) further explore perceptions between pedagogy and scholarship in rhetoric and composition, (2) discuss four studies on the ratio of male-to-female publishing, (3) present some problems that can prevent women from publishing as much as their male counterparts, and (4) offer some suggestions about publishing in rhetoric and composition journals.

Gender and Publishing

Boyer's research on publication shows that in all disciplines nationally males publish more than females. The fairly recent entry of females, in any numbers, into higher education, however, should be taken into account. In his survey of all categories of institutions in higher education, forty-two percent agree that it is difficult to achieve tenure without publications (the breakdown by type of institution: research, eighty-three percent; four-year, forty-three percent; liberal arts, twenty-four percent; two-year, two percent). Even in the four-year universities with their lack of doctoral programs (and sometimes limited resources for research) and in the liberal arts colleges where teaching is highly prized, tenure is still difficult without publication.

My own national survey in 1992 of over three thousand teachers of writing posed some forty-three questions about the professional lives of writing faculty, one section focusing on record of publication. Because I received smaller samples on this section of the questionnaire than the other sections, I can report only those percentages correlating to the number of publications for writing faculty in four-year and research universities (see Tables 1 and 2).

Table 1

No. of Published Articles by Tenure-Track Writing Faculty

No. of articles published	Four-Year		Research	
	%M	%F	%M	%F
None	31	69	43	58
1-5	50	50	5	95
6-10	48	53	45	55
11+	75	25	35	65

Table 2

No. of Published Articles by Non-tenure-Track Writing Faculty

No. of Articles Published	Four-Year		Research	
	%M	%F	%M	%F
None	30	70	33	67
1-5	12	88	0	100
6-10	53	47	42	58
11+	48	52	56	44

Statistics such as these indicate that the percentages of women in rhetoric and composition who have not published is significantly higher than the percentages Boyer found across all disciplines. Those tenure-track writing faculty in four-year universities who have published between one and ten articles are pretty equally divided by gender, but the writing faculty who have more than ten publications are predominently male.

The data show a different picture in research universities. Although tenure-track, female writing faculty in research universities publish more than their counterparts in the four-year universities, women still comprise fifty-eight percent of the professors at this level who do not publish. And far more women in research universities have published only between one and five articles as compared to their male counterparts. Tenured or tenure-track women who have published between six and ten articles, however, make up fifty-five percent of this group. One of the more striking statistics in the survey shows that of those research-university, tenured or tenure-track writing faculty who have eleven or more publications, sixty-five percent are female. These percentages suggest a possible correlation between the majority of women hired since 1987, who would have been heavily involved in scholarship in preparation for the promotion and tenure process during the sixth year of employment, most likely the year 1993. Overall, males are still publishing more; the gap, however, is narrowing as increasingly more women are being tenured. Women are doing exciting and vigorous scholarship; yet, of all those in four-year and research universities who do not publish, sixty-six percent are women.

In addition to this national survey that was the basis for a book on faculty lives and gender roles, I have researched the percentage of female-authored articles in rhetoric and composition journals since 1982. I was drawn to the topic first because more than other fields rhetoric and composition, at least until fairly recently, has been defined more by journal articles than by books. (Until recently, there were few avenues for publishing books other than textbooks. Until the early 1980s, there were few writing journals, too, but opportunities for publishing still were better there, especially in NCTE's official journals.) I was also drawn to the topic when I conducted an informal survey of scholarly and professional books in rhetoric and composition that told me that seventy-seven percent of our field's scholarly books (not including textbooks) were male authored. This informal survey of books in our field led me to think about gender and publishing in our journals because I believe our journals more than books reflect the various voices and conversations going on in our discourse community.

The first survey's percentages, from 1982-1988, were stark and shocking. In the journals that we consider our most scholarly, far more men were published than women. Inversely, in the journals we consider pedagogical, women published much more than men. When I first reported the percentages in 1990, I think journal editors were the most shocked: the ratio of male-to female-authored articles published in our journals began to change. I don't know whether the percentages were so shocking that more women started doing more research and thus suddenly began to submit more articles (though I don't really think this is the case; I know that *Rhetoric Review* continued to receive more submissions from men), or that some of the more traditional editors saw their roles as more than gatekeepers, or that some peer review policies and procedures were changed. We didn't know much more in 1990 except that the sparse data we did have suggested a slight majority of women in the field. Also, the research in higher education showed that women considered themselves to be teachers first, spending less time on research than men, who considered research and writing to be their "real" work.

I updated the journal article study, adding publication by gender for 1988 and 1990 to show just how much the percentages had changed. My interest to update this research was spurred in part by James Kinneavy's statistics based on the index to Winifred Horner's second edition of *The Present State of Scholarship in Historical and Contemporary Rhetoric*. Of the 366 items in the index, 250 are male authored compared to the eighty-one female authored. (The other thirty-five entries are journals.) That about one-fourth of the authors are women seemed an encouraging ratio to Kinneavy: "Very few disciplines can make such a claim—except, of course, specialized disciplines like nursing" (qtd. in Enos, "Gender and Publishing" 314). The comparison between the two disciplines bothered me somewhat because even though rhetoric and composition, like nursing, has more females than males, its knowledge-making through publications still comes from males more than females (with the one exception of writing faculty in research universities that I commented on earlier). In nursing it is the women who hold the positions of power and the males who are trying to break through the glass ceiling. In rhetoric and composition, women still do not have the power, pay, and real positions despite their numbers.

One change slowly taking place is a broadening of the definition of scholarship to better fit with what it is we do in rhetoric and composition. It is ironic that Boyer's definition of scholarship—discovery, integration, application, and teaching—has been the mosaic pattern of our work in rhetoric for twenty-five hundred years. Boyer argues against the traditional German model of research and quantitative evaluation (which U.S. universities adopted and have maintained throughout this century) as only part of the four-patterned mosaic of scholarship that he envisions and that is so familiar to us in rhetoric and composition. One result of the traditional model, because it is at odds with the unique act of rhetoric and composition—to theorize practice and apply theory—is that many writing faculty, in order to earn tenure, have had to do research and publication in literature or creative writing instead of in rhetoric and composition—their area of scholarly interest and expertise, and the area for which they were hired in the first place. Many faculty told me that only after tenure could they do the work in rhetoric that first attracted them to the field.

In updating the journal study, I found that the ratios of female-to-male publishing had changed significantly in three years; more women were getting published. In 1995 I again updated the survey, this time including 1991 through the available 1995 issues. The percentage of female-authored articles in our journals dramatically increased, the last column in Table 3 showing the increased percentage of women publishing.

Table 3
Percentage of Male and Female Authors

Journal	1980-88	1988-90	1991-95	Increase
*College English**[*]	31	36	43	12%
College Composition and Communication	37	41	55	18%
Rhetoric Review	31	30	37	6%
Journal of Advanced Composition	30	40	42	12%
Pre/Text	24	36	47	23%
Rhetoric Society Quarterly	19	27	30	11%
Journal of Teaching	44	57	66	22%
Journal of Basic Writing	58	51	69	11%

[*](Since Louise Smith took over the editorship of *College English* in 1992, the percentage of female authors has increased to forty-six percent.)

Women are being published more in our journals. Whether the number of submissions to journals in rhetoric and composition has increased so that the percentage of increase correlates to the increased percentage of publication, I don't know, but I *can* speak for *Rhetoric Review*. Female-authored submissions to *Rhetoric Review* have remained about the same (though there's been a sharp increase in 1995); I still get more male-authored submissions. And the double-blind peer review process I began in 1983 has remained the same. As women have done more sustained work in the history and theory of rhetoric and composition, we do have, in some journals more than others, a chorus of female voices ringing out. And for the first time, we have a female editor of one of the two major NCTE journals: *College English*. Given the nature of our area of study and of the majority of women in rhetoric and composition, however, *College Composition and Communication* should have been the first.

In the next sections, I want to present some problems that particularly attach themselves to our professional history in rhetoric and composition, perceptions about our intellectual work, the realities of women's burdens in administering writing programs and mentoring students, the consequences of finding a voice, and questions about collaborative work.

Distinctions between "Rhetoric" and "Composition"
Although gendered perceptions of work are changing as more women enter the field, men and women overall in the academy but particularly in rhetoric and composition perceive their "intellectual work" differently. To men, *real* work in the field more often than not has meant writing books, doing research; work to women usually has meant teaching. According to my

survey data, women writing faculty spend more time teaching than men. In the four-year university, women spend sixty-one percent of their time teaching compared to fifty-four percent for men. And in research universities, women spend forty-nine percent of their time teaching compared to forty percent for men.

The data show interesting correlations of time spent on research and both age and length of time tenured. Males spend more time on research than females overall (twenty percent to seventeen percent); by institution, however, there are significant differences. In two-year colleges, female writing faculty spend a little more time on research (eight percent) than do their male counterparts (six percent). In liberal arts colleges, the percentage is the same for both male and female writing faculty: thirteen percent. In the four-year universities, male faculty spend twenty-one percent of their time on research, while women spend only sixteen percent of their time doing research. In research universities, males spend twenty-nine percent of their time on research, while women's research takes up twenty-five percent of their time. According to the data, the older the faculty member and the longer tenured, the less research that person does. Those tenured in 1980 or before, for example, spend less time on research than those who were tenured later. And those age forty or less spend more time on research (twenty-two percent) than do faculty over forty (sixteen percent).

The pressure to publish in the early part of one's career in order to obtain tenure, and/or getting married and raising children (or not), surely affect an academic's scholarship. But the figures do suggest some correlation: if we know that those tenured in 1980 or after do the most research and if we know that more women than men have been hired in tenure-track positions since about 1987 so that women now are the majority in rhetoric and composition, then submissions by female writing faculty to journals would understandably increase. (Such data do not explain why female-authored publications rose to forty-six percent under Louise Smith's editorship of *College English*; editorial policy and politics also share a role in the increased publication of women.)

One problem with which we're increasingly having to deal is the very name of our area of study, most usually called "rhetoric and composition." The name calls up attitudes that can, and I think do, complicate our efforts to broaden the definition of what we do in rhetoric and composition. Although eighty percent of the survey respondents said their program or department made no distinction between "rhetoric" and "composition," twenty percent offered evidence that many English departments put the two terms into a dichotomous relationship. "Rhetoric" in some English departments means theory and history, rigorous scholarship, doctoral programs. "Composition" means service courses and association with only the undergraduate curriculum. The differing meanings of the two terms reflect an intellectual distinction, not a programmatic one. Rhetoric, a number of respondents said, is in their department more recognized as a discipline than composition, which is considered a service-oriented field.

Doing research on the theoretical and historical study of texts, style, structure, and persuasive use of language, and publishing in journals strongly associated with "rhetoric," have been the *sine qua non* for evaluating scholarship at most universities that have writing programs and especially doctoral programs in rhetoric and composition. No matter that "composition" already is part of "rhetoric"; no matter that rhetoric is not only the oldest of the humanities but also unique in that it is both a substantive art and a methodology. To do one's research in writing pedagogy is taking a career risk if the department does not have separate criteria for research in rhetoric and composition studies: it's harder to earn tenure if you're a specialist faculty in a research-oriented university, and it's harder to obtain a tenure-track position in either a four-year or research university if all your research focuses on pedagogy. Of those too few women who have made it to the "top" in the field, most if not all have done their work in the history and theory of rhetoric, not pedagogy. And they have published their work primarily in the journals considered the most scholarly. They are known for adding to our "body of knowledge"; their work is defined as knowledge-constructing.

Mentoring/Nurturing/Administrating—Women's Burdens

In my survey the subject of administrative work elicited more angry, despairing, bitter narratives than almost any other topic, the majority of these voices belonging to women. Too often women are less protective of their time than men, but too often the faculty members with the greatest authority to make demands are male. (Department heads and writing program directors in our larger universities still are mostly male.) Within rhetoric and composition, male faculty tend to hold the real administrative positions with real titles while women faculty tend to handle the many details of day-to-day running of committees and the nitty gritty work with students that does *not* get recognized because it is less organized, less associated with a "position."

Administrative duties for writing faculty are both heavy and wide-ranging. Although faculty in research universities spend more time on administrative duties than their counterparts in other colleges and universities, all writing faculty spend a large percentage of their time on administration: research faculty, thirty-three percent; four-year, twenty-five percent; liberal arts, eighteen percent; two-year, eighteen percent. For seventy-one percent, their administrative work counts for tenure and promotion; however, that leaves twenty-nine percent whose administrative work does not count.

Women writing faculty take on a heavy burden of administrative work—too often a heavier burden than our male counterparts and without the same status derived from formal titles and commensurate compensation. And we know that such administrative work does not have the exchange value it should in promotion and tenure decisions. In her letter of "support" during my tenure review, my former dean, avowing herself a victim of gender discrimination and for years nurturing a reputation as an ostensibly strong supporter of women, wrote disparagingly of the administrative duties I'd taken on as an overload for five years (associate director of composition and coordinator for our TA teacher training, a year-long credit-bearing preceptorship and colloquia). This dean called these heavy administrative duties and responsibilities "quasi-administrative work."

The practice of burdening *untenured* faculty with directing a writing program falls mostly to women. Many times an untenured assistant professor who is a woman is given the job of director of first-year English so that change is kept to a minimum. Many times she is expected, or forced, to act as a caretaker rather than become an innovative administrator because to step out of the drawn lines means risking alienating tenured members of the department who most likely have had some hand in shaping the program.

For all of us, the unique mix and heavy burden of teaching and administrative work, along with the expectations for research and publication, is onerous. For women who have families, the pressure becomes greater. Women still bear most of the responsibility for family and home; women faculty often are torn between teaching and a "life." One of the stories I hear quite often is that a woman who is not married and/or who does not have young children can leave campus as late as five o'clock and still can have five to seven hours to grade papers, write from her research, or even relax during some evenings. A woman with family responsibilities might have only a couple of late-night or early-morning hours to prepare her classes. This difference is not recognized in any way that I can see—certainly not in publishing circles or in promotion and tenure reviews.

Along with the heavy administrative work that too often is not connected to a real position, women still are given much of the work of mentoring and nurturing students within the department. Seventy-one percent of the women who responded to the survey said their careers had been nontraditional because of changed or interrupted careers or because they had had no mentors in graduate school and most often not even one female professor in their field of study. Many of these women now spend inordinate amounts of time nurturing and mentoring because of their own experience of bias in the early part of their careers. And more of them are now realizing the dangers of mothering in the academy.

Mothering in the academy—whether it's through the nurturer in the writing program or the maternal teaching model—can carry with it a danger. Such a model can lead to our silencing in situations in which we might still be uncomfortable, or unable to deal, with conflicting parts of our identity. To be separate, individual, and autonomous may be emphasized too much when we speak about and live in the male-dominated arena of much of our professional lives. But we live in this world of faculty where, despite our numbers, we may not have worked out for ourselves how to maintain separate identities. If we make ourselves too available, too maternal, too caring, we risk not achieving a balance between our very natures and our careers. They should be the same; alas, they are not. A number of respondents to the survey commented on these problems that so many women who teach writing face, expressing that perhaps we should learn to stop mothering in the academy and to better balance nurturing with autonomy in order to guard our time.

So we women faculty can and often do find ourselves in a dilemma. We like to work with students; we don't guard our time carefully. We're already overburdened by administrative work, work that does not have exchange value with traditional scholarship. Mentoring was not explicitly included in any of the many department or university criteria that I saw while conducting the survey. And, no surprise here, nurturing was not mentioned. But here's the rub: if women scholars don't assume the additional responsibility of mentoring—especially for our female colleagues and students—then how can we change some of the destructive discriminatory practices still going on in our departments and programs?

Knowledge-Constructing and Voice
As an editor who reads hundreds of manuscript submissions every year and as a teacher who works primarily with women graduate students, I know feminist theory well enough to see its siren-call to female graduate students who are working toward a career in rhetoric and composition in institutions of higher education and who already are trying to get published. Sometimes I think that "making knowledge" many times gets confused with "finding a voice." Let me tell a story to illustrate.

Several years ago I sent out for blind peer review a manuscript written by a woman who is known for her scholarship in the history of rhetoric. In the manuscript she had included a personal narrative about her mother trying to teach her to make cinnamon rolls when she was eight years old. I should say that this was a departure from the scholar's usual style, but part of her argument logically grew out of the narrative. It worked—I thought. When the reviews came back, one of the reviewers had objected to the narrative. This reviewer is male and is also well known for his work in the history of rhetoric. He is, furthermore—and I say this with conviction—extraordinarily supportive of women's work in the field. Although his review was overall supportive, he commented that the narrative should remain part of the "scholarly" manuscript on rhetorical history only if the author was one whose work was well known. That way, he said, the previous work would provide a context and make the personal part acceptable.

I suspect that a double-blind peer review system cannot eliminate bias—of course not, because the *words* are still there on the page. I'm not even sure that this would constitute gender bias anyway, though I know that the use of personal narrative can be viewed as "gender specific." Lately I have been rethinking the epistemological position that women's ways of composing are different from men's; women who have published the most might have a larger repertoire of "styles"—they've probably always had to be acutely aware of their audiences, given the economic, cultural, and social constrictions on them because of their sex. But it's not just women who use narration as a way of arguing, or personal narrative to create voice; the perception remains, however, that this is "female style," or that it is nonscholarly. I would have to agree with the peer reviewer who commented on the "cinnamon bun story" that indeed it's true, sadly enough, that the most highly recognized people in the field "get away" with having voice ride above content—and there are fewer women in the high-profile group of scholars in rhetoric and composition. James Corder, who is recognized for his style—his marvelous sense of voice—as well as his ideas, visited my campus in 1990 as part of our annual colloquia for writing faculty and TAs. Over coffee and pastries, graduate students were informally discussing with Jim his homespun, philosophical style. One student, who particularly admired Jim's writing style and who wished to be able to project as strong an ethos as Jim's, asked, "Could I write like you do and get published?" Jim answered, "probably not." We all laughed. We understood too. Jim talked about his problems years ago in getting published in *College Composition and Communication* and *College English* because the manuscripts he submitted weren't "scholarly" enough. He hasn't changed his style; his work is regularly published now, though. He has a name—and he has a voice.

Let me tell another story, this one about a manuscript submitted to *Rhetoric Review*, a feminist reading of Plato's *Gorgias*. The paper argued that "if a discursive practice exacts as its price for authorization the repression of feeling or of personal stakes in the practice, then that price is too high." The essay was based on an episode, told with much anger, about the female author's encounter with a "famous" male scholar at a conference who had, in his male way, dismissed her ways of thinking about authority and models of inquiry. The peer reviewers to whom I'd sent the manuscript all replied similarly: the piece set up binaries too neatly—and violently and angrily—without offering readers an alternative. One reviewer commented that the "conversational style and stream of ideas" was not the most effective way to present the point, this reviewer stressing that the author did have something important to share with readers. The reviewers thought voice got in the way, became more important than the argument.

The author subsequently revised and resubmitted the piece; she was not willing, however, to rethink the role voice and narrative played in the argument. I sent it to the same peer reviewers. The first reviewer to respond was "sorry not to be able to recommend publication," saying that the "personal narrative" was not appropriate for *Rhetoric Review*, that the essay "presents characterizations that are based on stereotypes. Those who disagree are giving into the power structures, male professors are authoritarian, efforts by others who are not in agreement with the author are 'moves,' etc." This reviewer went on to express the hope that the "author will see these comments as my fairest and most sincere effort to comment on areas of need and not any sort of statement prompted by any other reasons than the scholarly criteria used to adjudicate an essay's merits." Another reviewer said:

> While you privilege "feelings" (the song came to mind more than once as I spent a great deal of time on the piece) and the "personal" (not really presented in a way that I could understand, particularly considering the postmodern turn which you avoid even though it could help your case a lot), my reading saw a privileging of immediate sensation, not emotion or feeling. This privileging of sensation would ordinarily fascinate me, partly because I am in such great need of feminist responses. It does with, for example, the autobiographical work of Linda Brodkey and Marianna Torgovnick, whose autobiographical writing is so carefully, so thoughtfully, worked through. The series of sensations re-presented here are not really related to Plato.... They appear to be related to a desire to perform catharsis in front of the large audience of *Rhetoric Review* interpreters....
>
> Jasper Neel in *Plato, Derrida, and Writing* presents his great anger toward both Derrida and Plato. He does so in a compelling, lucid, provocative way that I can and have used over and over in my writing and in my graduate and undergraduate classes. I hope that you will study how his book is made. He started out with lots and lots of hard study and difficult encounters with other writer/speakers. I also recommend that you immerse yourself in Derrida's "Plato's Pharmacy." Derrida, too, is mad at Plato. Many have been mad at Plato. Your piece assumes the stance that expressing this anger is a new kind of event.... I hope ... that you will explore the difference between exposure of sensation to a supposedly public audience and exposure of insight to a group of readers.

Another reviewer who didn't "want to fall into traditional scholarly modes of critique" asked a graduate student to collaborate on the peer evaluation. But all of the reviewers had problems with the author's handling of, or confusion with, knowledge-construction and the expression of a particular view through voice. The author chose not to work with the four reviewers' suggestions; the manuscript, therefore, was rejected. Lest you are curious: two of the reviewers were female, two male.

We certainly need more research on how women's scholarship is evaluated. One of the few studies we have on this topic reports that women's scholarship in academia consistently is evaluated as being precise, thorough—and noncontroversial (Bernard). A few women who publish a lot and whose scholarship is perceived to be more in "composition," or the politics of composition, than "rhetoric"—women like Ann Berthoff, Maxine Hairston, Patricia Bizzell—have strong, political voices. They can be "controversial" in a way that traditional women scholars in the history of rhetoric, say Winifred Bryan Horner, are not. If a woman historiographer, however (Susan Jarratt, for example), "rereads" history, she can become well known, can become a controversial figure.

Women Scholars and Collaboration

Several years ago I reported on the amount of collaborative writing being published in rhetoric and composition journals. I was particularly interested in how many coauthored articles were by women working together. Belenky and her coauthors in *Women's Ways of Knowing* had described the collaborative process that produced their book as the wonderfully cooperative way in which women can work together. "It would seem," Elizabeth Flynn says in response to a published interview with Belenky, "that women are, in general, more cooperative than men, more connected to each other and hence more capable than men of collaborating successfully" (176). But women's emphasis on mutuality, concern, and support is difficult to implement in academia where conflict and competition are facts. Indeed, our educational structures have served to separate women from each other and from knowledge; new structures must be found that allow for connected knowing.

Also responding to this same interview, Marilyn Cooper comments, "It is a moot point whether competition is associated with men and collaboration with women because of innate differences or because of socially constructed ones; the current pattern is that women by and large prefer to work collaboratively and that because collaborative work is devalued and dismissed in institutions structured on the basis of competitive strategies, women's work is often devalued and dismissed" (180).

These comments by Flynn and Cooper generated my interest in examining the number of coauthored articles in several of our leading journals, especially since collaborative scholarship is perceived to be highly valorized in our field. What I found is that if women frequently collaborate in their scholarly work, much of it is not getting published. Although the number of female coauthored publications has increased slightly over the last two years, most of the collaboration that has resulted in publication since 1980 is with men—either two men working together or a woman with a man. So one obvious question that perhaps we should be asking, given Cooper's comment about women's work often being dismissed, is: Why then do women more often collaborate with men than with each other?

We know that in this country more males than females encounter difficulties with writing English in school, although more published authors are male. Research that has revealed ways in which males and females differ in their writing processes suggests that men delay writing while women plunge in. It would follow then that women would find it more difficult to coauthor with men than with other women. There's fertile ground here for integrated (and collaborative) studies of the gender politics involved in collaborative research as well as deeper research into writing processes themselves.

Overcoming Obstacles
Getting published means writing a lot, and disciplining our time. For women directing writing programs (and that's a great many of us) it's hard to give equal attention to teaching and research. Winifred Horner has been tireless

in her efforts to help women learn from events in her own academic history; we should heed what she learned regarding the heavy administrative burdens placed especially on women when they should be doing research and writing. She scolds and cajoles: If you take on heavy administrative work—especially before tenure—make sure that it is with the agreement that one day a week—or two afternoons a week—you will not be in the office. This is your research time. Stick to it; whatever you do, do not even think you can work anywhere in the building where the composition office is. Do not even try to work at home. Go to the library. Hide, so no one can find you—and they will try. The "problem" will always be there in your office waiting for you the next morning; it can wait till then.

Another long-time administrator reminds me often that women must learn to "say no": "Jobs stick to an administrator as ticks to a dog; every job performed well leads to requests for two more." We need to learn how to discriminate better between essential duties and peripheral chores that can be delegated. As mentors, most composition studies faculty are overworked because they are popular with graduate students. This is important and delightful work, though usually unrecognized and time-consuming. But too often more of the burden falls on female writing faculty for mentoring and role modeling because female graduate students now make up seventy percent of the typical program in rhetoric (Enos, *Faculty*). The burden is accepted female-to-female, often sacrificially, often preventing women faculty from pursuing their own research. In research universities, it takes women longer to get tenure than males: according to my survey, 6.9 years for women as compared to 5.7 years for men. As a result, for mentoring or (wo)mentoring—if it leads to delays in getting published—we are penalized *de facto* for our contribution to future scholars. One thing we can do is to define mentoring so that its activities are not split between nurturing (female) and "real work" (male). In addition, mentoring responsibilities must be both carefully delineated for and equally distributed among all faculty.

Even after having been a journal editor for fifteen years, I don't have any magic advice on how to get published; as teachers, however, I think we can do much to help demystify the publication process for our graduate students. Few of our seventy-two doctoral programs in rhetoric and composition offer their graduate students a seminar in writing for publication or a course in the rhetoric of scholarship (see Brown, Meyer, and Enos). Because courses like these focus on how knowledge gets disseminated in the field, they foreground the politics of publication: the discourse community of rhetoric and composition studies, knowledge-construction, editing and peer review roles, journal and article-type analyses, and the etiquette of submission. And, of course, such courses are a forum for ongoing invention, writing, peer response, revision. In our history and theory courses especially, if we're not already doing so, we need to start viewing the required graduate "research" papers as a succession of drafts. Despite our talk—and practice in the undergraduate writing classroom—of process and peer-group praxis, more of us can turn our graduate writing courses into discourse-discussion groups where research is seen as invention, where successive drafts of papers are brought in and discussed, rather than where the traditional semester-end research paper is produced (still our most usual practice, I suspect) and where the professor, seeing it for the first time, evaluates the paper to justify the seminar grade.

Creating an environment in which students are encouraged to shape their traditional research papers into publishable papers helps demystify the publication process and involves students in a conscious dialogue about distinctive journal "voices," thus dealing with real audience considerations. I would argue for this approach instead of faculty/student coauthoring. I do know that important publications have come out of collaboration between faculty and student, and I support collaborative work. To increase publishing opportunities, however, I think it better to create an environment where a "publishable" paper is the semester goal rather than the usual summative seminar paper, which by its very nature is a record of *what* the student knows instead of an essay showing *that* the student knows.

The essays in this volume offer much practical advice for professionals just entering the field. Although my primary purpose here has not been advising how one gets published, still I'd like to offer a few suggestions from experience. One of the steepest hurdles blocking knowledge-construction and publication is learning to gain a sense of situatedness. So, young scholars—more and more of you women—situate *yourself* in your research topic, and I can assure you that a voice will emerge that shows an active mind in the process of constructing. Always connect—learn to make connections that allow for exciting exploration so that all your written work in graduate school (or "before tenure" if you're in your first ranked faculty position) reflects a mosaic of discovery, integration, application, teaching. To make those connections, whatever your main interest (major period, figure, concept, application), *historicize*. Historicizing helps us to define and redefine rhetoric. Historical resonances help us to broaden our sense of ourselves as we challenge and then perhaps cross the limits of our frames of reference. Then theory and praxis more easily fit themselves into the expanded frame or new frames.

Suppose you most generally define rhetoric as, and identify yourself with, the teaching of writing. There's a whole range of issues there related to English studies at all educational levels and in all periods. A whole range of questions on how people actually read and wrote needs more research. Suppose you define rhetoric and composition as a theory of persuasion. Your research area is a universe populated by accepted theories—shaped by intellectual, social, economic, political, legal trends. Many commonly accepted institutionalized trends are waiting to be rewritten. Suppose you define rhetoric as socially constructed discourse. You have lots of ground to cover (and lots of company), and many choices about which discourse conventions to examine: who gets to speak, how they are allowed to speak, and what purposes discourse serves or, better yet, can serve. Treat each hurdle as a challenge rather than a barrier. I cannot promise you that the path toward publication smooths out completely; I can promise you that you will find much reward along the way.

Works Cited

Belenky, Mary Field, Blythe McVicker Clinchy, Nancy Rule Goldberger, and Jill Mattuck Taruale. *Women's Ways of Knowing: The Development of Self, Voice, and Mind.* New York: Basic, 1986.

Bernard, Jessie. *Academic Women.* University Park: Pennsylvania State UP, 1964.

Boyer, Ernest L. *Scholarship Reconsidered: Priorities of the Professoriate.* Princeton, NJ: Carnegie Foundation for the Advancement of Teaching, 1990.

Brown, Stuart C., Paul R. Meyer, and Theresa Enos. "Doctoral Programs in Rhetoric and Composition." *Rhetoric Review* 12 (1994). Special Issue.

Cooper, Marilyn M. "Dueling with Dualism: A Response to Interviews with Mary Field Belenky and Gayatri Chakravorty Spivak." *Journal of Advanced Composition* 11 (1991): 179-85.

Enos, Theresa. *Gender Roles and Faculty Lives in Rhetoric and Composition.* Carbondale: Southern Illinois UP, forthcoming 1996.

——. "Gender and Journals, Conservers or Innovators." *Pre/Text* 9 (1988): 209-14.

——. "Gender and Publishing." *Pre/Text* 11 (1990): 311-16.

Flynn, Elizabeth A. "Politicizing the Composing Process and Women's Ways of Interacting: A Response to 'A Conversation with Mary Belenky.'" *Journal of Advanced Composition* 11 (1991): 173-78.

Lauer, Janice M. "The Feminization of Rhetoric and Composition Studies?" *Rhetoric Review* 13 (1995): 276-86.

Shaping the Conversation:

Publishing Scholarly Monographs
and Textbooks

From Dissertation to Scholarly Monograph: Meeting Professional Expectations

MAUREEN M. HOURIGAN

"You are your dissertation," affirmed Paul Cantor at the Wayzata Conference on the future of graduate studies in English (12). The year was 1987, and expanding graduate programs and an improving job market had induced an atmosphere of cautious optimism among the conferees. Cantor was entreating directors of graduate programs and those who teach in them to help their students "keep the job market in mind throughout their graduate careers." In particular, he was discussing the central importance of the dissertation in screening and hiring candidates and the need for graduate advisors to make the connections between the dissertation and the job market "crystal clear" to their students (10-11).

While Cantor's remarks made sense at a time when a period of retrenchment in English departments seemed near an end, they make even more sense today when federal and state governments seem less able and less willing to fund higher education at even the reduced levels that have predominated in the early 1990s. Not alone is Robert L. Jacobson in concluding that "higher education will never return to the boom days of the 1980s" (qtd. in Holub 78). According to the experts he consulted, postsecondary institutions will simply have to do more with less: class sizes will increase, funding will decrease, and "creative solutions" (distance learning and an increased use of part-time teachers, from my experience) will be implemented to cope with needed but unfunded and unfilled positions (Holub 79, 81). The resulting depressed academic job market has created an increasingly professionalized class of graduate students and an anxious class of junior professors facing increased expectations of publication for tenure. Just as a well-chosen dissertation topic can improve a graduate student's prospects of obtaining a position in a depressed market, so, too, can a dissertation written for publication from the outset improve a junior faculty member's prospects of promotion and tenure in times of increasing expectations of scholarly productivity.

The Depressed Academic Job Market

Time has proved the wisdom of both the optimism and the caution that pervaded the 1987 Wayzata Conference, as Bettina Huber's recent analysis of trends in the modern language job market demonstrates. Indeed, the job market for Ph.D.s in English did improve dramatically in the 1980s. From 1983-84 to 1988-89, the number of positions advertised in the *MLA Job Information List* (*JIL*) increased by fifty-three percent, reaching a high of more than two thousand listings in 1988-89. Dramatic though the increase was, an even more dramatic decline, beginning in 1989-90, followed. By 1992-93, the number of positions advertised was forty-four percent lower than the high of 1988-89. In 1993-94, the number of listings decreased again; the 1,054 listings eclipsed the previous low point in modern language hiring. Moreover, while the number of positions advertised in *JIL* decreased, the number of job seekers increased. Between 1986-87 and 1991-92, the number of Ph.D.s awarded in English rose by thirty-five percent (88-89).

But news from the academic job market is not unrelievedly gloomy, especially for rhetoric and composition specialists. For one thing, good news greeted all job seekers in 1994-95: the number of positions advertised in *JIL* increased by eight percent ("Final Count" 1-2). For another, although the number of advertised rhetoric and composition positions dropped sharply between 1988 and 1992 (Huber 101), rhetoric and composition programs graduate far fewer Ph.D.s than literature programs do. A comparison of listings in the October 1992 *JIL* and the number of Ph.D.s awarded that year for each specialty will serve as an example. Although the 244 listings for literature professors outnumbers the 159 for writing specialists, literature programs awarded 965 Ph.D.s in 1992 compared with the 117 awarded by rhetoric and composition programs (Parham 6). While rhetoric and composition specialists may face less competition than literature specialists in the current depressed market, job listings for both specialties increasingly require engagement in professional activities.

The depressed academic job market has increased the stakes both for hiring and for promotion and tenure. "The highly competitive job market produces graduate students who have what it used to require to get tenure," laments one disillusioned graduate student in a June 1995 *Council Chronicle* article (Parham 7). An earlier generation of job seekers, now sitting on the opposite side of the interviewing table, agrees. Gene Young, chair of the English department at Sam Houston State University, for instance, tells of a "respected scholar" who looked up from a mound of applications and said in bewilderment, "Do you realize that none of us would be able to get the job we're interviewing people for?" Young continues: "It's an embarrassment of riches for eager departments like ours, but it's a horror story for the candidates on the market" (Parham 7). As newly minted Ph.D.s, particularly in literature, compete with unemployed, underemployed, and unhappily employed Ph.D.s for smaller numbers of positions, what becomes all too clear is that a tight job market will exist for quite some time and that graduate students who hope to have any chance of standing out in it will need to have published extensively. Frank Madden, a counselor for job seekers at the 1994 MLA convention, remarks, "I was saddened by the number of exceptionally well-qualified people who had not been called for a single interview—Ph.D.s in hand, several articles on their vitae, lots of adjunct teaching experience" (Parham 7). Despite numerous articles in *The Chronicle of Higher Education* and *PMLA* confirming the situation Madden describes above, Erik D. Curren, President of the MLA Graduate Student Caucus, reports,

> While it has become folklore that completing the formal requirements of a Ph.D. program is not enough these days and that graduate students need to participate in all sorts of professional activities to get in the running for a job at all, many students are still convinced that if they do what they are told, they will have a reasonable chance of getting a job comparable to many current faculty positions when the job market turns around.
>
> (58)

Even in the less competitive job market for rhetoric and composition specialists, graduates need a record of scholarly productivity, not just a degree. Gary Olson, Professor of English in the University of South Florida's rhetoric and composition program, cautions, "The piece of paper that says Ph.D. doesn't do it" (qtd. in Parham 6). Yet, students responding to a nationwide survey of graduate students in rhetoric and composition, compiled at Ohio State, knew little about the dissertation process or the successes or failures of past program graduates (Parham 8).

An analysis of the listings for rhetoric and composition specialists in the October 1994 *JIL* demonstrates the wisdom of both Curren's and Olson's admonitions. Consider, for example, the credentials expected for a *one-year renewable appointment* at a California university:

> *Composition Specialist: Academic Coordinator/Lecturer* in composition with major responsibilities in (1) training, supervision, and evaluation of instructors; (2) teaching composition; and (3) development of curriculum. Ph.D. required, *plus scholarly publications on composition and/or professional activity in some of the following areas*: curricular leadership and innovation; research in composition theory and pedagogy; writing and minority populations; basic writing; research and grant design, including some familiarity with statistical analysis. . . . (emphasis added)

Such are the effects of the severe economic downturn in California on hiring practices in higher education. While I have admittedly chosen a worst-case example from *JIL* to illustrate the increased expectations of publication for even non-tenure-track positions, more than forty percent of the tenure-track positions advertised for rhetoric and composition specialists specifically mention expectation of publication. Advertisement after advertisement for entry-level assistant professors included such phrases as "publications preferred," "publications an asset," "publications desirable." One advertisement for a writing center director required "a record of publications," and one for a "beginning" assistant professor stated that the successful candidate was "expected to publish at the national level."

Calls for better advising of graduate students by graduate programs reverberated throughout a series of articles in *Profession 94* addressing the collapse of the academic job market. In particular, graduate advisors are again urged to help graduate students select dissertation topics that will serve them well in a job search (Hutner 77; Curren 60). Graduate programs at New Mexico State University and the University of South Florida have responded to the job crisis by attempting to professionalize their graduate students. Graduate students at New Mexico State, for example, are required to take a professional practicum in which they analyze *JIL* lists; those at the University of South Florida are required to take a course in scholarly writing for publication and are encouraged to attend professional conventions (Parham 6). Graduate students who present papers at conferences can increase their chances of publishing their dissertations by visiting the exhibit booths of university presses and introducing themselves to the publishers' representatives, often acquisitions editors. Such contacts are invaluable when the time comes to publish the dissertation. As Paul Parsons reports, "Although no quantitative evidence exists, editors believe that prospective authors have a better chance of being published when the initial contact is a face-to-face encounter rather than a faceless query" (67).

But efforts to professionalize graduate students are controversial. Wendell V. Harris of Penn State University is concerned that graduate students in their race to publish quickly and prolifically read less widely and deeply, narrowing their focus to those texts and theoretical approaches that "can be quickly blended together into at least the outward shape of books and articles." Furthermore, he calls upon members of the MLA, particularly those who are not convinced "that the profession and the world are really better for the ever-increasing flow of printer's ink," to debate the issue of "excessive" publication expected of graduate students and junior faculty members and to judge "if things are the way they ought to be" (120-21). Even Janice Lauer expresses similar concerns in another chapter of this book. But Susan Wolfson, addressing the transition from graduate student to faculty member, points to the advantages—and not just "business" ones—that accrue to graduate students who publish. They discover the fun of the profession while creating the kinds of writing samples required by search committees. Moreover, graduate students often can find time to write more easily than can new assistant professors, and trusted mentors and fellow graduate students are still down the hall for critical dialogue (67-68).

One effect of increased qualifications for job seekers has been a concomitant increase in requirements for tenure. Explains Bernard Rosen of Ohio State, "It's as if you're grading on a curve, and now that you have all honors students, you're still giving the same percentage of failing grades" (qtd. in Lederman and Mooney A18). At Rutgers in 1986, for example, almost all junior faculty at mid-tenure review either had already published a book or had one under contract (Wolfson 67-68). Such early records of accomplishment have significantly raised the stakes for tenure. Domna Stanton, editor of *PMLA*, reports that "many universities require for tenure not only a book and a body of articles but also substantial progress on a second major project" (8). Recent surveys demonstrate that such substantial records of achievement for tenure are required not only at research universities. In the 1989 National Survey of Faculty conducted by the Carnegie Foundation for the Advancement of Teaching, thirty percent of the faculty at comprehensive colleges—which essentially have no doctoral programs and scant resources for research—ranked as "very important" the number of publications for granting tenure in their departments. At liberal arts colleges, too, where teaching has traditionally been valued more than research, almost a quarter of the faculty strongly agreed that it is difficult to obtain tenure in their departments without publication (Boyer 30, 11-12). A survey of writing program administrators conducted in 1992 reinforces the importance of research: sixty-three percent of those responding from doctorate-granting institutions cited research as the primary criterion for tenure and promotion (Barr-Ebest 58).

But just as tenure-track professors find themselves expected to publish more for tenure, they also find themselves facing larger classes and increased course loads, and, in the case of many rhetoric and composition specialists, assuming administrative responsibilities for a writing program, too. Gone are the days when a new tenure-track hire could expect a year or two of reduced course loads and university service commitments to enable him or her to conduct research and publish the books and articles required for tenure. By way of example, let me return to the October 1994 *JIL* to an advertisement for an assistant professor in English and composition. Consider how the successful candidate for this year-round position (with one month of leave per annum) at the University of Redlands' Whitehead Center for Lifelong Learning would find time to publish:

> The successful candidate will have the opportunity to set up and oversee a writing-across-the-curriculum program for Whitehead students. Beyond this curricular innovation and design, this faculty member will have the responsibility of recruiting, training and evaluating part-time faculty to teach in such a program and to train other full-time faculty in the implementation of the program in their respective disciplines. Other areas of responsibility include the teaching of courses in composition, writing, critical thinking and literature, and recruiting, training and evaluating faculty who teach in these areas. The University of Redlands also expects its faculty to maintain active scholarship and to serve the community in committee work and governance.

Almost thirty listings in the October *JIL* for assistant professors in rhetoric and composition likewise require writing program administration of some kind, a concern for women faculty especially. Sixty-six percent of untenured women responding to the 1992 survey of writing program administrators reported that writing program administration work had impeded their progress toward tenure (Barr-Ebest 59). What seems clear from report after report on current conditions in academe is that junior professors who hope for a long academic career must begin to publish early and consistently, ideally as graduate students. One time-honored strategy for achieving tenure in even dismal times is to revise one's dissertation and publish it as a scholarly monograph. The advice I offer on the process is based on my experience in quickly turning my own dissertation into a scholarly monograph and in serving as a manuscript reader for a university press.

The Transformation Process: At the Beginning
Transforming a dissertation into a scholarly monograph is a process best begun early, before the first word of the dissertation is committed to legal pad or computer screen. Crucial to the success of the process is the choice of dissertation topic and director. Graduate students in today's economically pressured university are themselves pressured to reduce the time-to-degree (currently averaging about eight years in the humanities) to five years (Curren 59; Stanton 8). As a result, many graduate students, when asked how best to choose a dissertation topic, will say, "You should pick as obscure a topic as possible, something no one has worked on before" (Cantor 3). However, both Cantor and Gordon Hutner point out that choosing safe, narrow subjects to investigate can ill serve graduate students in a job search. Obscure topics are less likely to fit the needs of potential employers and can result in "unemployed and brokenhearted" job candidates (Cantor 13; Hutner 77). Oftentimes, too, time-constrained doctoral candidates produce dissertations of no more than 150 pages of "undigested and unpolished" research that "must be seriously revised and expanded" before they can be transformed into scholarly monographs (Stanton 8). Both Robert Armstrong, some two decades ago, and Cantor and Hutner, more recently, point accusing fingers at directors for this situation. As Armstrong so succinctly puts it, "Excellence in works written for the degree often results from excellence of supervision" ("Dissertation's" 244). Thus, a director who has published extensively in the field of rhetoric and composition and whose advisees have a history of quickly turning their dissertations into monographs is exactly whom an astute graduate student should seek out. Such a director not only steers graduate students clear of dead-end dissertation topics that will define (and confine) them for the first years of their academic careers, but will insist on a coherent and cogent development of the topic. Moreover, when the time for publication comes, such a director can often provide introductions to acquisitions editors at university presses that specialize in publishing related scholarship.

Choosing a dissertation committee that agrees that a dissertation should be written for publication as a monograph from the outset is another step that a doctoral candidate can take before the writing begins. Such a committee, department consenting, is more likely to agree to the inclusion of the traditional extensive review of the critical literature in the dissertation prospectus rather than in the first chapter of the dissertation itself, where, according to most editors, it would have to be promptly removed when the time for publishing comes (Deats 144-45).

Once the dissertation director and committee are in place, the doctoral candidate usually writes, rewrites, and submits the formal prospectus, the chapter-by-chapter blueprint of the dissertation (and, with luck, a review of the literature). Some candidates, especially those who experience writing anxiety or writing blocks, may want to incorporate an intermediate step between the selection of the committee and the writing of the prospectus. Anxious or blocked writers who have had no experience writing so lengthy a project or even a plan for one are often encouraged to think of the project as no more than a series of related articles. While such a ploy may reduce anxiety or unblock a writer, it may result in a dissertation of disparate chapters, one whose unifying principle is at best fuzzy and at worst absent. Composing a short mini-prospectus before writing the formal one is one way a candidate can more clearly focus the purpose of the project and assume the command over the material that a scholarly monograph requires. Olson asks his advisees to write an informal, two-page letter to him, clearly explaining what the dissertation is intended to accomplish and what they think the research will show. Later, this two-page letter, polished and fleshed out with a detailed chapter-by-chapter description, becomes the formal prospectus.

Another technique is to write the "blurb"—the summary/sales pitch that will eventually appear on the back cover of the dissertation-turned-scholarly-monograph. "Nothing," claim A. Clay Schoenfeld and Robert Magnan, "will so rivet your mind to the task at hand; nothing will so keep you on track through months of labor" (265) as providing the following information (borrowed from the marketing questionnaire of one university press):

> Please provide one double-spaced page of promotional copy about your book. It should be written on a level that would be meaningful to a non-specialist and should cover all the selling points of the book. (Why would anyone wish to purchase it?)

As a bonus, writing the promotional copy at this early stage will rescue a writer from later having to write it hastily for the marketing department.

Doctoral candidates writing with publication in mind from the outset will want to take one last step before beginning the dissertation: setting aside an hour or so to read a series of articles on revising a dissertation for publication that appeared in *Scholarly Publishing* in the 1970s (Armstrong; Halpenny; Holmes). Here are identified the telltale signs of the dissertation that a writer must root out before submitting it to a university press for consideration: redundancy, an apologetic opening, excessive quoting, an over-abundance of discursive footnotes, and the like. Taken as a group, these articles provide a blueprint for what not to do in the months of dissertation writing that lie ahead.

The Transformation Process: After the Dissertation Is Complete

Rare indeed is the doctoral candidate who does not abandon the finished dissertation on the director's doorstep, wishing for yet another week, another month, another year to revise. Those who revise their dissertations for publication find their wish granted, for a university press often requires the revised manuscript to be delivered one year after the agreement to publish is signed. How long should a doctoral candidate wait before assuming the mantle of prospective author? Conventional wisdom dictates a "leisurely return" to the dissertation, anywhere from a few months to a year or more to acquire proper distance and maturity of perspective (Armstrong, "Revising" 43; Halpenny 112; Parsons 116). And newly-minted Ph.D.s, fearful of being uncovered as "frauds," fearful that their dissertations will not "make a contribution" (Boice 32), and distracted by preparations for their new careers in oftentimes geographically removed places are all too glad to have a reason to postpone assuming the new role. For several reasons, new rhetoric and composition scholars can no longer afford so leisurely a pace. Robert Boice notes, for one, that "professors who wait until they are fully ready and undistracted tend to do very little writing" (14). Furthermore, should they dally, they may share the experience of one modern drama scholar whose more mature perspective took a few years to develop. Not only had more than thirty-five works on his subject been written in the time between the dissertation and the proposed revision, the critical approach he had used (much like cognitivist methodology in composition in the early 1980s) had fallen out of favor. Most importantly, the weeks between the submission of the dissertation and the assumption of the role of junior professor are often the least constrained windows of time a new scholar is likely to experience between graduate school and the awarding of tenure.

Thus, I recommend that the doctoral candidate return to the dissertation no more than a week or two after submitting it to the committee. Now is the time for a long, hard, critical look. If the dissertation is truly no more than a collection of distinct chapters, it might best be mined for an article or two, then abandoned for another research project. But if it gleams hard and true at the center, now is the time—yes, before the defense, even—to query an acquisitions editor at a university press. Suggestions for appropriate presses, particularly those listbuilding in the subject area of the dissertation, may come from the dissertation director or members of the committee. *College Composition and Communication*, *College English*, the *Journal of Advanced Composition*, and other journals in the field often carry announcements of new book series in rhetoric and composition. Or a prospective author might query an acquisitions editor met earlier at an exhibition booth at a professional conference. Whereas many publishers claim to prefer a written query letter, I have found a telephone call more likely to elicit a positive response and immediate interest in a manuscript. "There is a distinct advantage," says one editor, "to a one-on-one conference. If I've met and talked with a prospective author about [his or her] manuscript, that is much better than a query letter and a written response. We can sit and talk about the work at some length, and begin to know each other as individuals as well" (qtd. in Parsons 67). A telephone call is the next best thing to a one-on-one conference.

The prospective author who chooses to send a query letter instead should craft it as carefully and as interestingly as a sales blurb, outlining the contribution the work will make to the field and to the press' publishing list. One good way to attract an editor's attention is to mention that a recognizable name (perhaps the dissertation director?) has suggested that the prospective author contact the particular press. One good way to lose it is to mention that the work under consideration is a dissertation. A prospective author who feels compelled to mention that the work is a dissertation is advised by one editor to slip the information into the third paragraph and mention that the dissertation has been extensively revised (Parsons 119). The query letter should be written on letterhead and addressed to the acquisitions editor by name.

Presuming the acquisitions editor has called for the manuscript and responded favorably to it, the manuscript will be sent to two or three readers for peer review. An editor usually asks a writer for recommendations for peer reviewers, partly as a test of the writer's knowledge of scholars in the field (Parsons 84). Waiting the month or more for the readers' reports is an anxious but not idle time for the prospective author. Not everyone agrees with me, but I recommend that the author spend this time diving into serious periodicals and scholarly journals (both rhetoric and composition journals and those in related fields), reading with an eye toward expanding the background to meet the needs and interests of a larger audience for the scholarly monograph. Given the present collapse of the academic job market and the shrinking market for scholarly monographs, I believe that one of the best things academic authors can do for themselves and the university is to write to an audience comprised of both academic intellectuals and intelligent nonacademic readers. (For a larger discussion of this issue, see both Curren and, especially, Cary Nelson and Michael Bérubé's recent and often cited article.) The prospective author can also begin compiling those lists of names and addresses that the marketing department will require later: lists of scholarly journals, institutions, programs, and individuals that should receive review copies (Schoenfeld and Magnan 270).

Presuming that the readers' reports favor publication, that the prospective author has responded to suggestions for revision, and that he or she has received and signed a contract, the time for revision has come. But first, a word about publishing options, particularly for prospective authors expecting the "prolonged relationship of considerable intimacy" with a manuscript editor that Armstrong describes ("Revising" 49). Today's university presses have been so adversely affected by shrinking university library budgets that only works likely to sell between three thousand and ten thousand copies receive extensive line-editing from senior editors (Thatcher B1; Marshall 17). In the face of the "light copyediting" an unknown author's manuscript will receive, an author who can provide camera-ready copy may wish to query the acquisitions editor about the possibility of an honorarium for doing so. Says one writer who has published both ways, "I found the camera-ready alternative was far less painful than delivering copy, reviewing the copy editor's marks and reading galleys" (Sihler B3). Providing camera-ready copy can significantly reduce production time and simplify indexing the work as well.

The Transformation Process: Re-vision
A new scholar considering revising the dissertation for publication as a monograph will find no lack of advice from editors and scholars on "what to get rid of." Whether an editor is pointing out the dissertation's "deadly sins" (Armstrong) or identifying telltale signs of the thesis that should be rooted out before publication (Holmes), the overriding recommendation is to revise the content, pace, and style of the dissertation with both the different purpose and the larger, less specialized audience of the book in mind. But recent composition scholarship demonstrates that adjusting one's discourse to the needs and interests of an audience is a more complicated process than these lists of "what to get rid of" suggest.

The purpose and audience of a dissertation and a scholarly monograph are indeed different. "A dissertation," claims one university president, "should be defined solely as evidence of the ability to do independent work" (Parsons 112). A book, on the other hand, is written to communicate something that matters to an audience who matters (not just to serve promotion and tenure, as curmudgeonly critics contend). The audiences of a dissertation and a book are different, too, and analyzing their differences in the light of recent composition scholarship provides the new author with one key to a successful revision. David Bartholomae was one of the first compositionists to point out how complicated the intertwined problems of purpose and audience awareness are. He states, "It is difficult to imagine how writers can have a purpose before they are located in a discourse, since it is the discourse with its projects and agendas that determines what writers can and will do." Moreover, he continues, "The writer who can accommodate her motives to the reader's expectations . . . must see herself within a privileged discourse. . . . She must be either equal to or more powerful than those she would address" (163). When a student is writing to a teacher, or a doctoral candidate to a dissertation committee, the problem becomes one of "power and finesse," for "the writer has to assume privilege without having any" (Bartholomae 164, 166).

Like the basic writers Bartholomae describes in "Inventing the University," the writer of a dissertation finds him or herself before an audience of skeptical experts who probably know more about the subject than the writer does. As novice writers try to assume privilege and establish themselves "rhetorically and stylistically" in a discourse that is not "'naturally' or immediately theirs, violent accommodations," especially at the beginning, occur (170, 178). The first chapters of a dissertation are often a case in point. Parsons, for instance, claims that much of what appears there amounts to no more than "defensive maneuvers designed to deflect aggressive questioning from the dissertation committee" (116). Quite often, the opening chapters contain exhaustive reviews of the literature, both to prove to the committee that the candidate has read widely and deeply and to situate the subject of the dissertation in the ongoing conversation of the discipline. Mina Shaughnessy's study of advanced writers helps to explain the stylistic "violence"—the jargon, the justifications, the numerous discursive footnotes and lengthy demonstrations—often found in dissertations. Advanced writers, she notes, "inherit the language out of which [they] must fabricate [their] own messages." In "taking over phrases and whole sentences without much thought about them," more facile writers often find themselves "in a constant tangle with the language, obliged to recognize its communal nature and yet driven to invent out of this language [their] own statements" (qtd. in Bartholomae 180). Sometimes a dissertation writer attempts to assume a position of privilege in scholarly discourse by using stilted language and the jargon of the profession. Ironically, the overuse of jargon ("dissertationese") that often ensues identifies the writer as an amateur (Armstrong, "Dissertation's" 241).

All in all, in order to successfully transform a dissertation into a scholarly monograph, a writer must be able to "both imagine and write from a position of privilege," in Bartholomae's words (163). Because the writer is now writing as the expert to novices instead of the reverse, he or she will need to write in a clear, strong, and confident voice. In my reading of many lightly revised dissertations for a university press, I often find the self-assured voice (unshackled by dissertationese) appropriate for the scholarly monograph surfacing only in the final chapters of the dissertation, when scholarly discourse seems more the writer's own. In revision, the writer will want to adopt this more confident tone in the opening chapters, too. Imagining oneself writing to a real individual, one who would be interested in but unfamiliar with the topic, as Parsons suggests, might likewise enable a writer to adopt a more confident and authoritative tone.

While this new, less specialized and less skeptical audience will require more background information than did the initial audience, the extensive review of the critical literature that helped establish the writer's authority for the initial audience will probably fatigue the audience for the scholarly monograph. Likewise, the new audience is likely to regard detailed demonstrations and lengthy discursive footnotes and quotations like sidebars in jury trials: sometimes interesting, but far more often tedious, intrusive, and bothersome. Most of the demonstrations and discursive footnotes can be deleted; essential details in the footnotes can be included in the text. Eliminating all but the most brilliantly crafted and insightful quotations permits the new audience to focus on the writer's meaning instead of on that of the "ghostly colleagues" (Holmes, "Part One" 345) and can save the writer hours of labor in the months ahead. Lengthy quotations require permission to republish from the copyright owner, and securing permission is usually the writer's responsibility. One university press, for example, requires permission to republish more than fifty words from a periodical article and four hundred fifty from a book. These permission requests often take three to four months to be filled, and the editor cannot turn a manuscript over to production until the permissions file is complete.

Now feeling comfortable with his or her rhetorical location in a discourse, the writer is ready to consider matters of style. Redundancies, dissonances, and overuse of passive voice and jargon practically jump from the page, now that the writer has appropriated and been appropriated by the discourse of the field. After cutting, whittling, and polishing the language, just three steps remain before the monograph is submitted to the press for production: a careful check and recheck for accuracy of every quotation, the compilation of the subject and author index, and a radical change of title. Anecdotal evidence suggests that some departments assign less weight to revised dissertations in tenure and promotion decisions. Radically changing the title of the monograph may forestall this practice.

It may seem that I have been emphasizing material motives for transforming a dissertation into a scholarly monograph at the expense of discussing the more intellectual pleasures of seeing one's monograph in print. Indeed, this emphasis may seem to confirm the notion that graduate students and junior professors publish primarily to advertise themselves, as Harris so cynically contends (121). But given the collapse of the academic job market and the increased expectations of publication for junior faculty, I believe that directors of graduate programs and those who teach in them must again make clear to their students the importance of the dissertation in establishing themselves professionally. Having said that, I also believe that while the material rewards—a position with released time for research, tenure, a merit increase, and the like—are welcome acknowledgments of a writer's hard work, they cannot compare with the pleasure of discovering that university libraries throughout the country have spent scarce funds to purchase one's monograph and that their patrons have checked it out. Kurt Vonnegut's blurb on a recently published monograph reads, "A lot of smart people...will read and admire you—and learn from you" (Marshall 17). Could any new scholar hope for more?

Works Cited

Armstrong, Robert. "The Dissertation's Deadly Sins." *Scholarly Publishing* 3 (1972): 241-47.

——. "Revising the Dissertation and Publishing the Book." *Scholarly Publishing* 4 (1972): 41-50.

Barr-Ebest, Sally. "Gender Differences in Writing Program Administration." *WPA: Writing Program Administration* 18 (1995): 53-73.

Bartholomae, David. "Inventing the University." *When a Writer Can't Write*. Ed. Mike Rose. New York: Guilford, 1985. 134-65. Rpt. in *Teaching Writing: Theories and Practice*. 4th ed. Josephine Koster Tarvers. New York: Harper, 1993. 159-85.

Boice, Robert. *Professors as Writers: A Self-Help Guide to Productive Writing*. Stillwater, OK: New Forums, 1990.

Boyer, Ernest L. *Scholarship Reconsidered: Priorities of the Professoriate*. Princeton, NJ: Carnegie Foundation for the Advancement of Teaching, 1990.

Cantor, Paul. "The Graduate Curriculum and the Job Market: Toward a Unified Field Theory." *The Future of Doctoral Studies in English*. Ed. Andrea Lunsford, Helene Moglen, and James E. Slevin. New York: MLA, 1989. 9-14.

Curren, Erik D. "No Openings at This Time: Job Market Collapse and Graduate Education." *Profession 94*. New York: MLA, 1994. 57-61.

Deats, Sara. "From Prospectus to Print: Editing Conference Papers and Publishing the Dissertation." *Writing and Publishing for Academic Authors*. Ed. Joseph M. Moxley. Lanham, MD: UP of America, 1992. 133-46.

"Final Count for *Job Information List* Ads, 1994-95." *MLA Newsletter* 27.2 (1995): 1-2.

Halpenny, Frances G. "The Thesis and the Book." *Scholarly Publishing* 3 (1972): 111-16.

Harris, Wendell V. Letter. *PMLA* 110 (1995): 120-21.

Holmes, Olive. "Thesis to Book: What to Do with What Is Left." *Scholarly Publishing* 6 (1975): 165-76. Pt. 3 of a series.

——. "Thesis to Book: What to Get Rid of." *Scholarly Publishing* 5 (1974): 339-49. Pt. 1 of a series.

——. "Thesis to Book: What to Get Rid of." *Scholarly Publishing* 6 (1974): 40-50. Pt. 2 of a series.

Holub, Robert C. "Professional Responsibility: On Graduate Education and Hiring Practices." *Profession 94*. New York: MLA, 1994. 79-86.

Huber, Bettina J. "Recent Trends in the Modern Language Job Market." *Profession 94*. New York: MLA, 1992. 87-105.

Hutner, Gordon. "What We Talk about When We Talk about Hiring." *Profession 94*. New York: MLA, 1994. 75-78.

Lederman, Douglas, and Carolyn J. Mooney. "Lifting the Cloak of Secrecy from Tenure." *Chronicle of Higher Education* 14 Apr. 1995: A 16-18.

Marshall, Jessica. "Inside Publishing." *Lingua Franca* 5.1 (1994): 17-22.

Nelson, Cary, and Michael Bérubé. "Graduate Education Is Losing Its Moral Base." *Chronicle of Higher Education* 23 Mar. 1994: B1-3.

Parham, Kathy, "Academics Take a Hard Look at the Current Job Market." *Council Chronicle* June 1995: 6-7.

Parsons, Paul. *Getting Published: The Acquisition Process at University Presses*. Knoxville: U of Tennessee P, 1989.

Schoenfeld, A. Clay, and Robert Magnan. *Mentor in a Manual: Climbing the Academic Ladder to Tenure*. Madison, WI: Magna, 1992.

Sihler, William W. Reply to Letter of Sanford G. Thatcher. *Chronicle of Higher Education* 14 Apr. 1995: B3.

Stanton, Domna. "On Multiple Submissions." *PMLA* 109 (1994): 7-13.

Thatcher, Sanford G. "The Crisis in Scholarly Communication." *Chronicle of Higher Education* 3 Mar. 1995: B1-2.

Wolfson, Susan. "The Informal Curriculum." *The Future of Doctoral Studies in English*. Ed. Andrea Lunsford, Helene Moglen, and James E. Slevin. New York: MLA, 1989. 60-70.

Getting Booked: Commodity, Confinement, Conundrum

JASPER NEEL

From Cover . . .

One of the most popular TV shows of the 1970s was a police drama entitled "Hawaii Five-0." Each week's installment ended with the main character, a detective named Steve McGarrett, telling one of his assistants, "Book 'em, Dano." The actor who played McGarrett wore a sweeping pompadour hairstyle and impeccably tailored suits. Even riding at high speeds in an open boat, his hair always stayed in place. He was the embodiment of masculine authority and control. No one who watched the show had any doubt that McGarrett and his crew would apprehend the culprits of the week. His directive, "book 'em," clearly signified conviction and punishment. When McGarrett "booked" a criminal, the criminal stayed booked. At least in the early 1970s, McGarrett was the one who solved the crime, reassured the victims, disciplined the criminals, and reestablished order. In the midst of Vietnam, Watergate, the Cold War, and various social liberation movements, the TV viewer of the early 1970s seemed to need a weekly booking that would set things right. McGarrett was just the sort of booker the moment seemed to require.

Twenty years before McGarrett booked for large TV audiences, James Baldwin had been booked into the Parisian criminal justice system. After he was released, he described his experiences in a *Commentary* essay. He was charged as a *"receleur,"* a receiver of stolen goods. One of his friends had stolen a sheet from a hotel and given it to him. As a New Yorker, Baldwin thought nothing of receiving linens with a hotel logo. When the police discovered the stolen sheet on the bed in his apartment, they arrested him and kept him in prison for several days, including Christmas Day, while the wheels of justice ground along very slowly. By the time he got word of his incarceration to a friend, Baldwin had decided that he would never again be free. When his cellmates teased him about paroled prisoners who were sent to the wrong line and guillotined by accident, Baldwin was so overcome with terror that he became nauseated even though he knew he was the butt of a prison joke. The police Baldwin describes were nothing like McGarrett—not in manner, wardrobe, or coiffure.

Another two decades before Baldwin was booked in Paris, Virginia Woolf's semi-autobiographical character, Mary, in *A Room of One's Own* was *un*booked at Oxford where she was driven off the lawns and denied admission to the libraries. *A Room of One's Own* grew out of an invitation to lecture on the subject "women and fiction," but the pathway to and through that topic forced Woolf to confront the impoverished, constrained status of women in 1929. In the process of writing the book, Woolf thinks first "how unpleasant it is to be locked out" and then "how much worse it is to be locked in" (24). As she works her way around her topic, she finds women "booked" in a variety of ways: they are "booked" out of economic power because their names usually do not appear in the books that record ownership of property, bank accounts, and symbolic capital. They are "booked" out of those fellowships and societies where money and rank associate. They are largely "booked" out of the writing of books themselves because, on the one hand, they have neither the leisure nor the space in which to write, while, on the other hand, they have no sentence bequeathed to them by the history of writing. The "police" in Woolf's world are the officious beadles in cut-away coats and the obsequious librarians in academic gowns. They are as different from McGarrett, Dano, and crew as they are from the terrifyingly reticent, impersonal, and ubiquitous Parisian police of the early 1950s.

McGarrett's TV show reassures by keeping the books straight, property secure, felons under control. On "Hawaii Five-O," as on other such TV police shows, no one seriously questions the outcome. None of the principal characters can be harmed except perhaps in some superficial way; no injury suffered by a main character carries over to the following week. The last two minutes of each installment show the principal actors in a state of tranquil resolution, usually sharing a big laugh as they enjoy the safe normalcy that has been restored. Baldwin's essay, in contrast, shows a terrified young man in a strange country where his command of the language is limited. Woolf's book, in yet a different contrast, shows an angry, middle-aged woman who cannot walk where the writers of books walk and who cannot read where the manuscripts of great writers are housed. Though Baldwin's reason advises calmness, he cannot stop worrying that he will spend the remainder of his life in a prison. Baldwin describes his experience as being like those portrayed "in movies I had seen":

> I was placed against a wall, facing an old-fashioned camera, behind which stood one of the most completely cruel and indifferent faces I had ever seen, while someone next to me and, therefore, just outside my line of vision, read off in a voice from which all human feeling, even feeling of the most base description, had long since fled, what must be called my public characteristics—which, at that time and in that place, seemed anything but that. He might have been roaring to the hostile world secrets which I could barely, in the privacy of midnight, utter to myself. But he was only reading off my height, my features, my approximate weight, my color—that color which, in the United States, had often, odd as it may sound, been my salvation—the color of my hair, my age, my nationality. A light then flashed, the photographer and I staring at each other as though there was murder in our hearts, and then it was over. (373)

As a matter of hard fact, says Woolf quoting Sir Arthur Quiller-Couch, nine of twelve major nineteenth-century British poets

> were University men: which means that somehow or other they procured the means to get the best education England can give. As a matter of hard fact, of the remaining three you know that Browning was well to do, and I challenge you that, if he had not been well to do, he would no more have attained to write *Saul* or *The Ring and the Book* than Ruskin would have attained to writing *Modern Painters* if his father had not dealt prosperously in business. Rossetti had a small private income. . . . We may prate of democracy, but actually, a poor child in England has little more hope than had the son of an Athenian slave to be emancipated into the intellectual freedom of which great writings are born.
>
> (107-08)

Writing, Woolf felt strongly (for purposes of this essay, I might say, "being bookable"), depends first on the writer's circumstances: "Intellectual freedom," as she puts it, "depends on material things" (108).

Commodity

The academic rage in the humanities these days is to write a book, particularly a "scholarly" book published (if at all possible) by a university press. One can define one's location in the academic pecking order by the number *and status* of books required for tenure at one's university. At Yale, generally speaking, one must publish two well-received books before achieving tenure (of course, one must have many other excellent qualities, but I want to keep the focus on books). As one moves downward in the pecking order, the next stop is "one book out with a second discernibly on the way" (that is what we insist on here at Vanderbilt). The next stop down is "one book, if not out, at least well into production and indisputably on the way out." The next stop is "essays significant enough to imply a book is on the horizon." And so on.

This book fetish is fairly new. When I finished my Ph.D. in 1975, one good book would have met the research requirement for tenure at any university in the land, and Baylor University, where I began my career, expected nothing more than "evidence of scholarship," evidence that one could amass with three or four well-placed journal articles or book chapters. Those who received their Ph.D.s in 1955, after all, could achieve tenure at a major university with far less than a book. Ratcheting the system up from an essay or two in 1955 to several essays in 1975 to two books in 1995 seems fairly intense to me. At that rate, my daughter, who is now seven, will need three books to achieve tenure at Yale (here at Vanderbilt she would probably be able to get away with 2.5; 180 miles east at the University of Tennessee she might get away with 2; 180 miles west at the University of Memphis 1.5 might do the trick).

Let me begin with Detective McGarrett's sure and certain movement toward resolution. In this frame of reference, everything functions as a commodity. The economic and political systems define acceptable and unacceptable locations and behaviors. McGarrett, for example, suffers no existential angst over his role in life. He does not wonder about the justice and wisdom of the laws he enforces; he merely enforces them. He does not fret over the social and personal histories of the criminals he arrests; he merely arrests them.

Had McGarrett pursued an academic career in rhetoric and composition, he would have attended the highest-rated graduate program that would admit him. While there, he would have learned the names and folkways of the top journals and most distinguished presses in the field. He would have tried to develop at least two of his seminar papers into essays for top-ranked journals. For his dissertation director, our rhet/comp McGarrett would have chosen a professor with a distinguished record of publication and a history of helping new Ph.D.s launch their publishing careers. McGarrett would have written a dissertation that could, within two years, be revised and developed into a book acceptable to a university press.

With the first book out, our McGarrett would have begun his second book. For starters, he would have written those chapters of the second book that could stand alone as essays. After completing two such chapters and sending them out to leading journals, he would have written the remainder of the book, making sure to focus it narrowly enough so that he could complete the entire book before the year in which his tenure vote would occur. Thus, at tenure time he would have the following scholarly record: two essays from his graduate seminars in print, a book developed out of his dissertation in print, two additional essays extracted from his second book in print, and his second book in circulation. With some luck he might even have a contract for the second book before his department voted on his credentials. His publications would not be commodities in themselves because none of them would have significant stand-alone economic value. Neither of the two books would be likely to sell more than three thousand copies, and each would be considered quite successful when sales passed fifteen hundred. The essays, of course, would earn no direct income at all. All these publications would, however, have made McGarrett himself into a highly desirable commodity. Not many people can achieve a Ph.D., not all of those who do achieve one can secure a tenure-track job, and only a small percentage of those on the tenure track can meet the 1.75 book requirement in six years. As a result, those who accomplish all these difficult tasks become extremely rare commodities, commodities whose value is not questioned by department, college, university, or board of trust. (Caveat: The books are not the only features whereby our McGarrett must distinguish himself in order to make himself into a commodity: he must be a good teacher as demonstrated by both student evaluations and peer review, he must be an adequate academic servant, and he must have sufficient interpersonal skills not to alienate his colleagues on the grounds of personal distaste. I do not take these matters up because I am writing about books, not about classroom teaching, academic service, and departmental politics.)

In behaving this way, our McGarrett is not behaving cynically (as that term is used pejoratively these days); he is merely inhabiting the role invented by Aristotle and his students at the Lyceum 2,300 years ago. One can see this role most clearly at the end of *Nicomachean Ethics* (1181^b) as Aristotle outlines the scholarly work he will do in the *Athenian Constitution* and the *Politics*. In explaining why he would have his students undertake the (no doubt arduous) task of gathering, comparing, and describing 158 different Greek constitutions, Aristotle describes the professional, scholarly voice through which knowledge is gathered, disseminated, and understood. "Collections of laws and constitutions," he says of the project that would become the *Athenian Constitution*, "may be serviceable to students capable of studying them critically, and judging what measures are valuable or the reverse, and what kind of institutions are suited to what national characteristics. But those who peruse such compilations without possessing a trained faculty cannot be capable of judging them correctly. . . ." In this passage Aristotle codifies for the West at least the following notions: (1) scholarship must be as thorough as possible, reviewing every available scrap of information; (2) scholarship depends on critical judgment and educated opinions; (3) scholarship can be undertaken and understood only by the professionally trained. A few lines later, as he outlines the work to be done in writing the *Politics*, Aristotle develops his notions of scholarship further:

> We will begin then by attempting a review of any pronouncements of value contributed by our predecessors in this or that branch of the subject; and then on the basis of our collection of constitutions we will consider what institutions are preservative and what destructive of states in general, and of the different forms of constitution in particular and what are the reasons which cause some states to be well governed and others the contrary. For after studying these questions we shall perhaps be in a better position to discern what is the best constitution absolutely, and what are the best regulations, laws, and customs for any given form of constitution.

This paragraph adds two additional criteria to the three already articulated: (4) scholarship begins with a review of the existing literature, and (5) scholarship in the human sciences has an ameliorative responsibility.

Aristotle, as the shelves of any library clearly show, wrote books. I have twenty-one of those books on my shelf (some, such as the *Rhetoric*, in multiple editions). His object was the definition and dissemination of knowledge. As far as one can tell, he felt no obligation to entertain his reader. Even the *Rhetoric* presents itself as a comprehensive, disinterested, scholarly study of persuasion; its appeal is entirely to the logos. None of Aristotle's apparently flamboyant personality comes through in his scholarship. The reader gets no hint of Aristotle's lavish dinner parties, his opulent clothes, or the gaudy, expensive jewelry that generated so much animosity toward him in Athens.

At the beginning of the modern era, one sees this same notion of books. Perhaps Matthew Arnold, that great defender of modern humanism, makes as good an example as anyone. Arnold also wrote books (as many as Aristotle I suspect, though I have only four of Arnold's, none in more than one edition). If our McGarrett had done a Ph.D. in rhet/comp, he would have taken his notion of scholarship right out of Arnold. In "The Function of Criticism at the Present Time," Arnold recasts Aristotle in modern terms: "Of the literature of France and Germany, as of the intellect of Europe in general, the main effort, for now many years, has been a critical effort; the endeavor, in all branches of knowledge, theology, philosophy, history, art, science, to see the object as in itself it really is" (258). A few pages later, Arnold presses this notion of "seeing the object as in itself it really is" by asking that critical scholarship not only compare ideas, but also rank them and then try "to make the best ideas prevail"; the watchword of this endeavor is that once-famous Arnoldian term, "disinterestedness" (261-70). Arnold preserves the elite, self-actualizing voice of Aristotelian scholarship when he admits that "The mass of mankind will never have any ardent zeal for seeing things as they are; very inadequate ideas will always satisfy them" (274). In the "Preface" to *Culture and Anarchy*, Arnold completes the definition of the modern humanities scholar by demanding both that he (I do not think Arnold anticipated many female scholars) be trained by and that he work within an Establishment (Arnold capitalizes the term): "The great works by which, not only in literature, art, and science generally, but in religion itself, the human spirit has manifested its approaches to totality, and a full, harmonious perfection, and by which it stimulates and helps forward the world's general perfection come, not from Nonconformists, but from men who either belong to Establishments or have been trained in them" (9-10).

One sort of book about rhet/comp then is the sort thought up and demonstrated by Aristotle in the 320s BC and then recast slightly for the modern university by Arnold in the 1860s. Our McGarrett would try to see the composing process, the function of pedagogy, and the history of rhetoric as they really are; he would try to help the best ideas in the field prevail; he would maintain a tone of neutral disinterest both in studying the field and in arguing for the best ideas; he would expect to do his work in the intellectual environment of a research university; and he would not be at all troubled by the comparatively cushy life available to him after he published three books and achieved the rank of full professor. Indeed, once tenured he would be a veritable gorgon at the gate, insisting that tenure candidates demonstrate clear evidence of establishment training, objective seeing power, and substantial production of scholarship. McGarrett would have booked himself, and he would have insisted that all who sought his station also be booked. He would have conducted himself with the same professional zeal and thoroughness as his TV namesake. For him, getting booked would have constituted the normal and necessary professional process, a process whose lineage goes back twenty-three centuries.

Confinement

Almost any sort of booking imaginable has the final effect of confinement. When it first appeared in English, the noun *book* implied not only a specific writing (and thus a specific object in which writing has been preserved), but also the capitalization of real estate whereby a certain parcel of the earth's surface is set aside for private use by a single individual. In general, though, as the *OED* confirms, a book is "a written or printed treatise . . . occupying several sheets of paper or other substance fastened together so as to compose a material whole." In modern terms, the *OED* continues, a book is a "whole being protected by a binding or covers of some kind." It is a "material article" whose pages can contain almost anything, or even nothing. In other words, a book with blank pages (at least according to that book of books, the *OED)* is still a book. When the definite article changes from "a" to "the," the *OED* continues, "book" signifies "the" Bible, or "the" copy of words to which music is set for an opera or a musical, or "the" recorded line on which one can place a wager.

The universal aspect of "book" (even "the Lamb's book of life" in which "saved" Christians have their names recorded) is its materiality. It is a physical object, usually containing written (or typeset) language. It must be produced, owned, and shelved. At least in a material way, its contents remain fixed inside; the contents do not and cannot leave; the order of the contents does not and should not change.

The thing most on James Baldwin's mind when the Paris police first arrested him was when he would eat his dinner. As the hours (and then days) wore on, he changed his aim from dinner to breakfast, from breakfast back to dinner, and so on in the regular order of meals. But then prison food and the terror of being held incommunicado in a strange land changed his focus from food to confinement. Once his name appeared on the books of the criminal docket and the police placed him "in the system," his physical being was shelved as tightly and effectively as any book in any library. Baldwin traces out his oscillation between rational hope ("What is the maximum time anyone could be locked up for accepting a stolen sheet?") and terror ("What is to prevent them from holding me forever?").

Getting booked, after all, signifies containment. In both *Phaedrus* (274-79) and "The Seventh Letter" (341-44), Plato complains bitterly about the way books "contain" thought. He was particularly alarmed that the container itself—that is to say the physical object, "book"—could make no judgments about who should and should not own it, read it, characterize its contents to the public at large. Once "booked," Plato complains, a "thought" is defenseless because it is both confined to endless repetition and helpless in choosing its audience. Twenty-five years ago, Derrida (in everything from *Of Grammatology* and *Speech and Phenomena* to *Writing and Difference* and *Margins of Philosophy*) was still complaining about booking an idea, or even an ethos. He wanted to use "book" itself to unsettle the confining, linear nature of a book. But in the wake of deconstruction, even Avital Ronell's *Telephone Book* is still a book, odd though it looks on the inside.

Our Baldwinesque rhet/comp person books and gets booked in a manner rather different from that followed by our McGarrett. Rather than navigating the river, our Baldwin gets swept up in its currents, often carried away against his will. Whereas the paradigmatic McGarrett would have been B.A. with an eye on graduate school by age twenty-one, Ph.D. with a tenure-track job and a nearly publishable dissertation by twenty-six, and firmly tenured in the Establishment by thirty-three, the paradigmatic Baldwin became interested in writing in ways that he still does not fully understand. He never intended to become an English major, he got started teaching writing as an M.A. candidate who entered graduate school largely because no attractive alternative presented itself, and he finally settled on rhet/comp as a specialization because it seemed the most humane, least ideological work he could find.

Our Baldwin does not complete college until his mid-twenties. After two years of unsatisfactory, demeaning jobs, he applies to graduate school, giving no thought to the implications of his decision and enrolling in the state university located in his home town. As a graduate student he teaches too many sections and thus does not complete his Ph.D. until his mid-thirties. There is no professional pattern in the courses he has taken, he writes no essays of publishable merit as a graduate student, and his dissertation takes too long to complete because it undertakes a task far too big for a single book. But because rhet/comp is still a relatively hot field and because he has paid no attention to the procedures and politics of the faculty in his graduate department, Baldwin follows the advice of his graduate school mentors and accepts a job at a major state university with a big doctoral program. He arrives on campus late one August utterly exhausted from a long, hot summer spent in a frantic attempt to draw a border around the mess that his dissertation finally became. He is not quite sure how he got where he is, he finds both the politics and the professionalism of his new department disgusting, and he knows he must get a book published within five years. Since there are two untenured faculty in rhet/comp, he feels constantly that he is competing with his colleague. He is quite sure that both rhet/comp specialists will not receive tenure, even though the search committee and the department chair have assured him that all tenure-track faculty are judged independently.

For Baldwin academic book writing is largely a mystery. Should he set his sights on a book with Southern Illinois, Pittsburgh, SUNY, or maybe South Carolina? University press books are, after all, the coin of the realm in his department. If he can place his book with Boynton/Cook, Ablex, or NCTE's new monograph series, will it count? How much of a risk does he take if he writes the book with his best friend from graduate school? Does a coauthored book count as only half a book? He cannot seem to get straight answers to his questions. His senior colleagues are frightened of legal action if they misadvise him; his dissertation director feels that her work was completed when he landed a tenure-track job in a big-time university.

Baldwin's writing process turns out to be almost comically romantic. He seems to be living in the "Preface" to Coleridge's "Kubla Kahn," waiting for inspiration to strike and hoping the person from Porlock will not interrupt. Diarrhea is a daily problem, as it was for Coleridge, and he is not above the occasional use of "controlled substances" to help him through some of his darker days. Though Baldwin's pedagogy reflects all the self-conscious strategies and interventions that one hears about at CCCC, his attempts to write a book come straight from such high romantics as Wordsworth and Coleridge—not because he is persuaded by romantic theory but because he has no clear notion of how to proceed other than to sit at the keyboard hoping for the best. When his writer's block becomes insurmountable, he goes to the library to read in hopes of finding new inspiration. He remembers Shelley's contention in "Adonais" that harsh reviewers killed Keats, and he sometimes wakes up at night in a cold sweat after horrible dreams of what the external reviewers have written about his as yet unpublished book.

Quite unintentionally, in the "Preface to the Second Edition of *Lyrical Ballads*" Wordsworth describes our Baldwin's predicament. Our Baldwin, who has never actually read any of Wordsworth's prose, wonders constantly to himself, "What is meant by the word *scholar*? What is a scholar? To whom does the scholar address him or herself? And what language is to be expected from the scholar?" Wordsworth's very words come back to answer these questions: A scholar is someone "endowed with more lively sensibility, more enthusiasm and tenderness, who has a greater knowledge of human nature, and a more comprehensive soul, than are supposed to be common among mankind." The scholar "has acquired a greater readiness and power in expressing what he thinks and feels, and especially those thoughts and feelings which, by his own choice, or from the structure of his own mind, arise in him without immediate external excitement." Worst of all for our Baldwin is the existential isolation, the ahistorical ignorance in which he, like Wordsworth, finds himself. "Aristotle, I have been told," writes Wordsworth, making clear that he has never read Aristotle, "has said that poetry is the most philosophic of all writing" (441). But our Baldwin is not so confident as Wordsworth. He is not at all sure that he is endowed with a greater knowledge of human nature, let alone a more comprehensive soul, than are most other people. His ignorance of the history of rhetoric worries him constantly. For Baldwin, getting booked is a process of confinement, not much different from a jail sentence. Our Baldwin finds himself in academe much as James Baldwin found himself in Paris—in a strange place where the language, the customs, and the crimes are hard to understand. Our Baldwin has accepted a tenure track job without giving much thought to its implications much as James Baldwin accepted the stolen sheet, and, as a result, our Baldwin lands in a predicament from which he has no notion how to escape.

But, as fate would have it, luck smiles. Our Baldwin is so frightened and insecure that he sits for three years at a word processor and, à la Coleridge, a sort of self-creating organic form organizes itself and emerges through the writing process: "it shapes, as it develops, itself from within, and the fullness of its development is one and the same with the perfection of its outward form" (471). Somehow, through an agonizing process as mysterious as dreams themselves, a wonderful book emerges. It wins a Shaughnessy Prize from MLA, a Book Award from CCCC, and the Winterowd Prize from ATAC. Suddenly, editors of collections begin to solicit manuscripts from our Baldwin, journals invite him to sit on their editorial boards, graduate students organizing panels at the CCCC and Rhetoric Society conventions invite him to participate in their sessions.

To his utter amazement, our Baldwin achieves tenure a year before his rhet/comp colleague—a wannabe McGarrett—gets fired. Almost simultaneously, our Baldwin is asked both to direct the writing program at his university and to sit on the college's tenure and promotion review committee, where he must review the scholarly record of each candidate in the arts and sciences. Our Baldwin goes to sleep each night and awakens each morning pondering what has happened to him, whether he has through some Kafkaesque metamorphosis become a member of the police force, if not an insect. All that constitutes high profile academic life seems like a betrayal of the political and social commitments he thought he was making when he enrolled in graduate school and chose the teaching of writing as a specialization. He rarely sees a first-year student anymore. Like faculty in most big Ph.D. departments, he is responsible for teaching only four courses each year, but he receives two courses released time for his administrative duties. Aside from this, he teaches a graduate seminar each fall and a composition pedagogy course for secondary certification majors each spring. After he unlocks the door to his office building at 7:00 a.m. each day, he stands for a moment and listens in the stairwell as the door closes with a chastening clang. He wonders what or whom the door locks out, or in.

From our Baldwin, a second sort of rhet/comp book has emerged, this time as a sort of unexplainable prodigy. Its effect is to grant its author sufficient privilege and financial security to imprison him. He is no longer able to risk the penury of his life before tenure. A guaranteed income of $50,000 a year together with generous fringe benefits is tantamount to a gold strike for our Baldwin, who has never really had anything like reliable, ongoing income before. And he receives an eleven percent bonus for his administrative work, bringing his salary to $55,500. But he is nagged by feelings of charlatanism, unable to believe in himself as a "professor." He has no idea really how he wrote his book and little confidence that he can write another. He fears that his ill-formed, monstrous, and largely useless dissertation reflects his true ability.

Conundrum

Our Woolf undergoes something of a transformation as an undergraduate. As a first-year student, she fled the label "feminist" as she would have fled the labels "communist" or "atheist." But her English major introduced her to ways of reading that she had not expected, and her courses in women's studies solidified her commitment to social transformation. This sentence from *A Room of One's Own* rings in her ears as she contemplates an academic career: "Nobody in their senses could fail to detect the dominance of the professor. His [is] the power and the money and the influence" (33). "The Professor" together with his "power," "money," and "influence" become an agenda, for our Woolf, a massive project of unworking. She reads the history of Western rhetoric—from Aristotle onwards—as one unending agon, a competitive struggle through which a few male voices manage to silence all the other voices.

Her dissertation stakes out a project of resistance. In particular, she wants her first book to resist the notions "control" and "privilege." Uncertain how the project will work, she turns to the computer-based world of electronic discussion as a way to write. Rather than a book between covers, a book of the sort that troubled Plato so dreadfully, she spends the last two years of graduate school and all six years of her tenure probation patiently bringing into existence a complex, open-ended, but extremely powerful home page. At the time of her tenure review she presents to her department a web site with a highly sophisticated navigational structure. Thousands of students and faculty, including nearly every important scholar in the field, have participated. Anyone in the world can log onto the page and discover thousands of course syllabi, thousands of classroom strategies, and a well-mapped labyrinth through contemporary discussions of both pedagogy and theory. The home page is so comprehensive and so navigable that it has become the point of departure for composition studies. As part of their introduction to teaching writing, new teaching assistants are introduced to it at every college in the country, and almost one thousand foreign scholars and teachers visit the page each day. An international community of distinguished scholars logs onto the page as part of their normal scholarly procedures. They know that this page will take them quickly to those sources, both primary and secondary, that will prove essential to their work.

The page becomes so powerful that our Woolf begins to use it to reshape the entire notion of composition studies. She creates an ancillary page on which she teaches HTML, and she begins to argue that writing in HTML will soon play a role similar to the role played by alphabetic writing after Gutenberg. The McNeil-Lehrer Report dedicates an hour to her new ideas, and her name begins to appear in *The New York Times* and in speeches by national politicians. In short, our Woolf turns out to be one of those visionaries who reshapes an entire field. The quality of her work is beyond question; the quantity of her work prodigious; the power of her intellect awesome. And she is very pleased to see that gender seems to play little or no role on her home page: users are fifty-two percent female; volume of use is fifty-four percent female; and the page is so regularly watched by everyone in rhet/comp that it operates as a true, open-ended collaboration. It is the place where anyone interested in teaching writing can find support, advice, and a vast wealth of information.

Less than a year after our Woolf achieves tenure, however, she finds, for the first time, that she is spending more time wondering about scholarship than updating and improving her home page. Her reputation has spread so quickly and her name has become so important that she is inundated with requests to serve as an outside reviewer for tenure and promotion decisions. Even more troublesome, nearly every month a major university contacts her to ask whether she would consider relocating. Increasingly, the phrase "endowed chair" comes up during discussions of such offers. As she responds to this wholly unexpected situation, she feels that she has become Virginia Woolf's own Mary Carmichael. Men are "no longer to her 'the opposing faction.'" She no longer feels herself constrained by them. Whereas fear and even a little hatred had governed her early work, she no longer feels either. As a scholar, she writes "as a woman, but as a woman who has forgotten that she is a woman." Even so, as she finds herself wooed by the profession, courted by her own university, and flattered by those who seek her advice as a consultant, she knows that "the bishops and the deans, the doctors and the professors, the patriarchs and the pedagogues all [are] at her shouting warning and advice" (92-93). Increasingly, she feels like a prize race horse who must pick her fences carefully and jump them at just the right moment, all the while beset with a gaggle of self-appointed advisors, none of whom has any idea how she developed or where she intends to go: "Hesitate or fumble," Virginia Woolf says to her, "and you are done for. Think only of the jump." But the moment our Woolf clears the fence, there is another fence beyond and then another beyond that (94). Suddenly she realizes she is in a competition, surrounded by other horses, all racing toward some uncertain finish.

As the pressures on her time and the demands for her opinion intensify, as students who seek her as a dissertation director or who simply want to bask in her reflected glory proliferate, she recognizes two habits of mind taking over her intellectual life. More and more she looks to the traditions of her field. When she reads new work or listens to new ideas, she compares them to what she already knows, and she finds that she has little patience with those who teach her nothing, those who do not refigure (or at least promise to refigure) the establishment in some important way. And she is acutely aware that the established modes of discourse are the criteria by which she judges new scholars. Though she has a political commitment to nurture those who repeat what she and others have already written, in fact, at the earliest possible moment she turns them over to one of her research assistants. Like her namesake, our Woolf feels compelled to create the sentence for the next generation of scholars; there is a sense of urgency about her intellectual life as she fends off any enterprise that does not contribute to shaping that sentence. When a student or colleague with limited ability comes to her for advice, she quotes Virginia Woolf, but she knows full well that Woolf (as *that* Woolf surely would have known, too) was repeating Matthew Arnold, who was merely reformulating Aristotle: "Think of things in themselves," our Woolf says (111).

A third sort of "book" grows out of our Woolf's political and social agenda. This "book" is intended as a vehicle for transformation. And it works. The entire notion of "book" is different after our Woolf. But the transformation comes at a price. By developing her home page, our Woolf created a new space and a new mode of scholarly discourse. But to her surprise, her success radically narrowed opportunities for new scholars. Before her home page, the scholarly world saw about thirty new scholarly books in composition studies each year. The history of rhetoric added another fifty new books. But composition studies and rhetoric together seem likely to sustain no more than a dozen truly useful home pages, and those pages, which are so fluid and dynamic, modify themselves at every instant in real time. Our Woolf finds herself as one of a dozen distinguished scholars who must redefine the criteria for judging merit in the field. But the very notion of "merit" implies privilege; it defines a commodity, confines the space or privilege to a few, and forces our Woolf into an exceedingly uncomfortable conundrum.

... To Cover

So, is it possible to book without getting booked? I doubt it. Are there bookers other than these three: the professional, the romantic, and the reformer? If there are, I have not met them. Must one choose? I doubt that one can. The professional could no more become the disorganized and uncertain romantic than the romantic could become the organized, calculated, and aloof professional. The romantic finds siblinghood with the reformer, but the reformer has a zeal, a certain commitment that the romantic, though filled with admiration, can never emulate. The reformer finds some solace in conversation with the romantic, but she could never live in a world where her writing process dictated to her what to write. The romantic, in contrast, has no notion how one proceeds to develop an idea or an agenda and then uses the writing process to sell the idea or promote the agenda. The professional and the reformer (once she has become a star) develop a grudging respect. Each tends to use the terms "rigor" and "responsibility" with almost religious devotion. The professional accepts the romantic because the romantic generates those brilliant bursts of insight that create for the professional whole new vistas of discussion.

Writing in the decade before Johannes Gutenberg's birth, Chaucer, at the end of his *Troylus and Criseyde*, articulated what all bookers feel about booking and getting booked: "Go litel bok, go litel myn tragedye." With the book away in the world, according to Chaucer, nought but prayer avails. The prayer he prays could, with modern spelling, have been written by any author finishing almost any book yesterday morning:

> And for ther is so gret dyversite
> In Englyssh and yn wrytyng of oure tonge,
> So prey I God that noon myswryte the,
> Ne the mysmetre for defaute of tonge.
> (5: 1786, 1793-796)

Works Cited

Arnold, Matthew. *Culture and Anarchy*. Ed. Samuel Lipman. New Haven: Yale UP, 1993.

——. "The Function of Criticism at the Present Time." *Lectures and Essays in Criticism*. Ed. R.H. Super. Ann Arbor: U of Michigan P, 1962. 258-86.

Aristotle. *The Art of Rhetoric*. Trans. John Henry Freese. Cambridge: Harvard UP (Loeb), 1991.

——. *The Athenian Constitution*. Trans. H. Rackham. Cambridge: Harvard UP (Loeb), 1981.

——. *The Nicomachean Ethics*. Trans. H. Rackham. Cambridge: Harvard UP (Loeb), 1990.

——. *Politics*. Trans. H. Rackham. Cambridge: Harvard UP (Loeb), 1977.

Baldwin, James. "Equal in Paris." *The Art of the Essay*. Ed. Lydia Fakundiny. Boston: Houghton, 1991. 367-80.

Chaucer, Geoffrey. *The Complete Poetry and Prose of Geoffrey Chaucer*. Ed. John Hurt Fisher. New York: Holt, 1977.

Coleridge, Samuel Taylor. "Kubla Khan." *The Norton Anthology of English Literature*. Ed. M.H. Abrams. 6th ed. Vol. 2. New York: Norton, 1993. 346-49.

——. "Shakespeare's Judgment Equal to His Genius." *Critical Theory Since Plato*. Rev. ed. Ed. Hazard Adams. New York: Harcourt, 1992. 469-71.

Derrida, Jacques. *La voix et le phénomène: Introduction au problème du signe dans la phénoménologie de Husserl*. Paris: Presses Universitaires de France, 1967.

——. *De la grammatologie*. Paris: Les Éditions de Minuit, 1967.

——. *Margins of Philosophy*. Trans. Alan Bass. Chicago: U of Chicago P, 1982.

Plato. *Phaedrus and Letters VII and VIII*. Trans. Walter Hamilton. New York: Penguin, 1973.

Ronell, Avital. *The Telephone Book: Technology—Schizophrenia—Electronic Speech*. Lincoln: U of Nebraska P, 1989.

Shelley, Percy Bysshe. "Adonais." *Shelley: Selected Poems, Essays, and Letters*. Ed. Ellsworth Barnard. New York: Odyssey, 1944. 386-415.

Woolf, Virginia. *A Room of One's Own*. 1929. New York: Harcourt, 1981.

Wordsworth, William. "Preface to the Second Edition of *Lyrical Ballads*." *Critical Theory Since Plato*. Rev. ed. Ed. Hazard Adams. New York: Harcourt, 1992. 437-47.

The Edited Collection:
A Scholarly Contribution and More

GAIL E. HAWISHER AND CYNTHIA L. SELFE

Dear Cindy and Gail:

Enclosed is the draft of my chapter. Be kind.

Yours truly, HT

Dear Gail and Cindy:

At last, here is my revised manuscript. Again, my apologies for being so late. This is *not* my usual style! Your editorial comments were very helpful, and I have tried to do what you suggested. I may not have succeeded!

Thanks, JM

Several authors have asked for deadline extensions—nag them unmercifully! This volume is going out on schedule.

Your coeditor

Dear Colleagues:

We have some great news. We received a contract for the *Critical Perspectives* text. . . . For your timely response to our suggestions and for getting your chapters back to us in tip-top shape, we are extremely grateful.

Cindy and Gail

As teacher-scholars in composition studies who began contributing to professional conversations in the 1980s, we place great value on the edited collection as a scholarly publication and more. Although authored texts were important to each of us in our early graduate school days in rhetoric and composition (for example, Edward Corbett's *Classical Rhetoric for the Modern Student*; Janet Emig's *The Composing Processes of Twelfth Graders*; James Kinneavy's *A Theory of Discourse*) and remain critical to our thinking today, the edited collection was also a crucial component of our introduction to the field. Charles Cooper and Lee Odell's *Evaluating Writing* and Gary Tate's *Teaching Composition: 10 Bibliographical Essays* gave us a sense of an ongoing dialogue; they encouraged us to eavesdrop, to listen in on the important conversations of the field as we plunged headlong into our studies. Since that time, we have come to value the edited volume not only as an introduction to a field of inquiry but also as a genre capable of sustaining serious debate on critical issues within a discipline.

There is no question that over the years the anthology as a genre has proliferated in composition studies. The genre seems especially critical to those fields we would label as relatively newly-constituted disciplines, such as cultural studies, film studies, literacy studies, and, we would argue, composition studies. By bringing to scholarly conversations voices that might not otherwise be heard, the edited collection defines and broadens fields of inquiry, while at the same time identifying issues that demand attention. A short list of landmark edited texts in composition studies doesn't exist today; there are far too many excellent collections to present a tally of those we find noteworthy. We can, however, name at least two that the profession has honored by bestowing upon them the MLA Mina Shaughnessy Award (Connors, Ede, and Lunsford's *Essays on Classical Rhetoric and Modern Discourse*) and the CCCC Outstanding Book Award (Bullock and Trimbur's *The Politics of Writing Instruction: Postsecondary*). Certainly, there are also other superb collections worthy of the profession's attention. Many, like the two award winners, take as their subject one aspect of a larger area of study, be it classical rhetoric, the politics of teaching writing, cultural studies in English classes (Berlin and Vivion), feminist issues (Phelps and Emig), or computers and workplace literacy (Sullivan and Dautermann), to mention a few.

But that's not to say that all anthologies are the same. Like the authored book or the article, many falter and beg for improvement. Several make us wonder why the particular group of essays appear under one cover; a few make us wonder why they were published at all. And, in many respects, the edited collection *is* different from other academic genres, presenting problems and challenges that are absent in other kinds of authorship or at least are less of a problem. How do you make "single" essays into "chapters?" How do you get chapters "to talk" to one another? How do you ultimately make the book cohere? And, moreover, what kind and degree of coherence are you really seeking in trying to represent complex subjects in as accurate a way as possible? Of course, there are also the somewhat more everyday but nevertheless important considerations we've highlighted in the excerpts that begin this chapter: How do you convince the best possible scholar-teachers (and often the busiest) to join you on a project that will inevitably require time, effort, and some frustration before ultimately yielding productive results? How do you respond "kindly" but effectively to colleagues' writing in ways that will encourage them to do their best work but not push them beyond the limits of their professional good will? How do you ensure that contributors submit their drafts and revisions to you in a timely manner when they are faced with a raft of other professional deadlines of their own (such as, responding to student papers in a timely fashion, maintaining departmental and university committee schedules, completing work for the CCCC, MLA, and NCTE)? And how do you secure an appropriate publisher?

Over the years, with seven collections of essays under our combined belts, we have developed a set of approaches that we think contributes substantively to the genre and helps address a few of the common problems associated with it. These approaches do not, of course, make the task of editing such collections challenge free. The problems we have already identified are so complex, so dependent on the characteristics of individual scholars and the wide range of interpersonal relationships that characterize professional life, that no one set of approaches can completely or satisfactorily anticipate them all. In the rest of the chapter, however, we offer our common experience as a guide, and we outline the characteristic challenges associated with publishing edited collections, along with suggestions for possible ways of addressing these challenges. We offer them in the spirit of collegiality and with the hope that the field's newcomers, and not so newcomers, will also find them helpful.

A Few of the Things We Have Managed to Get Wrong: A Story

We begin with a story. The excerpts from letters that introduce this chapter were extracted from the correspondence of two of our earliest collaborative efforts: the first was begun in 1986 and resulted in the publication of *Critical Perspectives on Computers and Composition Instruction* in 1989; the second was begun in 1989 and resulted in the publication of *Evolving Perspectives on Computers and Composition Studies: Questions for the 1990s* in 1991. With each of these edited collections, there were numerous problems, but we learned as we worked on them and were finally rewarded for our efforts.

Perhaps because it was our first collaboration (and first edited collection), we encountered more, or at least different, problems with *Critical Perspectives* than with other volumes we have recently edited. In retrospect, we seemed to do almost everything *wrong*. We began, for instance, by writing to possible contributors and collecting full, completed essays that grew out of papers presented at the 1986 Computers and Writing Conference. In this effort, given that we had no indication from a publisher that such a collection would be of interest, we depended entirely (and naively, we now recognize) on the good will of friends in the profession. In asking these generous colleagues to contribute papers before we had sent out a prospectus, we could not even provide them the intellectual direction offered by a carefully considered overview of the project. Later, we discovered just how fortunate we were in collecting a series of chapters that focused on the theme of critical perspectives on technology, a common thread we drew upon from the conference presentations. We could well have ended up with a much more loosely and less successfully focused set of essays on that first venture.

Continuing in this less-than-informed fashion, we then sent out the completed manuscript to approximately twelve publishers (we blush at the number), only three or four of whom were appropriate for the project at hand. We did not take the time to do our homework on each publisher and to learn about the kinds of scholarly work on which these houses focused their existing series or efforts. In this approach, we were driven, like most beginners, by faith in the casting-the-broad-net approach. We hoped that one publisher would recognize the brilliance of our as-yet-not-clearly-formed ideas and immediately fire us off a contract—what a more experienced colleague later called a "cold contact," reminding us that these seldom yield the desirable results. We were so focused on ourselves that we were not capable of perceiving the acquisitions editors of these publishing companies as professionals with their own important agendas. To excuse our behavior, we can only note that we had never met a real "live" publisher at that point. (Publishers were not exactly knocking on our doors; ten years ago technology issues weren't of much interest to those in composition studies). Hence, to us the publishing world was populated primarily by those academic colleagues who wrote books. The acquisitions editors (and the production editors, developmental editors, project assistants, reviewers, clerical staff members, copyeditors, and compositors who would later help us with our projects) were only mythical, albeit highly powerful, individuals we did not know. As a result of these perceptions, we also did not take the time to establish an initial personal contact through a face-to-face conversation at a professional conference or a simple telephone call. (Both strategies, of course, terrified us as neophytes; why would we want to get close enough to actually *meet* the people who were going to be rejecting us, we reasoned?)

We also failed to understand that publishers generally prefer a prospectus (or full manuscript) to be sent only to one of them at a time, or to a very limited number of competitors. Nor were we likely to have learned this astounding fact; after all, we were afraid to ask any of our more experienced colleagues for help in publishing for fear of sounding ignorant and naive—even though we were, understandably, both. Of course, we have since learned that it's acceptable to submit a prospectus to more than one publisher, as long as it is clear in your cover letter which other publishers you have contacted.

It was not surprising, given these unintentional gaffs, that we received rejection letters from most of the twelve original publishers on that first project. Indeed, in retrospect, it continues to astound us that three very generous and experienced editors forgave our fumbling approach and expressed interest in the project. Subsequently, one of the three decided against publication, and we chose from the two remaining. Even today, it amazes us that the book was published in as timely a fashion as it was, and we credit the professional efforts of good editors and the generous contributions of talented colleagues for that fact. About the only thing we did right was to be persistent. Regardless of how many rejections arrived in our mailboxes, we believed that the book was a good and necessary one for compositionists, and we knew that the contributors to the volume had written, in many cases, groundbreaking essays. Our belief in the importance of the book was justified, fortunately, and that made all the difference.[1]

Common Challenges and Strategies for Addressing Them

What should we have done differently? What would we suggest that you do as you begin the task of proposing an edited collection to a publisher and convincing colleagues to join you on such a project? The following suggestions are offered as guides. We know that they will not suit the special constraints of all projects, the needs of all individual editors, or the personal styles of all contributors. Nevertheless, they remain for us a good starting point when we embark on a project, and we hope they provide you with similar assistance. Please note that the suggestions appear in only a rough order and that several factors must come together simultaneously to ensure a first-rate project. The process of putting together an edited collection is not nearly so simple as our discussion suggests.

Find the Right Project

Our first piece of advice to editors of collections is to find the right project—a more complicated task than it seems. Good projects must be complex enough to hold your interest as an editor (and to hold contributors' interest as participants) and focused enough in content for you to provide the necessary context and direction to all contributors. The project you choose, for example, should be in an area that you know well—well enough, in fact, to be able to review all of the relevant competing texts for the prospectus. We believe it is a mistake to choose an area in which you may have a moderate or limited interest simply because you think that it will spark publishers' interest or that it will sell well. Neither prediction is likely to come true unless you have the expertise to contribute.

We would suggest, as well, that you choose an intellectual focus for which you can clearly articulate the key professional issues, especially those already identified by other colleagues who have published in related areas. The first sign of naive editors, we have learned, is an inability to set their projects (and their intellectual work) in the contexts of ongoing professional conversations, to recognize that their work has benefitted from the thinking that has gone before them and is connected to other current issues in the field. The best homework we have found for this stage of the project is to review the last five years of several professional journals in the area under consideration or to read several recent scholarly books that focus on the topic. This strategy helps us identify those issues and themes relevant to the proposed project. For some editors, drawing a map of the intellectual relationships represented by these conversations helps a great deal to conceptualize the field of play.

A final suggestion is to choose a rich topic area that lends itself to the multiple voices inherent in edited collections. One of the benefits of such collections is their multiplicity and the variety of perspectives with which they represent a theme, problem area, or set of issues. Choosing a focus that takes advantage of these multiple voices is not always an easy task, and balancing this concern for focus and coherence with the responsibility of representing a rich range of perspectives on a topic makes the task doubly difficult. The best projects, in our minds, are those that are controversial enough to merit serious attention, interesting enough to appeal to several relatively broad-based groups of people in the profession (for example, people who teach composition courses in community colleges, teacher educators, or writing program administrators), and complex enough to benefit from the richly textured layering of multiple voices. Finally, choose a project you believe is important for others to study—and be able to tell others, succinctly, why it is important. The process of compiling an edited collection is frustrating enough; spending time on a project that doesn't merit your effort is counterproductive. We suggest testing your thinking by consulting with colleagues and asking for their views on issues. The very process of talking and writing about the topic will help you consolidate your own thinking and confirm (or refute) your judgment. We'll suggest more about this network of contacts in the next section.

Build a Network of Colleagues

All publishing projects depend on the efforts of many people, and nowhere is this truer than for the edited volume. Indeed, even before you begin editing a collection, you will want to build the initial professional network to help your project get off the ground. Good colleagues whose work you respect are your first important resource. Although colleagues at your own institution are one source of professional contacts, we believe in the importance of extending a network and including individuals from other institutions with similar scholarly interests or with interests that are unfamiliar and generative. National professional conferences and summer seminars are excellent venues for encountering interesting work, generally because we can focus on those sessions and colleagues that share our specific areas of interest. As journal editors, we have also learned to ask an interesting question or two at the end of every session in an attempt to give presenters the opportunity to explain more of their work; we try to meet colleagues whose papers we have enjoyed to let them know we were listening and learning; we write notes to people after conferences telling them how much we enjoyed their presentations and sending along related papers of our own in exchange; we agree to serve as chairs of sessions so that we can find out what projects bright colleagues are working on. Of course, conferences aren't the only place to create a scholarly network of colleagues. We also try to cultivate professional relationships via e-mail and often write others about chapters they have written for books and about articles they have published in journals as well.

We have begun to see in these scholarly encounters not only potential contributors for future edited collections, but also potential reviewers to suggest to editors, valued resources for exchanging help and advice, and, most importantly, interesting friends. Experienced colleagues can also help by providing sample copies of successful prospectuses—often a real help for those who are just making the transition from graduate student to assistant professor.[2]

Editors of publishing houses are additional professional contacts that we have learned to value. We now sometimes introduce ourselves at the exhibition booths of conferences if we think we have an especially promising project for them, often asking for a few minutes of time to sit down (away from the crowds) and describe the kinds of projects we are working on. (You'll notice that this is the same kind of advice that Maureen Hourigan provides in another chapter of this book.) We have learned that many of these individuals know a great deal about our field and, moreover, that they are generous and helpful in their advice. We recognize, of course, that editors are more willing to make time for us as we get more successful publications under our belts, but we have observed them being quite responsive to junior colleagues who have published less but who have interesting projects that are likely to attract the attention of the profession.

One caution might be useful here. It's not wise to confuse the personal intellectual interest of editors with their professional judgment. Although publishers might be personally encouraging about and interested in your work, they will also be very frank, if asked, as to whether their particular publishing house is appropriate for your proposed project in the form in which you think it should be published. We have learned to listen to these assessments and to value them; they are generally right on the mark.

At a basic level, in-person meetings give publishers a face with which to associate your written product, and they provide you with the opportunity to decide whether the editors are people with whom you can work. You can also find out at these meetings exactly what the editors would like to see in a prospectus. Most publishers require a five- to ten-page document that provides an overview of the book, a description of the targeted audience, a discussion of market competition, a table of contents, abstracts of chapters, an identification of the approximate number of manuscript pages, and a timeline for completing the project. Most also require two exemplary chapters that typify the kinds of essays you will be featuring in the collection. In many cases, a publisher may ask for less, but remember that your prospectus is usually being sent out for review and the referees need to see enough of your project to make a fair judgment. Chapter contributors will also benefit from a fuller prospectus as they work on their manuscripts. For many of these colleagues, isolation from other contributors, not knowing what other authors are doing or thinking or reading, can be a factor that contributes to raising their anxiety about writing. A good prospectus, along with a great deal of communication with the collection editor, can help alleviate these concerns. Finally, our own experience as series editors tells us that too often colleagues send off a prospectus for an edited volume without any chapters from the book. For us, the chapters are crucial because they give us an in-depth view of the volume's possibilities. It is also useful to attach a cover letter to the prospectus indicating your willingness to work with the publisher and suggesting several well-known professionals—individuals experienced in the field—who might be willing to review the project.

Identify an Appropriate Publisher

The preliminary steps we have suggested thus far should prepare you to think about suitable publishers for your collection; you should, at this point, know which houses are publishing collections on a particular subject, which topics are ripe for further analysis and exploration, and which editors seem like the kind of people with whom you want to work and who would be willing to work with you. The next part of the problem—finding a publisher who will make sure your project sees the light of day in a timely fashion—is not always easy to come by for edited collections. Even if the press has a reputation for its excellent production crew, you must also depend on the schedules of your contributors. With each of the books we have edited, we began with more authors than finally came to populate the collection; those who had to drop out found the time constraints to be the most difficult demand. One reason why we suggested that you send your contributors the timeline along with the prospectus is to ensure that everyone knows upfront your and your publisher's schedule. (You will also be signing a contract with the publisher stipulating the date by which you must submit the full manuscript.) Although inevitably you will fall behind the schedule you set, at least you give your contributors fair warning. As you probably already guessed, the "nagging" we highlighted in the excerpts at the beginning of this chapter doesn't always produce the desired results. The second text we worked on (*Evolving Perspectives*), while it certainly improved on our record, took two years from start to finish; we were hoping, like most collection editors, for a much faster turn around.

When you are talking directly to the publishers, consider also the procedures that their house follows for working with edited collections. Researching this kind of information is an unfamiliar task for most authors, but the investment in time ensures that you will have no surprises as you ready the book for publication. You need to ask about standard royalty contracts for collection editors and contributors; the formats required for final copy; advertising and marketing strategies; and support systems for indexing, seeking permissions, and accepting electronic text from authors. In another chapter of this book, Michael Keene and Ralph Voss provide useful advice on these issues.

Also of interest should be the production schedule typically followed on a project and the people it involves. Most publishers of edited collections, for example, begin projects when an acquisitions editor identifies a book that potentially fits the work of the particular house and agrees to work with a collection editor who seems able to deliver the material in a timely fashion and a readable form. In ideal situations, acquisitions editors are looking for people with interesting and marketable ideas and who show an insightful understanding of the professional issues, who have solid publishing track records, and who have the ability to involve notable contributors. They do not always find their ideal project editor, however, and often take chances on authors who demonstrate a willingness to work hard even if they have not had extensive publishing experience.

Once acquisitions editors receive a prospectus, they send it out for review to individuals whom they consider knowledgeable in the subject area of the project. This process, given academic schedules and the demands of professional obligations, often takes eight weeks or more and should be figured into your prospectus timeline. If the reviews are positive, the acquisitions editor receives a firm go-ahead on the project and may assign it to a developmental editor. The developmental or acquisitions editor is responsible for ushering the collection through the rest of the prepublication process—receiving the completed manuscript and sending it out for the review that will guide the revision of the manuscript. When you submit the final revised manuscript to be published, a production editor takes over. He or she supervises the copyediting and works with you on the cover and art design. Depending on the arrangements you have made, the production editor then sends you or your contributors the copyedited chapters to which each contributor responds. Only when all these chapters are returned to the production editor is the book ready to go to press. Staying in close touch with the production editor (even when things are not going wrong) and serving as a liaison between the production editor and the collection's contributors is one of the collection editor's most important responsibilities.[3]

Most publishers can provide a timeline for this production process; generally, you can estimate ten to twelve months for the process after you deliver a final manuscript to the project editors. This process always goes faster, however, if the collection editor assures that authors have made final checks between internal-text citations and bibliographical entries, adhered to the publisher's style sheet, and returned copy in a timely fashion. We have also found that electronic communication can speed up the process in several areas, especially in eliminating the creation of a second generation of typographical errors by compositors. E-mail has also simplified the business of keeping in touch with contributors about their work. One edited project to which we both contributed set up an e-mail discussion list about the collection itself that allowed authors to stay in touch with each other, to share leads on readings and research, and to engage in the rich exchanges that provide a collection internal synergy.

Balance the Delight in Multiple Voices with the Urge for Coherence
One of the most difficult tasks a collection editor faces is that of balancing the richness of different voices, perspectives, and representations

inherent in an edited collection with the natural urge to establish a focused topic area, a set of issues, or a problem around which to organize the chapters. And danger lies on either side of this balancing act. Editors who force too much coherence on a collection run the risk of producing a lackluster conversation in which all voices sound the same, perspectives are flattened, and disagreements based on the natural contradictions of human existence are resolved or erased. In contrast, editors who provide too little direction, too little common ground for contributors to inhabit or examine, often find they have helped produce a loose collection of independent views on too broad an area that has no internal synergy—chapters neither acknowledge, nor recognize, nor build on, nor play off of each other. Such collections are better suited to a thematic issue of a scholarly journal that can be published in a more timely fashion.

Given the many challenges of our first edited collection, we worked hard on this balancing act in our second collection, *Evolving Perspectives on Computers and Composition Studies: Questions for the 1990s*, trying to provide contributors a focus and considerable guidance in writing their chapters, while also encouraging them to use their own distinctive voices and intellects to explore areas that they felt important to the collection's discussion. Our goal for the collection was a clear one: to provide graduate students and seasoned scholars in computers and composition studies a richly textured, multiply layered series of research questions that they could use as a basis for their inquiry during the decade. The collection was important to us because it grew directly out of the questions that graduate students and colleagues from all over the country were asking us wherever we went to visit or talk: How are computers used in English composition classrooms? How does computer use affect writers, students, instructors; their composing processes; their written products; their teaching; the social and educational contexts within which they work? What are the ideological dimensions of computer use that are important for composition teachers to consider? By focusing all the chapters on a set of issues that needed to be defined and a set of research questions that needed to be addressed, we provided the collection needed coherence and purpose. By asking authors to choose an area of investigation that was important to their own work, and to which they could lend their own perspective and representational shape, we allowed the multiplicity of voices inherent within edited collections to take shape among the participants. The result, we still believe, is a positive one, and one of which we are exceedingly proud as a contribution to the field. Here are the instructions we gave to each author:

> **Book Purpose:** To identify theoretical, pedagogical, and research questions in computers and composition studies for the next decade.
>
> **Chapter Purpose:** To identify and define one particular area of exploration that needs to be undertaken. Chapters should not describe a specific, localized study, lab,

classroom, or program. Rather they should be explorations of generalized areas of study that are important within broad professional contexts, that encourage other researchers and scholars to realize the importance of further work in the field, and that sketch some of the directions that such work might take.

Chapter Structure and Organization: Please make sure that your finished manuscript is fifteen pages or less—double spaced. Please construct your chapter around the following three-part organizational guidelines:

- Begin with an introductory overview of your topic or area of scholarship (hypertext, evaluation of computer-based text, computers and gender, etc.). In this section, also be sure to foreground the importance of this area of study by placing it in a clear context of larger professional trends and concerns in such fields as composition studies, linguistics, literary studies.

- In the second part of your chapter, please include a review of the literature, but also use this section to expand on the important issues within your topic area that you introduced above. Explain or explore them in detail so that you can set up the questions you will identify in the third part of your chapter.

- The third part of your chapter should list a coherent set of unanswered questions that grow out of the issues and the topic areas you have identified in parts one and two of your chapter.... This is one book that will value the "asking" of questions more than the answering of them. We encourage you to think of questions that span theory, research, and practice.

Although you may choose to give your authors less guidance, you do need to conceptualize the shape of the book fully and to convey to the contributors your sense of the major goals of the collection. This work is often best done in the prospectus to the volume, which is of as much use and gives as much information to the contributors as it does to the publishers who are considering it. There are also, of course, additional ways of addressing the balancing act we have just described. Nancy Grimm, for example, has told us about a collection she is contributing to in which the editors have arranged times at several professional conferences during which contributors will meet face-to-face to exchange ideas. Michael Pemberton has told us of editors who ask all contributors to join them on IRC.[4] And, as mentioned earlier, we also know editors who have used e-mail discussion lists and even MOOs to engage participants for this purpose.[5]

Over the past several collections we have put together, we have identified strategies that help us ensure the balance between coherence and the vitality that stems from multiple-voice collections. For example, we generally ask particularly experienced scholars to write substantive overviews of sections, or we choose to write them ourselves. We give these overviews to all authors in the sections before they write their final drafts for the collection manuscript. We also provide all the authors in a section with copies of the other chapters in that section so that they can highlight areas of agreement and difference and create those important cross references (we like to think of them as the print version of hypertext links) that lead readers from one essay to other related contributions. We have also become fond of asking the book's contributors or additional contributors to write substantive responses to the pieces in a section, with the purpose of pointing out both their divergence on key issues, the relationships between the various authors' approaches, or the less evident connections inspired by the theory and practice that informs individual chapters. Such coherence can also be achieved—always with the consideration of honoring differences—by enlisting the help of colleagues. For the *Evolving Perspectives* collection, for example, we asked a panel of six "consulting editors" to read and help us comment on contributions. We chose these consulting editors for their broad experience in the field and their understanding of the ways in which key issues in computers and composition studies were related. Even as we chose them, however, we assured them that they would be featured as consulting editors and that their names and affiliations would appear prominently right after the title page. If you ask colleagues to help you with the editing, they need to be recognized in more than a brief acknowledgment. These consulting editors also gave us a sense of perspective on the contributors. From them, we realized the importance of identifying contributors who write well (we caution you not to ask a colleague whose writing you have not read), who complete their manuscripts by a firm deadline, and who are knowledgeable scholars who have already been published in the field or whose writing and scholarship shows great promise. Finally, to ensure some sort of visual coherence (and coherence of resources), we ask authors in all of our collections to follow a common format and to ensure that their chapters are approximately the same number of pages as you saw in the directions to contributors above.

Consider the Personal and Political Implications of Your Publishing Activities
Over the last decade, composition scholars have become committed to assuming responsibility for addressing the political issues associated with literacy education and for participating in ameliorating the inequitable power relations currently oppressing various populations of teachers and students in a range of academic settings given the conditions of racism, sexism, ageism, and classism. Among the edited critical works—and chapters within them—that have provided our profession with important and sound intellectual guidance in these efforts are Patricia Harkin and John Schilb's *Contending With Words*, David Downing's *Classroom Practices*, Anne Ruggles Gere's *Into the Field*, and Andrea Lunsford, Helene Moglen, and James Slevin's *The Right to Literacy*, as well as many excellent single- and collaboratively authored texts. There are times in the last decade, however, when the two of us have found our own professional gaze focused so tightly on politics with a capital *P*—those grand social issues that represent large-scale tendencies accruing from operant cultural, social, or ideological formations—that we have lost sight of the politics associated with personal

relationships (writ with a small *p*, we suppose), our ability to apply political concerns to the often mundane features of our own professional lives as we live them with individual students and colleagues, staff members, and, even, publishers. The challenges in this recognition appeal to both of us and provide additional reasons for enjoying and maintaining the work of compiling edited collections. We have come to value the importance of those collections that give voice to so many fine professionals and provide help to so many readers, teachers, and scholars. We continue to struggle, however, with making sure that our political actions as editors are ones of which we and others can be proud.

One set of issues on which we continue to work, for example, is our ability to make room for additional voices that at various times have been silenced in other professional venues. A landmark decision of our collaboration, for example, was to create a press (Computers and Composition Press) that is devoted to publishing work on technology use in English classrooms—a topic area that other presses were not particularly keen on in the 1980s and that professional journals often managed to overlook. A second decision was to initiate and edit two book series (NCTE's Advances in Computers and Composition Studies, and Ablex's New Directions in Computers and Composition Studies) designed to encourage and support additional farsighted scholarship in this important area of study, which we did not see happening in other publishing efforts. Not all of our challenges have been addressed as successfully, however; we continue to struggle, for example, to identify and include underrepresented authors in the collections we publish—the voices of scholars of color, of newly graduated professionals, and of women are still all too rare in this technology-rich area.

We also struggle with many more mundane matters. The self-discipline required to set realistic deadlines for publishing projects is tremendous, and we frequently err on the side of optimism, even after many years of experience. And while this characteristic generally means that our collections get finished and published, we continue to try to refine our sense of the possible in order to be increasingly responsible to our colleagues and the fine editors with whom we have had the opportunity to work. We know, for example, that contributors to edited collections must make a giant leap of faith—signing on to a project, committing time and energy to it—even before a contract has been signed. And because we have assembled collections that have taken time to place with the right publisher, we know that contributors must make difficult personal decisions about the timeliness of a contribution and the point at which they must withdraw a contribution—under the pressure of a tenure decision, for example—and seek a more immediate airing of their work. For these colleagues, we can offer only a continual stream of frank information as to where the project stands; when we hear something from a publisher that concerns contributors, we pass the information on to them as quickly as possible.

There may be no such generalizable strategies available for the other politicized decisions that seem to be associated with compiling a collection, however. How, for example, can editors remain open to the suggestions of contributing authors and appreciative of the unexpected directions their chapters frequently take, even when we have a strong editorial vision for the collection and even while we are engaged in providing the same individuals with an understanding of the overall shape of the collection and the nature of their chapter's contribution to it as we see it emerging? Being as frank as possible about these relationships, the nature of the collection as a whole, the responsibilities we have to the publisher and to readers, the relationships we hope for with contributing authors, our sense of when a piece is ready and when it isn't—all these shape the nature of our political action in the realm of the personal, but they don't ever eliminate the problems. And we are now used to, or at least somewhat comfortable with, the other more difficult decisions in this area. For example, we continue to struggle with the hardest decision of all in an edited volume: when to tell a colleague that his or her contribution does not fit with a particular collection, when to drop a late chapter and the contributions that we know it could make in order to salvage the rest of the collection, when to let bad writing go rather than editing it to death.

Wrapping It Up

Maybe the most valuable discovery we have made in the process of editing collections together is how much greater the sum is than the parts. A carefully crafted collection can bring multiple perspectives and a range of intellectual contributions to bear on difficult problems. In some cases (although, we recognize, not all), these problems would be represented much differently by a single author—more focus and depth but, often, less range; more agreement and the opportunity for a sustained argument, but less perspective; more coherence, but less vigor and multiplicity. Thus, we see edited collections and their many distinguishing characteristics, in most cases, as good for the contributors, for the editors, for the publishers, and for the profession.

And the recognition of efforts multiplied extends to our own collaboration—which we have also come to value more with our recognition that it is so unusual. As coeditors we build on this relationship carefully and every day: Gail does the first draft of this chapter and e-mails it to Cindy with an apology ("I'm calling from a roadside park on the way to Chicago; I'm sorry the draft for Olson and Taylor is less complete than I'd like. I've sent them an e-mail message, saying that it's coming. Now if you could just ..."). Cindy e-mails it back with six more pages shoehorned in between a retreat for department heads and a memo to Michigan Tech's president on the accomplishments of the department's scholars. Gail steals time from her University of Illinois WAC workshop and upcoming Center review to add more and to correct the obvious errors. And both of us—recognizing that this kind of project is both finished and never finished to our satisfaction—know that Gary and Todd will also have a strong vision for the emerging collection to guide us in revising the chapter. As we write and struggle to make the chapter a worthy contribution to the collection, we remember something we have forgotten: edited collections are scholarly contributions and more—with the right editors, they are also intellectually challenging and a great deal of fun.

Notes

[1]In a review for *College Composition and Communication*, Bruce Edwards was kind enough to support our belief in the collection. He characterized each essay in the book as "a model of lucid prose," and he argued that the volume would remain current beyond its time "as the first significant book-length contribution to our understanding of what we need to know *next*" about teaching with computers (342-43).

[2]Graduate students with whom we consulted on this chapter—Margaret Faler Sweany, Sibylle Gruber, and Bill Williamson—noted the difficulties of an unknown graduate student approaching a better known and more experienced colleague from another institution who might be in a position to help. They noted that they always felt much better about these encounters—which involve power differentials that can provide great pause for thought—when they had some additional and previous contact with the individual and when they had already worked with them in some positive professional context. We consider this to be additional evidence for starting to establish a network of contacts early on. As examples of such work, Margaret and Sibylle have frequently cited their contribution as associate editors of the *CCCC Bibliography of Composition and Rhetoric* as providing a valuable entré for such encounters, and Bill has cited his work as an associate editor for *Computers and Composition*. Both of these editing roles put these graduate students in the position of knowing and working with contacts that they deemed valuable and of having something to contribute to a relationship—what Pierre Bourdieu, in *Outline of a Theory of Practice*, might call cultural capital.

[3]The seven sets of publishers we have worked with over the years all have slightly different procedures. There have been times on the various projects when we have entered the copyeditings for the whole of the book (something you need to avoid doing), other times when we have responded to the copyeditor's suggestions for each contributor's chapter, and other times when we have even functioned as design editors. The more common request from publishers, however, is that you index the book or pay a professional indexer out of the royalties.

[4]IRC stands for the Internet Relay Chat system, which is a part of the Unix environment and provides participants with the opportunity to meet synchronously online regardless of their location.

[5]MOOs are virtual textual spaces that are technically Object Oriented MUDs, Multi-User Dungeons. Like e-mail, MOOs are conducted through phone-lines connected to the Internet, but, unlike e-mail, participants create virtual rooms, cafés, hotels, or other e-spaces in which they interact with one another synchronously.

Works Cited

Berlin, James A., and Michael J. Vivion, eds. *Cultural Studies in the English Classroom*. Portsmouth, NH: Boynton, 1992.

Bordieu, Pierre. *Outline of a Theory of Practice*. New York: Cambridge UP, 1977.

Bullock, Richard, and John Trimbur, eds. *The Politics of Writing Instruction: Postsecondary*. Portsmouth, NH: Boynton, 1991.

Connors, Robert, Lisa Ede, and Andrea Lunsford, eds. *Essays on Classical Rhetoric and Modern Discourse*. Carbondale: Southern Illinois UP, 1984.

Cooper, Charles, and Lee Odell, eds. *Evaluating Writing.* Urbana: NCTE, 1978.

Corbett, Edward P.J. *Classical Rhetoric for the Modern Student*. 1965. New York: Oxford UP, 1971.

Downing, David. *Changing Classroom Practices*. Urbana: NCTE, 1994.

Edwards, Bruce L. "Rev. of *Critical Perspectives on Computers and Composition Instruction*." *College Composition and Communication* 41 (1990): 342-44.

Emig, Janet. *The Composing Processes of Twelfth Graders*, Urbana: NCTE, 1971.

Gere, Anne Ruggles. *Into the Field: Sites of Composition Studies*. New York: MLA, 1993.

Harkin, Patricia, and John Schilb, eds. *Contending with Words: Composition and Rhetoric in a Postmodern Age.* New York: MLA, 1991.

Hawisher, Gail E., and Cynthia L. Selfe, eds. *Critical Perspectives on Computers and Composition Instruction*. New York: Columbia U Teachers College P, 1989.

——, eds. *Evolving Perspectives on Computers and Composition Studies: Questions for the 1990s*. Urbana: NCTE, 1991.

Kinneavy, James. *A Theory of Discourse*. New York: Norton, 1971.

Lunsford, Andrea, Helene Moglen, and James Slevin, eds. *The Right to Literacy*. New York: MLA, 1988.

Phelps, Louise Wetherbee, and Janet Emig, eds. *Feminine Principles and Women's Experience in American Composition and Rhetoric*. Pittsburgh: U of Pittsburgh P, 1995.

Sullivan, Patricia, and Jennie Dautermann, eds. *Electronic Literacies in the Workplace*. Urbana: NCTE (forthcoming).

Tate, Gary, ed. *Teaching Composition: 10 Bibliographical Essays.* Fort Worth: Texas Christian UP, 1977.

Planning and Producing a Traditional Rhetoric Textbook

Michael L. Keene and Ralph F. Voss

Despite the burgeoning of research in recent years, the field of composition remains remarkably driven by its textbooks. For anyone wanting to make a mark on the field, publishing a textbook thus becomes an obvious—although not the only—course to follow. The traditional rhetoric textbook, perhaps most generally exemplified by James McCrimmon's redoubtable *Writing with a Purpose*, serves as a benchmark for the whole composition textbook industry and is thus an obvious exemplar for would-be writers. Our purpose in this chapter is to offer composition textbook writers a short primer especially focused on the traditional (or "mainstream") rhetoric, and to share some thoughts on our own experience as textbook authors along the way.

A textbook writer, like any good rhetorician, needs to know the subject (including which elements are traditional and which are innovative), the audience (both teachers and publishers), and the situation (including the need for a particular project and how its timing fits the evolution of the subject in other texts). Specifically, would-be textbook authors need to know *why* they are producing a textbook, what both the market and the publishing world are like, what success in this market might mean—and then how to approach writing their book.

Purpose: Why Write a Textbook?

In some university English departments, a textbook is not regarded as a publication of high enough quality to reap such rewards as tenure, promotion, and raises, but for complex reasons this is not as widely true as it once was. In the departments the two of us work in today, our colleagues recognize that publishing a textbook requires solid knowledge of the subject, both its theory and its practice. Moreover, our colleagues know that the review-before-publication process conducted by most commercial textbook publishers is often very rigorous. Consequently, publishing textbooks has helped the two of us along the way to tenure and promotions. Publishing a textbook can very likely help you in the same way, though it's a good idea to inquire about how such a publication is viewed in your own department. (If you are in a department of writing rather than a traditional English department—as a growing number of writing teachers are—we're much more certain that publishing a textbook would help you, for obvious reasons.)

There are other good reasons why you might want to try to write a traditional rhetoric for writers. The book or books you are now using, or have used in the past, may seem to be lacking in some important ways, and perhaps you believe you can write a better one yourself. That's what we decided to do. As faculty in 1985 we saw the same problems with texts that we had seen as graduate students in 1970—such as the failure to integrate reading and writing as essentially complementary acts—so we decided to try to address these problems through our own textbook. Perhaps you have the same kind of "this is such an obvious thing to do, why hasn't anyone done it yet?" perception about current textbooks. If so, and you think you can make your ideas real in the form of a textbook, we encourage you to go for it.

Subject and Audience: The Traditional Rhetoric Textbook Market
The key word here is *traditional*, because although the market for college-level composition textbooks continues to splinter into ever widening varieties of texts, it is still at base a very traditional—and in that sense *conservative*—market. Thus, if you wish to write a highly innovative textbook, we do encourage you, but this section of our chapter may not be as helpful for you as it might be for others. The market for traditional rhetoric textbooks is conservative for many reasons, but the most important is the conservatism of writing teachers themselves, a conservatism that may seem surprising given the advances made in composition studies in the last thirty years. The reasons for that conservatism have to do with composition teachers themselves, the subject of composition, and commercial academic publishing.

The Conservatism of Writing Teachers
Over thirty years have passed since D. Gordon Rohman first wrote that "writing is usefully described as a process," twenty-five years since Janet Emig published her pioneering *The Composing Processes of Twelfth Graders*, and twenty years since Carl Klaus challenged those attending the 1976 CCCC convention in Philadelphia by saying that "we have, in fact, only a handful of professionally trained writing teachers in the entire country"—three important events that signaled the rise of "writing-as-process" and the field-building scholarship in composition studies that followed in its wake. But the "revolution" in composition pedagogy that Maxine Hairston discerned as underway in her 1982 article, "The Winds of Change," has yet to be completely triumphant. Revolutionaries may be in charge in the capital, and they certainly control many of the communication centers, but out in the countryside, people are still living and working pretty much the same way they always have. They seem to assume that whatever worked for them yesterday will probably still work today and tomorrow.

In fact, theory has flourished and moved on through several revolutions in the last thirty years, but pedagogical practice, as experienced by most of the four million or so students who take first-year college composition every year and as enacted by their teachers, remains recognizably close to where it was before the revolution started. While the cutting edge continues to slice its way through theory after theory, many writing teachers continue to rely heavily on grammar drill and practice, error avoidance, analysis of belletristic prose models disconnected from students' own composing, and other techniques long questioned by most of the scholars who publish in the leading composition journals and many of the teachers who read those journals.

Our point here is not to disparage any of our colleagues, but to explain why the market for rhetoric textbooks is conservative. Consider the numbers: the total of those who teach composition at the high school and college entry levels far outnumbers those who maintain *active* membership in professional organizations concerned with writing (such as NCTE and CCCC) or read such publications as *English Journal, College Composition and Communication, Teaching English in the Two-Year College*, and *Rhetoric Review*. And of those who do read the journals, how many put into practice in significant ways the innovations they read there? In our experience, the vast majority of writing teachers are quite dedicated and hard-working and do a good job of helping students learn to compose more effectively; however, often they are simply too busy and/or too focused to devote much time to studying newer ways of teaching. Some are skeptical of alternatives to their current methods, particularly if those alternatives are endorsed by prominent scholars publishing in major journals. Many are part-timers; others are in non-tenurable positions; still others are graduate students, often working on degrees in areas other than composition and rhetoric. Many are under the pressure of student "proficiency" exams and other kinds of externally imposed "instruments." How willing to take a risk on a new pedagogy are such teachers going to be? Even if they are willing, how free are they to do so?

Such instructors teach the overwhelming majority of the composition classes in this country, and they also choose most of the textbooks for those classes. Though most might expect to see new textbooks that at least pay lip service to composing as a process, and many might expect to see some attention paid to collaboration and writing workshop practices, and some might hope for at least a touch of a constructionist approach or some hint of awareness of the role of intertextuality in student writing, these teachers expect most of all to see textbooks that cover familiar territory, albeit territory often now considered by composition scholars to be much less important than it once was.

The Conservatism of the Subject

What does that familiar territory look like? It almost certainly must include the venerable "modes of discourse," which seek to convince teachers and students alike that most good writing somehow observes patterns of comparison and contrast, definition, cause and effect, description, narration, and so on. Though Robert J. Connors made a noble, even prize-winning attempt to inter these modes some years ago, the report of their death was decidedly premature. In fact, in our own rhetoric for writers, early reviewers of our plans for the book made it clear that we not only had to include chapters on the modes in our first edition (we compromised by explicitly using them for invention, not arrangement), we also were urged by the book's adopters and near-adopters to add more chapters on modes for our second edition.

Also, familiar territory almost certainly includes treatment of sentences and sentence style in traditional terms relevant to clausal structures (simple, compound, complex, compound-complex). A handbook section will likely be expected, treating the most common kinds of errors students make, ranging from sentence structure problems like run-ons and parallelism, through agreement problems in number and gender, to the conventions of spelling and punctuation. No one seems to ask for a generative grammar (although we included one anyway), much less a functional grammar.

"Rhetoric" is understood to mean many things in today's culture, but in the territory of traditional writing textbooks it is expected to include the classical canons of invention, arrangement, and style. Though these canons may be presented in a wide variety of ways, they can be omitted only at the risk of failing to attract teachers willing to adopt the textbook. Feedback from teachers using our first edition made it clear that in their eyes we had not paid enough attention to the concept of "thesis"; moreover, in the opinion of many of our adopters, we had not used the word *thesis* itself enough. We scoured our first edition and found what seemed to us to be abundant uses of the thesis concept, but often we had used synonyms like *point* and *main idea*. More than the concept, it was the word itself our adopters wanted. And it was the word itself that our adopters got in the second edition.

The Conservatism of Commercial Publishing

Another important reason traditional rhetoric textbooks are conservative is the nature of commercial publishing. Textbook publishers are business people: they not only expect to but *must* make a profit on the books they publish. If a textbook fails to make money, it will almost certainly be discontinued. This bottom-line attitude drives commercial textbook publishing more every day, especially as increasingly more of our publishing imprints are owned by fewer and fewer conglomerates. While the day when a senior editor can take a chance on a long shot is not entirely gone, we are certainly seeing the shadows of that day lengthen. And whether new media will provide a significant outlet for innovation remains to be seen. Thus, so long as most teachers "out there" demand a conservative rather than an innovative textbook, publishers will provide conservative textbooks.

We are not suggesting that publishers will avoid all innovation. If market conditions promise even modest profit, an innovative text has a chance to be published, although each round of review will serve to routinize the text more and more. But the composition textbook market is large, and the possibility of substantial profit exists if a textbook "takes off." The possibility of enormous sales lies mostly with conservative texts that will appeal to a wide range of composition teachers. Until there are enough truly blockbuster successes among non-traditional texts, a publisher's safest course of action is to continue to try small innovations within the existing genre rather than risk creating a new genre.

The Possibility of Success

Earlier, we discussed how writing and publishing a textbook might affect your career within your department. If your textbook is successful, it will also affect your career beyond your home institution. The recognition of colleagues around the country is something you can appreciate; all of us can occasionally feel underappreciated in our own institutions, and few will deny that being known elsewhere provides a feeling of accomplishment and satisfaction. Such acknowledgment can occur, by the way, even if your text isn't particularly successful in terms of adoption and sales.

Of course, there's always the money. While only a few of the many traditional rhetoric textbooks for writers have been exceptionally profitable, the level of success of those few suggests that it's still possible to publish highly profitable books. Achieving the highest level of commercial success depends upon at least three major and innumerable minor factors, many of them beyond your control, and thus it seems to us that any one book's financial fate is largely a crapshoot.

Content. Publishers like to say that the single greatest factor determining a book's success is the quality of the content, and they've definitely got a point. Unless you do good work—include the right material, organize clearly, write well, respond to reasonable input from reviewers, know when to hang onto your original vision and when to negotiate—your book won't have the kind of content that makes success even remotely possible.

Promotion. But excellent content is only one part of commercial success. After you have produced the best content you can, your publisher still has to make the book attractive and advertise it vigorously; your publisher's sales representatives have to pound the pavement, knock on doors, and *then* be convincing; competitors have to oblige by missing a step here or there; and the printers have to get your project out on time for spring adoption consideration. The most excellent content still needs professional production, effective promotion, and successful sales efforts—and those are not your responsibilities. The traditional rhetoric landscape of the last thirty years is littered with excellent books by terrific authors that never made it into a second edition. There's more to the game than content.

Kairos. Moreover, there's more to the game than publishing and promotion: to be a major success, your book also has to match some kind of groundswell demand in the field. This element of *kairos* is something that you as the writing expert are responsible for gauging, that your acquisitions editor is responsible for gauging as well, but that is difficult for even the most expert market analyst to predict. Basically, you have to get lucky. Still, the fact remains that some textbook authors have made far more money with repeated editions of just one successful book than they have on their teaching salaries.

Okay, I'm Convinced; How do I do it?
First, you need to decide whether to write your book alone or in collaboration with someone. Collaboration has its advantages, chief among them division of labor and, usually, specialization of knowledge and talent; that is, each section of the book can be written by the collaborator best suited for producing that section. Other good "fits" are possible; for example, in our case one of us is a much more thorough reader/researcher, and the other is a more rapid and better composer.

Collaboration is best when different strengths are complementary and the quality of friendship is high and durable. Collaboration with someone better known—hitching your wagon to a star, so to speak—can be a mixed experience, for it might mean one person's doing almost all the work in exchange for the other's name recognition on the cover. Still, such an arrangement might well benefit you more than collaboration with those whose careers are roughly comparable to yours. Moreover, some more senior and well-known colleagues believe in helping younger colleagues along, and collaboration is a respected as well as generous way to do just that.

In all cases, you should be certain you want to collaborate, be clear on how that will work (the two of us rewrote each other's chapters), and find out how collaborative publications are viewed by those who will eventually evaluate your credentials for tenure and promotion. Despite the proliferation of collaboratively written publications, single authorship often impresses review committees most. At one major university where one of us taught, the only kind of publication that counted less toward tenure than something on pedagogy was a coauthored publication. Combining the two, in 1980 anyway, put one of us beyond the pale in that department.

Once you've decided whether to proceed alone or in collaboration, you need to think rhetorically again and analyze your situation and project. First, survey the competition, closely examining not only the text you may be using now, but also the market leaders. What do they have in common? (You'll notice that they have much in common; the differences will be largely matters of degree.) Most will have some feature or features that set them apart, making them different, maybe even distinctive. What are these features? You may also want to note the page layout, print size, use of color, recurring designs, physical size, and number of pages. Which strike you as most attractive, as "reader-friendly"? One technique is to draw up a comparative list of all the books you examine.

Now think about your own book. What must it include? What will you add that is uniquely your own? An editor once told us that all rhetoric textbooks must follow a seventy/thirty rule: seventy percent or more should be coverage you could find in all other competing books (and, given the market, that coverage *must* be there); the trick is coming up with something truly distinctive and highly useful for the remaining thirty percent. We have found this to be good advice. You'll need to decide how much of each aspect of "familiar territory" you are going to provide and how you are going to treat this material. For example, how much rhetoric will you include? How technical will your rhetorical terminology be? How thoroughly will you treat the modes? Will you include samples of different kinds of writing by both students and professionals? Or will you minimize samples, assuming that those who adopt your book will choose a "reader" to accompany it? And so on. Then you'll need to bring your own, fresh material into the mix to make your textbook distinctive and attractive. What's this thirty percent going to be? Perhaps you have a new way of describing and illustrating coherence. Or maybe you have developed some humorous and excellent ways to explain fallacious reasoning. Maybe you will be the one to integrate both collaboration and intertextuality into the traditional rhetoric text's approach. Whatever your distinctive thirty percent is, it needs to be good, and you need to have some confidence in it.

Besides coverage, you have other decisions to make. For example, what voice will you establish? How do you want to "sound" to your student readers as well as to the teachers who are your potential adopters? Though the principal readers of a textbook are students, the first and most important readers of your textbook are their teachers. *They* must like what they read and be able to imagine their students responding to your authorial voice. Once you've decided on your voice, you'll need to keep that voice consistent as you go about producing your manuscript.

After formulating the overall idea and general plan for your book, your next step is *not* to begin writing. It's not wise to write an entire textbook, particularly a full-blown traditional rhetoric, before you begin to test the publishing and marketing waters. If you've got your full book in mind, you're almost ready to approach publishers. Most publishers wish to examine a prospectus, a written overall plan for your book, including an explanation of how your book will be both different from and competitive with other market leaders. A tentative outline should accomplish this explanation, along with, say, two or three sample chapters. At least one chapter should show your treatment of "familiar territory"; at least one should show your unique material (and its promise). A good sampling is all you need at this point because it's the concept of your book you're pitching, not the book itself. If a prospective publisher asks to see more, you can always supply it. Most major publishers will provide you with a set of instructions for how to prepare such a prospectus. Although the instructions may seem to be holy writ, what you finally submit as a prospectus is up to you. And yes, it's acceptable to submit your prospectus to more than one publisher at once.

How Do I Approach Publishers?

Publishers love to have successful textbook writers approach them with ideas for new books. They assume, often rightly, that someone who's done well with one textbook can do well with another. Our advice in this chapter assumes you have no such track record, that you're approaching publishers as virtually an unknown, at least in terms of previous textbook publishing. If you happen to have a fairly well-established reputation in composition scholarship it can help, but not nearly so much as a fairly well-established name in textbook writing, which can be and often are different communities altogether. The person you will most likely talk to will be the "acquisitions editor."

Acquisitions Editors and Initial Reviews

Your local book sales representatives are always on the lookout for potential authors for their companies, so they'll be glad to put you in touch with their acquisitions editors. Notice we are using plurals here. That's because you shouldn't approach just one publisher at a time. Potential publishers should understand that they are in competition with other publishers for your textbook. It is to your advantage for acquisitions editors to know you have shown the prospectus to other publishers.

You'll want to meet with these acquisitions editors if possible. Some will come calling on you; others will want to meet you at professional conferences. Let them buy you lunch, and show them your prospectus. If they like your prospectus, most acquisitions editors will want to send it out for initial review and then make a decision about whether to discuss a contract with you. Here are some things you ought to know about this review process.

In sending out your prospectus for review, most acquisitions editors are seeking more than just a reaction to your book idea. They prefer to obtain initial reviews from professors whom they see as potential textbook adopters. While they want these reviewers' opinions of your prospectus, they also want to cultivate a working relationship with these professors in case one of them proposes to write a textbook too—or, equally if not more important, in case one of these professors is in a position to make an adoption of one of the textbooks published by the editor's company. That's why a standard question reviewers are asked is, "If this book is published, would you consider it for adoption? Why or why not?" It's a fair question, one whose answer must be taken seriously.

Most initial reviewers are in the early stages of their careers and are therefore likely to provide a conscientious review for a relatively small honorarium. Reviewers who direct composition programs are especially attractive to acquisitions editors because they often control large adoptions. Such reviewers can command larger honorariums for reviews, but they are often tapped later in the review process, usually to participate as focus group members at professional meetings, where they respond to larger portions of books already under contract.

The reviews your acquisitions editor receives initially, then, may well be conscientiously and constructively done—or they may be quickly and carelessly tossed together by someone who needs a new pair of shoes. The reviews are likely to be mixed; and some may even make you wonder if the reviewer read *your* prospectus or was sent a different one by mistake. Regardless, you should pay as much attention to these reviews as your acquisitions editor does. If the editor wants changes and another round of reviews before discussing a contract, consider that option. At this point, it's the contract you're interested in, and the book itself is likely to undergo changes anyway. If, on the other hand, another editor with a different (but perhaps still mixed) set of initial reviews wants to talk about a contract, then be prepared to negotiate. Even though you may be a first-time textbook author, everything is negotiable. And if you happen to have two or more editors wanting to talk about a contract for your book, then go for the best deal you can negotiate.

Contracts

While you may be a fine writer and quite knowledgeable about composition pedagogy, at first you may not know much about how commercial textbook publishers operate. You probably also don't know much about how books are produced and at what cost, about how the publishing bureaucracy works once a book is under contract, or about book contracts themselves. All of the things you don't know can hurt you. Note that what we offer here isn't a complete guide to such matters, but it's a serviceable start; negotiating textbook contracts is worthy of a chapter all by itself. Note too that we are not contract lawyers (although with seven or eight textbooks between us we are experienced with contracts), so you'll need to temper our advice with your own good judgment and other appropriate counsel.

Again, remember that everything regarding your book is negotiable, even though as a first-time textbook author you may not be inclined to think about negotiating to your advantage. You should first determine what you want in your relationship with a publisher, even though you may not be able to obtain everything you'd like. It's wise to discover what terms are fairly standard in a contract between an established publisher and a first-time author. For example, it may be that a particular publishing company offers a first-time author a royalty of ten percent (figured on the price the bookstore pays the publisher, not the price the students pay the bookstore). But nothing prevents you from asking for fifteen percent. Should the company want to sign a contract, it might be willing to offer you more than ten percent, or to offer you ten percent on a certain number of copies sold, scaling up to a higher percentage on copies sold above that number. The point here is that the percentage of royalty is negotiable, though first-time authors often don't know this. If what you request is reasonable, you just might get more than you otherwise would have.

Some first-time authors are reluctant to accept an advance on their royalties, fearing that something may eventually prevent the book from being published. Nevertheless, it's a good idea to accept an advance, even if you plan only to invest it and draw off the interest until the book is in print. As a first-time author, you won't be offered a large advance, anyway, but it *is* up-front money for signing with the company, and if a company has invested money in a book, it may very well work more diligently to produce and market it (this is not always true, however). Advances are paid back out of your royalties; if the book makes money, you repay the advance out of the money the book made you. If the book doesn't make you money, you typically do not have to pay the advance back; it's the company's loss.

If you use the work of other authors in your book, permissions will be required. Obtaining permissions requires both paperwork and money; the paperwork involves securing written legal permissions, and money is required for fees paid to the publisher, author, or the author's agent. Most first-time authors can't get publishers to agree to do the paperwork and pay these fees, but nothing prevents you from asking them during contract negotiations to do so, and by asking you might win some concession. For example, you might arrive at an agreement in which you do the paperwork but they'll split the permission costs, or they will pay the permission costs up front, collecting them later out of your royalties. If a publisher wants to sign your book, it costs you nothing to try to negotiate such aspects of your contract, and you may very well win some concessions along with your book deal. The point is that more of these matters are up to you than you probably realize, so make some decisions about what you want and then try to negotiate.

Points for Negotiation

The three most important aspects of a textbook contract are royalties, advances, and grants. Obviously, you want the best royalty percentage you can obtain, perhaps on a sliding scale (called an "escalator") tied to sales. And you want advances on your royalties, even if such payments are tied to your turning in successive sections of the text. And you want a grant (up front money that the publisher gives you outright and that is not linked to your royalty payments), perhaps to cover the price of a new computer, printer, modem, or fax to facilitate not just producing the text but also communicating with the publisher. But there are a number of other negotiable points as well, which for reasons of length we can only list here:

- *Agreement on the overall concept of the book.* A formal agreement on the overall concept of the book is very important but often is not included in the contract itself. If you can obtain such an agreement in a letter of understanding to accompany your contract, you will be helping yourself in the long run. If the publisher is reluctant to agree to some kind of written statement of the concept during contract negotiations, imagine what might happen later—as reviewers quibble, as editors change, as the market evolves.

- *Contract negotiations.* When and where do contract negotiations take place? Do you show a draft to a lawyer? What time frame governs the negotiations?

- *Manuscript review.* Try to make sure that the reviewers the editor will send your manuscript to have credentials in your target market. Discuss in advance how the reviews will be handled, especially if they turn out to be either irrelevant (for example, if you wind up with a reviewer for your handbook who states that he or she has never used a handbook and never will) or negative. (In particular, are your incremental advances contingent on receiving *positive* reviews? Who decides what *positive* means?)

- *Number of pages.* Too many contracts do not specify how many typed, double-spaced manuscript pages you are obligated to produce. Such an important factor should be agreed upon and stated clearly in your contract.

- *Deadlines.* You'll work better if you have several small, incremental deadlines rather than two or three large ones. If your publisher suggests penalties for missing deadlines, try suggesting bonuses for beating them.

- *Permissions.* Whose responsibility is it to handle the paperwork involved in requesting permission to reprint previously published material? Who pays the permission fees?

- *Ancillaries, supplements, and derivatives.* Will you also be required to prepare a teacher's manual? Other pedagogical materials? What about a teacher who wants to use your chapter 4 by itself? What about an online version?

- *Design.* Will the book be hardback or paper? What page size will it have? Will there be color? What type size will it use? Do you have any right of consultation or refusal on any of these items?

- *Index.* Who prepares the index? On what schedule? If someone else works on the index (which usually means you pay for it out of your royalties), will you have the right of refusal if it is done poorly?

- *Marketing strategy.* Will you be consulted on the marketing strategy the publisher will use to promote your book?

- *Agreement on subsequent editions.* Does your contract bind you for all subsequent editions, or can it be renegotiated?

- *Reneging.* Finally, most (probably all) contracts state that if the author fails to deliver the product as specified all advances must be returned to the publisher. But is that a two-way street? Is it possible for you to complete the whole manuscript, on time and in accord with reviewers' reasonable suggestions, and have the publisher at the last minute decide not to publish? If so, what happens to your advances? Who owns the manuscript?

If you obtain verbal agreements on these points, that's fine, but remember that *nothing counts unless it is written down*. Get as much of the agreement written into the contract as you can, and try to include the rest in a letter of agreement to accompany the contract. And, of course, when the company mails you your contract and letter, make sure that what you've negotiated for is in fact in them.

Finally, we strongly suggest you take the position that your contract is for a single book—not for anything else you might write in the future. Should you decide later to write *another* book, then that book is wholly separate and should be approached that way. In other words, signing for one book with one publisher does not obligate you to sign your next book with the same publisher. You have signed a book contract, not a personal services contract. We say this because some publishers include a clause in their contracts specifying that they have the right of first refusal on any subsequent books you may write. If that is the case, you can negotiate to have such a clause removed.

What Else?

We wish we could tell you that negotiating a contract is the last difficult passage between you and success, but we can't. Problems can arise. Perhaps most common is the author who never finishes the manuscript. Maybe the next most common is the editor who changes jobs. And perhaps the next most common is the marketplace that suddenly decides that your *kind* of approach is hopelessly outdated (no matter what you write, at least one reviewer will sneer that it isn't "cutting edge"). The first problem is within your power to avoid. The second may in fact have killed more book projects than any other, but the course of other people's careers is impossible to control. Perhaps the best way to avoid that problem is to make sure *numerous* people at your publishing house have bought into the project, have tied their careers in some way to its success (just as you have), so that no one person's departure can remove your sole means of support. The third problem, the marketplace that decides your approach really isn't cutting edge, is one to which the kind of book we discuss here is relatively resistant: you are writing a cutting edge approach to basically the same material presented in most other books on the market. Thus, if what constitutes the cutting edge changes radically tomorrow, it's more the approach you take to your material that you'll need to change than it is the material itself.

Even though so many of the factors that doom many good textbooks to only one edition (and many more manuscripts to never getting published at all) are beyond their authors' control, in balance the two of us have found writing a mainstream traditional textbook to be a rewarding experience. We've been well paid—although we're both still driving Fords, not BMWs; we've received recognition both by our departments and by the profession; we've worked with some great people in publishing and met many more interesting writing teachers than we ever would have otherwise; we've been able to add a new, rich dimension to our friendship; and, perhaps most important, we've been able to produce a good piece of work as writers. Ultimately, for both of us, writing is what it's all about. That need—to create, to create on paper, to see how our work reads (for us and for others), and then to create some more—is what drives textbook writers like us, maybe like you, just as we hope it can come to drive the students who use our book—or yours.

Works Cited

Connors, Robert J. "The Rise and Fall of the Modes of Discourse." *College Composition and Communication* 32 (1981): 444-55.

Emig, Janet. *The Composing Processes of Twelfth Graders*. Urbana: NCTE, 1971.

Hairston, Maxine. "The Winds of Change: Thomas Kuhn and the Revolution in the Teaching of Writing." *College Composition and Communication* 33 (1982): 76-88.

Klaus, Carl. "Public Opinion and Professional Belief." *College Composition and Communication* 27 (1976): 335-40.

Rohman, D. Gordon. "Pre-Writing: The Stage of Discovery in the Writing Process." *College Composition and Communication* 16 (1965): 106-12.

Making Essay Connections: Editing Readers for First-Year Writers

Lynn Z. Bloom

> 'Tis the good reader that makes the good book; in every book he finds passages which seem . . . unmistakably meant for his ear; the profit of books is according to the sensibility of the reader; the profoundest thought or passion sleeps as in a mine, until it is discovered by an equal mind and heart.
> Ralph Waldo Emerson, "Success"

It is fitting that the rationale for reading should come from an essay by Ralph Waldo Emerson, America's patron saint of self-reliance. While Emerson asserts that reading is essential for success in general, contemporary American composition teachers assert that reading well is essential for writing well. The rationale of Donald Hall, himself a distinguished essayist and poet, for the seventh edition of *A Writer's Reader* epitomizes the current consensus: "Reading well precedes writing well. Of all the ancestors claimed by a fine piece of prose, the most important is the prose from which the writer learned his craft. Writers learn craft, not by memorizing rules about restrictive clauses, but by striving to equal a standard formed from reading" (xxi).

Hall continues, "A composition course, then, must be two courses, one in reading, another in writing." College students, he says, have been reared on television and "bad prose" in newspapers, popular fiction, and textbooks; and they are taught to believe that "words merely stand in for ideas, or carry information on their backs" the way superhighways carry traffic. To become active readers, students must engage the writer's ideas in skeptical, questioning dialogue while learning from the prose of distinguished belletristic essays an intimate, textual integration of idea and expression, "rhythm and image, metaphor and syntax, order of phrase and order of paragraph" (xxi-xxii).

The Recent Lowly Status of Essays in the Academy

After spending nearly a century relegated to the dank basement of the House of Literature, essays—a.k.a. literary nonfiction, creative nonfiction, belletristic nonfiction, or personal essays—are coming upstairs. Essayists such as Joan Didion, James Baldwin, Stephen Jay Gould, Virginia Woolf, and Alice Walker now join their illustrious predecessors—Montaigne, Bacon, Swift, Addison and Steele, Emerson, and Holmes—as authors of a genre regarded once again as first-class, first-rate. That the status of the essay, the Cinderella of the literary world, was dubious throughout most of the twentieth century is reflected in E.B. White's self-deprecating observation that "the essayist, unlike the novelist, the poet, and the playwright, must be content in his self-imposed role of second-class citizen" (vii). With the critics (the ugly stepsisters in this tale) in the ascendancy, the essay was treated in the academy essentially as a utilitarian, efficient means of communicating technical information, its authority and aesthetic quality devalued. How essays were reduced to such a lowly state is not a pretty story.

We could blame Coleridge and his colleagues, who drew a distinction between "the *active* concerns of rhetoric and the *contemplative* ones of literature" (Bizzell and Herzberg 639). We could blame the British university system, for by the mid-nineteenth century, says Donald McQuade, "the British began to formalize this distinction by dividing instruction in rhetoric from belles-lettres, and American universities (led by Johns Hopkins and Harvard) did much the same" (487). We could blame our colleagues. McQuade explains how the academy in the early twentieth century demoted the essay from "a *primary* form of literature" to its standing "as a *secondary* source," often as "a commentary *on* literature" (490). Literature textbooks, such as Brooks and Warren's *Understanding Poetry*, shaped the ethic and aesthetic of literary study for decades.

And we can blame ourselves for cooperating with, if not condoning, the same value system. For example, in 1988 Chris Anderson's "Hearsay Evidence" explores the issue of why, as essayist Joseph Epstein says, "it is a sweet time to be an essayist" outside the academy "when the opposite is the case inside" (411). Anderson, himself a sophisticated essayist as well as a composition specialist, concedes that "Coming to the essay we know that we will not be subject to the metafictive and fabulist demands of much contemporary fiction and poetry or to the difficult, mind-jarring analyses of these demands in a [theoretical, critical] commentary" (307). Taking heart from Virginia Woolf's claim that the essay "is the medium which makes it possible for people of ordinary intelligence to communicate their ideas to the world" (150), Anderson finds "the essay an increasingly compelling model" and is willing to accept "second-class citizenship in exchange for freedom of movement" (307).

As a consequence of the prevailing values, McQuade explains, during the twentieth century the standard first-year composition course reduced the essay's "importance as an emerging subject of independent study" and required students "to produce models of correctness—in spelling, punctuation, syntax, grammar, and expression—that displayed the products of rigorously controlled analyses of literature drawn from a designated list of standard authors" (490). The resulting assumption—"that there is an irrevocable distinction between composition and literature," that literature is "elegant and elite, composition commonplace and déclassé"—still dictates the curriculum, as well as the academic pecking order, in numerous American high schools and colleges (490, 491).

Until the past decade, this view also provided the rationale for the existence of essay anthologies, and for their contents. In the English curriculum, the reading of essays has been relegated to first-year composition courses—where it largely remains to this day, except for critical essays read in literature courses. The essay has been "taught" primarily as an exemplary model of "service" writing in a course that is still identified as a "service" course, so like Cinderella viewed by the stepsisters, the essay has been perceived as a handmaiden to all the other academic disciplines in the university but devoid of literary merit of its own.

A Genre Whose Time Has Come

The main change in today's English curriculum is not the status of the first-year composition course, whose funding, rationale, and staffing to a large extent are still subject to the familiar hierarchical priorities. The difference lies in the fact that the course materials of first-year composition—essays still and always—are experiencing a renaissance and rehabilitation. There are several reasons for the fact that within the past decade essays, particularly personal essays, are now receiving new respect in the academy. English faculty—critics and composition specialists alike—are discovering what the cognoscenti, lovers and writers of belletristic essays, have always known. Current literary and rhetorical theories—of any and all persuasions—acknowledge the constructed nature of all literary texts, including literary nonfiction. Critics and teachers now understand that the techniques of good writing are as applicable to autobiography and essay writing as to fiction; as a consequence, critical studies of literary nonfiction have increased astronomically in the past two decades (see Bloom and Yu).

Likewise, critical knowledge is translated into pedagogical practice as composition teachers give sophisticated personal writing assignments that reflect what all serious writers know (see Bloom, *Coming*). Writing such essays enables students to understand the innumerable versions in which a particular experience or understanding can be rendered; the relation of style to substance, style to self; the significance of emphasis, omissions, gaps, erasures; the ethical, intellectual, and aesthetic difficulties of dishonesty; the importance of each word, each syntactic structure, each punctuation mark, in every text; the critical rigor that undergirds writing well for an external audience; the necessity, aesthetic and personal, of rewriting (see Bloom, "American"). As Douglas Hesse observes, "The power we hold out to students when we encourage them to essay is the power to be like other essayists, to write like authors their teachers read in serious leisure" (141).

Another reason for the current attention being paid to essays, particularly personal belletristic essays, is their recognized utility in addressing the political, cultural, and social issues that first-year composition promotes in initiating new students into the university. Belletristic essayists collectively function as purveyors of political correctness and a multicultural perspective. Indeed, nearly all contemporary essay collections for composition courses reflect a range of multicultural authors, balanced according to gender, ethnicity, class, religion, and sexual preference.

Consider the range of authors in just one representative essay collection from the approximately one hundred first-year composition readers published in 1993 and 1994, *The Presence of Others: Readings for Critical Thinking and Writing*, edited by Andrea Lunsford (a liberal) and John Ruszkiewicz ("an academic and political conservative," xiv): Adrienne Rich, Camille Paglia, Shelby Steele, bell hooks, Martin Luther King, Jr., Sojourner Truth, William Least Heat Moon, Leslie Marmon Silko, Rosario Morales, Linda Chavez, Norman Podhoretz, Mike Rose, P.J. O'Rourke, and Allan Bloom. The writing of such authors is intellectually complex, technically sophisticated, and provocative. *The Presence of Others* includes five of the dozen most frequently anthologized essayists appearing in the contemporary pedagogical canon: Joan Didion, Maxine Hong Kingston, Lewis Thomas, Alice Walker, Virginia Woolf. Omitted are seven more of the top twelve: Russell Baker, Annie Dillard, Loren Eiseley, Nancy Mairs, N. Scott Momaday, George Orwell and E.B. White (see Bloom and Myhal).

Why Edit Yet Another Reader?
Given the new legitimacy of essays in the academy, as well as their preponderance in the first-year composition curriculum, the prospect of editing a collection of essays seems enticing, especially if a publisher is projecting sales of forty to fifty thousand copies over four years. An easy task, good money, a soupçon of scholarly respectability, enhancement of one's teaching—who could resist? Dream on. Or, since I will address these reasons below, read on.

I want to become a better teacher. Improving one's own teaching may be the only certain outcome of editing any textbook. To edit a reader responsibly, the editor needs to have a clear sense of what constitutes good writing—in print and in class, even if this changes over time—how good writing can be achieved, and a variety of ways in which it can be taught. Thus, the prospective editor needs to have a sense of at least four key concerns in order to make appropriate selections and to determine how to use them. First, the editor needs a coherent philosophy of the ideal course to which the anthology pertains. Will the course emphasize critical thinking, argumentation, multicultural understanding, a particular topic, style, or rhetorical strategies—and will the course emphasize these things in general or as they reflect a particular disciplinary area? Second, what materials will best reinforce this philosophy? The work of major thinkers, belletristic writers, social commentators (including or excluding journalists), public speakers? Is this philosophy best addressed by a historical spread of authors, or by contemporary selections? By men and women equally? Will it include exemplary student papers? Will it contain fiction, poetry, artwork or photographs? If so, which ones? Why?

Third, which potential selections are teachable and for what reasons? Some good reasons for inclusion (or rejection) are the following:

- Appropriate level of difficulty for the intended teachers and readers. How much does one have to know or learn in order to teach this book and understand its contents?

- Appropriate length—that is, the essay's original length. (To maintain the integrity of an essay's form, content, and rhetorical design—and one's own integrity as an editor—one should *not excerpt*.) Is the book designed for long analyses of long pieces, short analyses of short pieces, or some mix? Will a given essay be used as an exemplary rhetorical model, as a stimulus to discussion, and/or in connection with other pieces in the book—say, to form a cluster for argument?

- Relevance of the topic or point of view. Does the piece address "enduring" truths, or topics of more limited or ephemeral interest? If the latter, how quickly is it likely to go out of date? Does it have resonance—intellectual and aesthetic—with other selections in the reader? Is it politically correct? Should it be?

- Rhetorical versatility—for reading, discussion, and writing. Any essay enriches a textbook if it can be used in a variety of ways. Indeed, Hall and Emblen point out the difficulties of arbitrary classification: "No piece of real prose is ever so pure as our systems of classification." They continue,

  > Although an essay may contain Division, or Process Analysis, or an example of Example, the same essay is likely to use three or four other patterns as well.... Thematic organizations ... have similar flaws; is E.B. White's theme in "Once More to the Lake" Mortality? Aging? Youth and Age? or, How I Spent My Summer Vacation? [Or, one could add, Parent and Child, Father and Son, the Self in the Setting, Once More to Self Discovery....] (xxiii)

Fourth, what instructional apparatus will the collection include? How concise or elaborate will it be? Apparatus, however minimal or extensive, consists of some or all of the following: discussions of how to read, think, and write critically; discussions of rhetorical principles; biographical, rhetorical, and/or critical introductions to the authors and selections; study questions on individual selections, focusing on such matters as content, rhetorical strategies, form, and style; suggestions for reading, discussion, and writing on individual selections or related pieces; a glossary of rhetorical terms; textual glosses; workbooks, in print or computer form; an instructor's guide. If the collection will include an instructor's guide, will this guide contain answers to the study questions? Interpretive essays on the book's themes or rhetorical issues? Suggestions for teaching? Discussions of current research in composition studies, and citations of professional literature? Sample student papers?

As with any expert performance, the polished result—in this case, a gleaming, state-of-the-art reader—looks deceptively simple. Yet, as with any expert performance, each new book requires an enormous amount of work—let's say, a minimum of one thousand hours. The genuine pleasure comes in the initial task: spending over three hundred hours to survey the field, discover what the competition is doing, and read potential materials. Then comes the work: at least ten hours to edit each selection (most essay anthologies contain sixty-five to eighty selections) and write and rewrite and rewrite and rewrite the apparatus—totalling some six to eight hundred hours. This does not include time spent reading the relevant professional literature in composition studies; learning to write clear, unambiguous, friendly prose that neither preaches nor condescends to teachers or students (let me count the ways you can say *you* or *I*); or trying out portions of the manuscript on one's own or others' students. Nor does it include time spent locating biographical, rhetorical, and critical information; tracking down original sources and securing copyright permissions; copying and preparing the manuscript for publication; editing and proofreading the page proofs; and—a final, time-consuming burden—preparing for the publisher's advertising department a market report that analyzes one's own book in relation to the competition. The meter is still running; better add on another five hundred hours. That's thirty hours of work per week for fifty weeks; or, more realistically, fifteen hours per week spread over two years. How could one's teaching fail to benefit from such a stupendous investment of time and thought?

I want to make an original contribution to the field. Don't count on it. Textbooks do not usually invent knowledge: they transmit existing paradigms and information. Textbooks are thus reactive repositories of the current state of knowledge in whatever discipline they represent; teachers aren't likely to adopt a reader with a largely unfamiliar table of contents. A reasonably familiar textbook is comforting to teachers who are assigned the course at the last minute, as many are, with little opportunity for advance preparation. Moreover, some uniformity of content is desirable in an introductory, multi-sectioned course where large numbers of students change sections during the first few weeks and where students are held responsible for some core body of knowledge and development of skills at the semester's end. So there is pressure, from within the field and from publishers, to clone texts that already have a following rather than to invent works *de novo*.

Thus, the innovations textbooks offer, if any, are much more likely to be pedagogical and pragmatic than theoretical. For example, two conspicuously innovative rhetoric books translated rhetorical theory into pedagogical practice: Edward P.J. Corbett's Aristotelian *Classical Rhetoric for the Modern Student* (1965), and Young, Becker, and Pike's application of tagmemic linguistics, *Rhetoric: Discovery and Change* (1970). Both books have profoundly influenced teachers, but they were too intellectually sophisticated and required too much background knowledge from the teacher to gain widespread use in first-year composition. The Corbett text, in fact, is more often taught in graduate courses, as is Donald Murray's simpler *A Writer Teaches Writing* (1968). Peter Elbow's *Writing Without Teachers* (1973) and Ken Macrorie's *Telling Writing* (1970), both expressivist rhetorics, are exceptional among innovative pedagogies that have had widespread adoption in first-year composition courses. They're reader-friendly; they're written with clarity, simplicity, and good humor; and they contain abundant illustrations. Yet all five of these books are rhetorics, not readers, and have much more space to expand on their subject than readers do. That all of these works were published between 1965 and 1973 implies that trade publishers were more willing to risk publishing innovative works a quarter century ago than they are now.

I want this reader to be a powerful influence in the field. The nature of anthologies—which are, after all, compilations of other peoples' writings rather than the editor's own—makes it hard for any editor to make a major impact on the field. Essay collections of any sort are a means of providing brief glimpses (usually the highlights) of a vast field of which the anthology's readers might otherwise be unaware: the reader's introduction to the field is comparable to studying art through viewing the Mona Lisa's smile, Botticelli's scallop shell (with or without Venus), or Michelangelo's touching fingertips of God creating Adam.

To make a powerful and innovative selection, the editor must cull essays, book chapters, and illustrative paragraphs from a wide range of works. Anthologies, even pioneer ones, are usually a mix of fifty percent familiar readings, twenty-five percent new or unfamiliar works by familiar authors, and twenty-five percent new works by unfamiliar authors. The depth of the editor's knowledge of the field (including authors, genres, individual writings, as well as pedagogical theory and research in composition) and the opportunity to be both innovative and influential is apparent both in unusual selections and in how all the selections are treated.

There are three possible avenues for substantial editorial innovation, and hence the greatest likelihood of long-term influence. The first is to be the first compiler of much-needed material in the field. Knowledgeably selected readings from a vast body of primary material will often be the student's (and perhaps the adopting teacher's) only exposure to that material. For example, Bizzell and Herzberg's *The Rhetorical Tradition: Readings from Classical Times to the Present* intends in 1266 large, tightly packed pages ("fifty-six selections from forty-four important figures," from Gorgias to Cixous and Kristeva) to provide—primarily for graduate students and teachers—"a thorough survey of the tradition of rhetoric," reintroducing out-of-print and inaccessible authors, and "eliminating the need for separate paperbacks" (book jacket). Although somewhat comparable collections have appeared since *The Rhetorical Tradition* was published in 1990, to be first with the most establishes a powerful priority of place. There is no comparable, widely used first-year anthology, except perhaps Lee Jacobus' *World of Ideas*, a book intended to enable "students in first-year composition courses ... to read and write about challenging works by great thinkers" (v). The current edition of this work contains thirty-five unusually long selections (averaging fifteen pages, as opposed to five in most anthologies) by Plato, Aristotle, Machiavelli, Thoreau, Darwin, Marx, Freud, Lévi-Strauss, and Simone Weil.

The second route to innovation is to be the innovator of a unique pedagogical method embedded in the reader and its instructional apparatus, in the introductions to the subject(s) and authors, and in suggestions for reading and writing about the anthologized material. When such a work is widely adopted, its attendant pedagogy is adopted as well. Though it has little apparatus, William Smart's *Eight Modern Essayists* incorporates a strong pedagogical philosophy: to expose students to clusters of writing by modern authors memorable for their style and trenchant point of view and to expect some semblance of emulation in form and style. David Bartholomae and Anthony Petrosky's *Ways of Reading* has a much more directive pedagogy. It not only introduces students (and many of their teachers) to "serious" writing—"long and complicated texts" by Gloria Anzaldúa, John Berger, Michel Foucault, Paulo Freire, and Adrienne Rich—it also provides a method of reading text against text that invites students "to be active, critical readers" by "open[ing] up the familiar world and mak[ing] it rich and puzzling" (vi).

The pedagogical philosophy of Bartholomae and Petrosky directly contradicts that of most first-year composition readers currently in print, except perhaps Jacobus': "We avoided the short set-pieces you find in so many anthologies" because they "misrepresent the act of reading." Such commonly anthologized essays "can be read in a single sitting; they make arguments that can be easily paraphrased; they solve all the problems they raise; they wrap up Life and put it into a box" (vi). By turning reading "into an act of appreciation" rather than a critical dialectic, such short selections imply that students, too, should "write a piece that is similarly tight and neat and self-contained." Instead of implying that the only thing student readers need to do is to "get the point," Bartholomae and Petrosky see students as beginning "with confusion and puzzlement" to "put together fragments," gradually creating a coherent text of their own through "writing and rewriting" (vi).

The third avenue for innovation is to be the first (or most knowledgeable) compiler of material on a topic of consuming interest, current or perennial. In the 1950s and 60s, casebooks of primary materials appeared, focusing on such topics as the Salem witch trials (implicitly analogous to the 1950s political witch hunts), on the Sacco and Vanzetti case, on the nature of justice in general, on Melville's *Billy Budd*, and on Faulkner's *The Bear*. At intervals other topical compilations (often called "mono-thematic" readers) are published; for example, currently there are readers on gender and on ecology. None has been in print longer than a decade, a duration which, short though it is, seems to denote a potential textbook classic.

The Incredible Intertextuality of Readers
Nevertheless, innovation of any of these three kinds is more the exception

than the rule. Approximately fifty readers are published each year, divided evenly between new and revised works (see Smitten, Webb). To call attention to their conspicuous intertextuality is a polite way of saying that many of these works, however intellectually and pedagogically sophisticated, have a strong family resemblance; canonical authors, even canonical essays (such as Martin Luther King, Jr.'s "Letter from Birmingham Jail" and E.B. White's "Once More to the Lake"), comprise at least fifty percent of any given textbook. Another twenty-five percent of most current textbooks is devoted to distinguished writings by other ethnic and minority authors only slightly less familiar—Judith Ortiz Cofer, Zora Neale Hurston, Amy Tan, Louise Erdrich, Gary Soto, among others. Bartholomae and Petrosky have accurately characterized the set-piece pedagogy of these works. Is it possible or even desirable for yet another editor to work so long and hard to replicate yet another Son of Reader III?

The answer is, yes, if the prospective editor wants the book to be published commercially. Publishers' offerings are analogous to automobile manufacturers' models, from the bottom to the top of the line: each publisher has a stripped-down, basic model; a general-purpose model; a minivan; a truck; a sportscar; and an elegant, fine-tuned top-of-the-line model. In a sense, each publisher's sales representative is promoting books that compete not only against other publishers' comparable models, but against other works in the publisher's own line. Indeed, when publishers sign a book, they do so to fill a particular niche in their line. They don't want books that are totally different from the competition; they want books that resemble the competitors in significant ways while making some changes. Promises notwithstanding, textbook editors cannot expect monogamous fidelity from their publishers, who are more likely to cast a host of competing books to the winds to see which ones fly.

I want to achieve academic recognition for my essay collection. Whether textbooks "count" as evidence of research or of pedagogy (or neither) depends on the evaluators' criteria, institutional and individual. Untenured faculty might consider devoting that fifteen hundred hours to shoring up a research publication record, delaying anthology editing until their scholarly reputation is assured by other means.

I want to make money from my edited textbooks. It's not wise to count on making money from edited collections. Publishers commonly estimate that to warrant reprinting, a book must sell between twenty and forty thousand copies over the lifetime of its current edition, usually three to four years. This sales expectation is unduly optimistic. Conservatively, the two hundred anthologies in print in any given year would have to sell one to two million *brand new* copies per year to reach this level. Even if one million students took first-year composition each year—a very high estimate—and seventy-five percent of these were enrolled in courses requiring a reader, at least two-thirds would buy used books, which generate no new sales. Thus, a more realistic estimate of annual sales of new copies of all readers combined is a quarter of a million copies per year—averaging 1250 copies of any given book, or five thousand total new sales over a four-year period. With customized publishing, desktop publishing, and the capability of any teacher or any bookstore to generate a custom-designed anthology, I assume that even this total sales figure of five thousand is being substantially eroded even as I write this.

If one's royalty were a generous two dollars per copy, that ten thousand dollars might be a welcome supplement to an academic salary, even though it represents approximately six dollars per hour of time spent on a first edition. (The hope is for a book to go into a second and subsequent editions, which happens infrequently. In later editions, which contain only twenty-five to thirty percent of new material, the time spent on revision is considerably less than on the first edition, and the remuneration is proportionately higher.) But wait! Publishers deduct anywhere between fifty and one hundred percent of the permissions costs from the editor's royalties. If most of the material is copyrighted (and most will be) the costs will average between three and four hundred dollars per item; seventy selections would cost between twenty-one and twenty-eight thousand dollars. Thus, royalties vanish; most essay anthologists are lucky to break even. That editors of anthologies have become the publishers' unpaid laborers is apparent only in retrospect.

A Coda

I offer a coda to this cautionary tale from my perspective as editor of three essay collections for first-year composition over the past thirty years. Two of these anthologies have remained in print (in various editions) for longer than the crucial initial decade; the votes aren't in on the third yet. Like most commercially viable readers on the market, these works are state-of-the-art in implied theory, sound in pedagogy, engaging to read, provocative to teach from. My professional reputation is largely independent of these antholo-gies, as is my bank account. I have worked with some of the best editors in the business, knowledgeable, assiduous and pleasant, and my books have been promoted better than most of the competition. Yet if I had it to do over again, I emphatically would not. I'm in this profession for life, and for fun (which for me includes good scholarship and good writing). E.B. White understands where these commitments reside when he observes, "The essayist . . . can pull on any sort of shirt, be any sort of person, according to his mood or his subject matter—philosopher, scold, jester, raconteur, confidant, pundit, devil's ad-vocate, enthusiast" (Foreword). White does not include editors of essay anthologies on this list of roles; I'd guess that nowhere on earth are people born lusting to be essay anthologists when they grow up.

Editing anthologies, in which the editor's creativity and innovation can generally be measured out in the most minuscule of coffee spoons, is (unless one hits the jackpot) ultimately unrewarding—intellectually, professionally, and financially. What one learns about teaching composition drops precipitously after the first edition of the first anthology. One can make many more substantial contributions to the state of professional knowledge by conducting original research, by writing belletristic essays that other people can edit, or by offering cautionary tales such as the one you are now reading. And one can have a better time.

Works Cited

Anderson, Chris. "Hearsay Evidence and Second-Class Citizenship." *College English* 50 (1988): 300-08.

Bartholomae, David, and Anthony Petrosky, eds. *Ways of Reading: An Anthology for Writers*. 3rd ed. Boston: Bedford, 1993.

Bizzell, Patricia, and Bruce Herzberg, eds. *The Rhetorical Tradition: Readings from Classical Times to the Present*. Boston: Bedford, 1990.

Bloom, Lynn Z. "American Autobiography and the Politics of Genre." *Genres of Writing: Mapping the Territories of Discourse*. Ed. Wendy Bishop and Hans Ostrom (publisher pending).

——. *Coming to Life: Reading, Writing, Teaching Autobiography*. Englewood Cliffs, NJ: Prentice (forthcoming).

Bloom, Lynn Z., and Robert Myhal. "Literary Nonfiction: The Current Pedagogical Canon" (in progress).

Bloom, Lynn Z., and Ning Yu. "American Autobiography: The Changing Critical Canon." *a/b: Auto/Biography* 9.2 (Fall 1994): 177-90.

Corbett, Edward P.J. *Classical Rhetoric for the Modern Student*. 1965. New York: Oxford UP, 1990.

Elbow, Peter. *Writing Without Teachers*. New York: Oxford UP, 1973.

Epstein, Joseph. "Piece Work: Writing the Essay." *Plausible Prejudices*. New York: Norton, 1985. 379-411.

Hall, Donald, and D.L. Emblen, eds. *A Writer's Reader*. 7th ed. New York: Harper, 1994.

Hesse, Douglas. "The Recent Rise of Literary Nonfiction: A Cautionary Assay." *Composition Theory for the Postmodern Classroom*. Ed. Gary A. Olson and Sidney I. Dobrin. Albany: State U of New York P, 1994. 132-42.

Jacobus, Lee A. *A World of Ideas: Essential Readings for College Writers*. 4th ed. Boston: Bedford, 1994.

Lunsford, Andrea A., and John J. Ruszkiewicz, eds. *The Presence of Others: Readings for Critical Thinking and Writing*. New York: St. Martin's, 1994.

Macrorie, Ken. *Telling Writing*. Rochelle Park, NJ: Hayden, 1970.

McQuade, Donald M. "Composition and Literary Studies." *Redrawing the Boundaries: The Transformation of English and American Literary Studies*. Ed. Stephen Greenblatt and Giles Gunn. New York: MLA, 1992. 482-519.

Murray, Donald M. *A Writer Teaches Writing: A Practical Method of Teaching Composition*. 2nd ed. Boston: Houghton, 1985.

Smart, William A., ed. *Eight Modern Essayists*. 6th ed. New York: St. Martin's, 1995.

Smitten, Paige Dayton. "Bibliography of Writing Textbooks." *Writing Program Administration* 16.3 (1993): 80-99.

——. "Bibliography of Writing Textbooks." *Writing Program Administration* 17.3 (1994): 75-94.

Webb, Suzanne S. "Bibliography of Writing Textbooks." *Writing Program Administration* 14.3 (1991): 84-108.

——. "Bibliography of Writing Textbooks." *Writing Program Administration* 15.3 (1992): 78-98.

White, E.B. *Essays of E.B. White*. New York: Harper, 1977.

Woolf, Virginia. "Addison." *The Common Reader*. First and Second Series. New York: Harcourt, 1948. 137-51.

Young, Richard E., Alton L. Becker, and Kenneth L. Pike. *Rhetoric: Discovery and Change*. New York: Harcourt, 1970.

Negotiating the Conversation:

Examining Issues in Scholarly Publishing

The Consequences of Theory
for the Practice of Writing

Thomas Kent

From the outset, I should confess that the title of this essay is somewhat misleading, for I intend to endorse Stanley Fish's claim that theory possesses no direct consequences for practice, and I will argue that as a consequence of theory's inconsequence, theory can neither shape nor control the practice of writing in any meaningful way. If theory does not shape or control the practice of writing—if, as Fish claims, "Theory is an impossible project which will never succeed" (320)—then my title clearly misleads, for *no* consequences, no *practical* consequences of theory exist for the practice of writing. However, to say that theory possesses no consequences for the practice of writing does not mean that theory possesses no consequences at all. Theory does possess political and institutional consequences, and, finally, I believe that these political and institutional consequences are the only consequences that matter, especially for those of us publishing theoretical scholarship. Therefore, by endorsing Fish's thin and unrobust view of theory, I do not mean to claim, as Fish does, that "theory's day is dying," nor do I mean to suggest that theory, as a disciplinary pursuit, should be abandoned (341). I mean to suggest only that we waste our time when we attempt to justify our practices by appeals to theory and that we—especially those among us who are newcomers to the field of composition studies and who are interested in publishing speculative, theoretical kinds of scholarship—would be better served to understand theory itself as a kind of practice that helps us survive within our academic environments.

On the surface, the claim that composition theory shapes, informs, or reforms writing practice seems completely reasonable and even unassailable, and to deny such an idea may seem peevish. Because research in writing practice generally discovers its authority in some aspect of composition theory, we naturally assume that some deep correspondence exists between the two. For example, almost every influential history of composition studies may be read as an account of theory's influence on writing practice. Martin Nystrand, Stuart Green, and Jeffrey Wiemelt rightly point out that important historians of composition studies such as Lester Faigley, C.H. Knoblauch, and James Berlin see a clear relationship between theory or particular theoretical perspectives and the practice of writing. Commenting on the work of James Berlin, for instance, Nystrand, Green, and Wiemelt claim that "Each theoretical perspective [identified by Berlin] forms a certain 'epistemic complex' of writer, reality, audience, and language that informs our understanding of invention, arrangement, and style in composing" (269). In fact, in their own history of composition studies Nystrand, Green, and Wiemelt assume that theory shapes practice, as when they argue that certain influential theories of composing such as sociocognitive theory have "affected recent research on basic writing" (309). Of course, the assumption that theory shapes writing practice not only informs our historical accounts of composition studies; this idea also influences scholarship in practically every area of composition studies. Mary Lay explains, for example, that a clear link exists between feminist theory and writing practice: "Finally, feminist theorists can help technical communicators provide new models of effective collaboration—models that help collaborators break out of gender roles" (364). We could add to this one example myriad other claims regarding the apparent connection between theory and writing practice, claims made by structuralist theorists (Emig; Moffett; Flower and Hayes), expressivist theorists (Elbow; Murray; Macrorie), social-constructionist theorists (Bruffee; Bizzell; Brodkey), and Neomarxist theorists (Trimbur; Berlin; Giroux).

The pervasive idea that theory shapes writing practice possesses particular exigence in the area of pedagogy, where many beginning instructors of writing frequently hear that they must ground their teaching in a theory of composition that both justifies and provides a coherent account of the practical advice that they impart to their students. In turn, these writing instructors pass on to their students the dictum that some sort of theory generates or undergirds the practice of writing, so students come to believe that, in order to write well, they must internalize a specific theory of writing that will guide their composing decisions. In addition, we often legitimate "theory" courses by arguing that these courses inform or shape the practice of writing; we argue that theory courses help students sharpen their practical reading and writing skills by providing them with a framework or schema that will help them become more self-consciously aware of their own assumptions as they read and write.

In composition studies, then, theory is seen to possess great consequences; it shapes our writing practices and informs the decisions we make about writing instruction. When we deny this contention, we destabilize one of the key foundational assumptions of contemporary composition research: the assumption that practice must be validated by theory. In the discussion to follow, I will attempt to outline some of the ramifications of this destabilization, and I will begin by relating the significance to writing practice of the "anti-theory" argument as it is developed by Stanley Fish and by Stephen Knapp and Walter Benn Michaels. I will next discuss two of the political and institutional consequences that theory, as a kind of practice, holds for conducting and publishing research in the discipline of composition studies, and I will conclude by suggesting some general guidelines for the institutional practice of publication in the area of composition theory.

The Anti-Theory Argument

In a nutshell, the anti-theory argument claims that we have it precisely backward when we think that theory shapes practice. Theory does not shape practice; rather, practice shapes theory. By "theory" I mean something similar to the definition proposed by Knapp and Michaels: "By 'theory' we mean a special project in literary criticism: the attempt to govern interpretations of particular texts by appealing to an account of interpretation in general" (723). As it relates to the issues under consideration here, I believe that Knapp and Michaels' definition may be modified without harm to read: By "theory" I mean a special project in composition studies: the attempt to govern the writing act by appealing to an account of the writing act in general. Stated a bit differently, the project of theory attempts to construct a generalized account of writing practice that remains uncontaminated by practice itself. Standing isolated, outside, or, more appropriately, above the hurly-burly world of human interaction, theory provides a formalized structure of understanding to which we may appeal in order to justify and validate our advice to students, our place at the academic trough, and our mission as teachers.

In his discussion of the consequences of theory, Fish identifies two kinds of theory, foundational and anti-foundational theory, and, for very different reasons, neither of these two kinds of theory shapes or informs practice. Foundational theory, according to Fish,

> can be seen to govern practice in two senses: (1) it is an attempt to *guide* practice from a position above or outside it . . . (2) it is an attempt to *reform* practice by neutralizing interest, by substituting for the parochial perspective of some local or partisan point of view the perspective of a general rationality to which the individual subordinates his contextually conditioned opinions and beliefs. (319)

For Fish, the example *par excellence* of a foundational theory is Noam Chomsky's project to isolate the underlying rules of the language system. In Fish's view, Chomsky seeks to discover rules that

> are not acquired through experience (education, historical conditioning, local habits) but are innate; experience serves only to actualize or "trigger" them. They have their source not in culture but in nature, and therefore they are *abstract* (without empirical content), *general* (not to be identified with any particular race, location, or historical period but with the species), and *invariant* (do not differ from language to language).
> (317)

Because Chomsky's theory of language is abstract, general, and invariant, someone who invokes Chomsky's theory "gives himself over to the theoretical machine, surrenders his judgment to it, in order to reach conclusions that in no way depend on his education, or point of view, or cultural situation, conclusions that can then be checked by anyone who similarly binds himself to those rules and carries out their instructions" (319).

The problem with this kind of foundational theory resides in the fact that the theoretical machine itself constitutes a cultural phenomenon; no theory transcends the culture in which it is fashioned. According to Fish, "This, then, is why theory will never succeed: it cannot help but borrow its terms and its contents from that which it claims to transcend, the mutable world of practice, belief, assumptions, point of view, and so forth" (321). Consequently, theory does not guide practice; rather, practice guides theory (for a similar view, see Toulmin and Vitanza). Fish explains that "Theory cannot guide practice because its rules and procedures are no more than generalizations from practice's history . . . and theory cannot reform practice because, rather than neutralizing interest, it begins and ends in interest and raises the imperatives of interest—of some local, particular, partisan project—to the status of universals" (321). Because theory derives from our practices, it is always interested and always implicated in our beliefs, assumptions, and points of view. Theory cannot provide, therefore, the god's-eye-view that foundationalists seek, for theory cannot transcend the everyday practices from which it springs. Fish calls this desire for the god's-eye-view "theory hope": the hope that knowledge and belief can be grounded in something other than "the accidents of education and experience" (322). To relinquish this hope requires us to relinquish along with it the hope that our practices may be justified and legitimated through an appeal to theory—the hope that we can appropriate a theory and then apply that theory to a set of practices in order to provide a justification for those practices (for a critique of this position see Goleman 93-122).

Although the hum of the theoretical machine may be heard across the entire terrain of composition scholarship, the appeal to theory in composition studies usually follows one of three general paths: scholars frequently employ an already established theory in an effort to authorize or explicate certain writing practices, or they appropriate aspects of different theories in order to generate a new theory of composition, or they apply the ideas of a master-theorist in order to authorize or explain some aspect of practice. One example (among many that might be cited) of the attempt to apply an already established theory to some aspect of practice occurs in an essay by Deborah Brandt that attempts "to translate the language of Flower and Hayes' cognitive theory of writing into a more thoroughly social vocabulary" (315). Brandt tells us that

> What [her] essay sets out to do is to explain the basic tenets of ethnomethodology, examine its connections to current thought in composition studies, and then apply ethnomethodological principles in an analysis of one writer's composing process. The overall goal of the discussion is to begin to develop a more thoroughly social conception of the cognition of writing than has heretofore been offered. (318)

In an effort "to develop a more thoroughly social conception of the cognition of writing," Brandt applies these abstract, general, and invariant "ethnomethodological principles" or rules to analyze "one writer's composing process." In so doing, she gives herself over to the theoretical machine; she surrenders her judgment to it and reaches conclusions that in no way depend on her education or point of view or cultural situation, conclusions that can be checked later by anyone who similarly binds him or herself to these ethnomethodological rules and carries out their instructions.

Of course, scholars do not need to limit themselves only to the direct application of a specific theory to the practice of writing as Brandt does. Elements from one theory or from a variety of theories may be employed to generate other theories. For example, Carol Berkenkotter and Thomas Huckin appropriate elements from several theories in order to develop their own theoretical framework for a sociocognitive theory of genre. They explain that

> Over the past several years our perspective has been informed by a number of disciplines and by various writers' theoretical constructs. These include structuration theory in sociology, rhetorical studies, interpretive anthropology, ethnomethodology, Bakhtin's theory of speech genres, Vygotsky's theory of ontogenesis, and Russian activity theory as it has shaped the movement in American psychology called "situated or everyday cognition." From our research and from this literature we have developed five principles that constitute a theoretical framework." (478)

In this example, theory begets further theory that may be applied down the road to the practice of writing.

The third and perhaps most pervasive application of the theoretical machine occurs when the scholar makes an overt appeal to concepts authorized by a master-theorist. In this move, the researcher extracts a concept or two from the works of a germinal thinker—someone like Marx or Freud or Derrida, for instance—and then applies the concept to some aspect of practice. For example, in a recent essay in *College English*, Alice Roy explains that she intends "to 'use' Burke and in particular his concept of scene as container for acts and agents" (183). When Roy proceeds to explain that her "focus is not on Burkean theory itself, but rather on current scenes and discursive practices that it can illuminate," she makes explicit her assumption that theory—in this case Burkean theory—shapes or, as she puts it, "illuminates" practice (183). The movement from the claims made by a master-theorist to claims about writing practice occurs so effortlessly and regularly in composition studies that the connection between theory and practice appears unproblematic, self-evidently reasonable, and even natural. We read, for example that Vygotsky's theory of learning "claims that these assisted interactions occur within the 'zone of proximal development,'" so "The implication of this theory for learning to write is that students must be engaged in social interactions that center on writing tasks that they cannot accomplish alone but can accomplish with assistance" (Freedman 76). Or, when we are told that "The means to form such an understanding [of reading and writing] can be found in Mikhail Bakhtin's theory of dialogism," we are not surprised to discover this aspect of Bakhtinian theory applied to a specific case: "In this essay, I'd like to show how Bakhtin's understanding of discourse offers us a way of reading Linda's text beyond the boundaries of the content/ form and personal/public dichotomies, a way that asks us to listen and speak back to a student's many voices as he or she searches for the means to form experience in the contentious social arena of writing" (Welch 494). In each of these examples, a link is established between the ideas of a master-theorist and some aspect of writing practice, and this link provides the justification and validation for the authors' claims about the practice of writing.

These three attempts to shape or to guide practice through an appeal to theory—the attempt to apply directly some sort of theory to practice, the attempt to generate a new theory by employing elements from other theories, and the attempt to justify or to authorize certain writing practices by an appeal to a master-theorist—demonstrate clearly a special project in composition studies: the attempt to govern the writing act by appealing to an account of the writing act in general. However, as Fish points out in his discussion of Chomskian linguistics, this project is doomed to fail because theory cannot transcend the practices it seeks to govern. All theory partakes of history; no theory resides above or outside historical contingency. In composition studies, for example, no empirically-based theory such as sociocognitive theory provides a god's-eye-view of writing practice because empiricism itself is an historical phenomenon deeply rooted in our beliefs about science, objectivity, and truth. So, empiricism does not transcend our contingent beliefs and practices; it derives from these beliefs and practices. Of course, since no theory escapes historical contingency, it would be nice to think that a theory of history—a Marxist theory or a Habermasian theory—might provide us with a perch high enough to enable us to view and to make sense of writing practice. Unfortunately, no such perch exists or could exist because no totalizing theory of history can provide us with a foundation or a framework that is not already constructed from the very beliefs and practices that the theory wishes to rise above. Because no god's-eye-view of writing practice exists or could exist, our attempts to govern the writing act by appealing to an account of the writing act in general simply cannot succeed.

To this point, I have been discussing foundationalist theory: the attempt to discover an Archimedean point outside of our contingent beliefs from which writing practice may be explained, authorized, and codified. In recent composition studies, however, a great deal of scholarship has focused on anti-foundationalist theory, although foundational theory still clearly dominates the field. Anti-foundationalist theory denies the basic tenet of foundationalist theory, the claim that a foundation exists from which we can acquire a god's-eye-view of writing practice. In other words, anti-foundationalism teaches that nothing outside our contingent beliefs, hopes, and desires justifies our practices. Because the justification for one of our beliefs will always appear in the form of another belief, nothing exists outside this web of contingent beliefs that could provide the epistemological foundation required either to shape or to justify the beliefs we hold.

What goes for belief also goes for practice: nothing exists outside of our practices to justify these practices. Because anti-foundationalism does not constitute a positive theory—it offers no program nor does it posit a generalized set of rules that guides or shapes practice—anti-foundationalism tells us nothing about the origin or essential nature of our practices and beliefs, so, as a result, it can tell us nothing about writing practice other than to make the innocuous and circular claim that we will endorse those writing practices that seem to work well in practice. So we see that both anti-foundationalist and foundationalist theory transport us (albeit from different directions) to the same destination: neither possesses consequences for writing practice. As Fish tells us, "Foundationalist theory has no consequences because its project cannot succeed, and anti-foundationalist theory has no consequences because, as a belief about how we got our beliefs, it leaves untouched (at least in principle) the beliefs of whose history it is an explanation" (325). Since nothing outside practice can justify our practices, practice may be seen to shape and to govern theory and not the other way around. If this is the case, practice possesses great consequences for theory, while theory possesses none for practice.

The Anti-Theory Argument
Because the claim that theory possesses no consequences for writing practice may seem overly contentious, I would like to address what I take to be the major and most obvious objection to this position. Fish formulates the objection in this way:

> Why restrict theory either to foundationalist attempts to ground practice by some Archimedean principle or to anti-foundationalist demonstrations that all such attempts will necessarily fail? Why exclude from the category "theory" much that has always been regarded as theory . . . works whose claims are general and extend beyond the interpretation of specific texts to the uncovering of regularities that are common to a great many texts? (325)

Rephrased, this question asks: Why exclude from the category "theory" a text such as Linda Flower's *The Construction of Negotiated Meaning: A Social Cognitive Theory of Writing* or Janet Emig's *The Composing Processes of Twelfth Graders*, texts that uncover general features of writing practice and then employ these features to construct an account of the writing process?

The answer to this question is twofold. First, a generalization derived from empirical data does not constitute a *theory* in any strong sense of the term. If every empirical generalization constituted a theory, then every general observation we made about writing would become a theory, and, as a consequence, theory would relinquish its power to do any real work for us. For example, Flower maintains that the "great question for cognitive rhetoric" is "How do individual writers (or readers) . . . carry out . . . diverse literate acts?" According to Flower, the answer to this question derives from "observation-based theory":

> For cognitive rhetoric, this question rises as an irresistible, necessarily empirical question. By *empirical*, I do not mean as a matter that can be resolved by the simple accumulation of facts, but, as I have argued elsewhere, as a question that calls for observation-based theory building grounded in the investigation of actual writers in specific contexts and for a willingness to be surprised and challenged by the unpredicted, by the data of experience. (42-43)

If I understand correctly Flower's notion of "observation-based theory building," a notion that she develops in detail in another chapter of this book, she seems to call for the kind of uncoerced and apparently open inquiry that we usually associate with research conducted in the natural sciences. Researchers in the area of cognitive rhetoric, she seems to say, should emulate the activities of the physicist or biologist by investigating the practices of actual writers in specific contexts and then proceed to build a theory based on these observations, a theory that is justified by the "data of experience" and that will change as researchers are "surprised and challenged by the unpredicted." Certainly, Flower's call for uncoerced inquiry—the belief that our observations about practice should be continually open to modification and change—represents a clearly laudable ethical goal. However, it is difficult to understand how Flower's observations—her empirical generalizations—about writing practice qualify as *theories* in any meaningful way. If our observation-based theories change each time we change our minds about what we are observing, our theories become little more than transitory descriptions or imitations of practice, and "theory" becomes synonymous with "model" or "exemplar." Of course, nothing stops us from employing the term "theory" to cover these imitations or models. Fish points out the obvious fact that

> If we like, we can always call such imitations of a powerful practice "theory," but nothing whatsoever will have been gained, and we will have lost any sense that theory is special. After all, it is only if theory is special that the question of its consequences is in any way urgent. In other words, the consequentiality of theory goes without saying and is, therefore, totally uninteresting if *everything* is theory. (326)

A second answer to our question concerns the misconception that every practice is always already theorized and that no unmediated—no untheorized—practice exists. This claim rests on the self-evident assertion that every practice becomes intelligible only within a set of assumptions or beliefs that describe the practice, but it does not follow from this idea that a *theory* articulates every practice. For example, Flower's observations about writing practice that she derives from her investigations of actual writers in specific contexts make sense only within a framework of beliefs that she and we already hold.   In other words, her beliefs inform her observations. However, a belief is not a theory.   Fish explains that

> A theory is a special achievement of consciousness; a belief is a prerequisite for being conscious at all. Beliefs are not what you think *about* but what your think *with*, and it is within the space provided by their articulations that mental activity—including the activity of theorizing—goes on. Theories are something you can have—you can wield them and hold them at a distance; beliefs have you, in the sense that there can be no distance between them and the acts they enable. (326)

When Flower observes writers in specific contexts, she already holds beliefs that help her make sense of what she observes, and, in turn, from her observations about writing practice, she either confirms or modifies these beliefs. But no reason exists to call these new beliefs a "theory." Certainly, as I have pointed out, we may call these new beliefs a "theory" if we so desire, but when we do so, we trivialize the concept and make meaningless the question of its consequences. So, when we attempt to extend the boundaries of theory to include a text (such as Flower's book) that uncovers general features of writing practice, we stretch the concept of theory so thin that it serves the same function as an empirical generalization or new belief *about* practice, and, as a result, theory fails to possess any specific consequences *for* practice.

Theory as a Kind of Practice
However, as I indicated at the beginning of this discussion, to say that theory possesses no consequences for writing practice does not mean that theory possesses no consequences at all. Theory possesses consequences because theory itself is a form of practice. Although theory does not guide or determine practice by standing outside it or above it, theory nonetheless forms part of the discipline of composition studies, and as part of this discipline, theory possesses great political and institutional consequences. Fish, for example, admits that "theory has consequences," but not because

> it stands apart from and can guide practice but because it is itself a form of practice and therefore is consequential for practice as a matter of definition. . . . As a practice, theory has all the political and institutional consequences of other practices. Those who do it can be published, promoted, fired, feted, celebrated, reviled . . . . But although these are certainly the consequences of theory, they are not theoretical consequences; that is, they are not the consequences of a practice that stands in a relationship of precedence and mastery to other practices. There is a world of difference between saying that theory is a form of practice and saying that theory informs practice: to say the one is to claim for theory no more than can be claimed for anything else; to say the other is to claim everything. So, even though the thesis that theory has no consequences holds only when the consequences are of a certain kind, they are the only consequences that matter, since they are the consequences that would mark theory off as special. (336-37)

Because theory constitutes a form of practice, Fish imagines a time when theory will disappear:

> Will theory stop? Certainly not as a result of arguments against it, mine, or anyone else's. . . . Theory will stop only when it has played out its string, run its course, when the urgencies and fears of which it is the expression either fade or come to be expressed by something else. . . . There will come a time . . . when the announcement of still another survey of critical method is received not as a promise but as a threat, and when the calling of still another conference on the function of theory in our time will elicit only a groan. That time may have come: theory's day is dying; the hour is late; and the only thing left for a theorist to do is to say so, which is what I have been saying here, and, I think, not a moment to soon. (340-41)

Although Fish forecasts the death of theory and even desires to speed up its demise, I do not share his view that the only thing left for a theorist to do is to admit that "theory's day is dying." Of course, Fish must be correct when he makes the commonsense observation that "Theory will stop only when it has played out its string," for clearly every practice changes and finally stops when it has no more to offer us. Unlike Fish, however, I do not believe that theory's day is done; I believe that theory remains alive and well, and its work remains unfinished.

As a practice, theory performs at least two important functions in composition studies. First, and perhaps most important, theory performs a political and institutional function by helping to empower composition studies as a recognized and legitimate area of study. In most universities, the obvious power inequities between composition studies and other academic disciplines, including literary studies, may be overcome only through the practice of theory. Unless we can demonstrate that composition studies is more than a service discipline—the handmaiden to literary studies or to the business college or to the engineering school—we stand little chance of overcoming its current condition: an under-rewarded, over-worked, and generally under-appreciated career path. One of the strategies to demonstrate institutionally that composition studies possesses the same kind of intellectual rigor claimed by other disciplines and to argue that composition studies offers more to the university than simply service to other disciplines is to emphasize the practice of theory. By "theory," I certainly do not mean a particular brand of theory—Marxist or feminist or cognitive or social-constructionist theory. I mean only that scholars in composition studies need to align themselves with the activity of doing *some* brand of theory, for only through this activity can researchers meet the expectations of intellectual rigor and appropriate scholarly achievement established for them by the university. We may chafe quite rightly at the fact that the kind of theory we do seldom matters to review committees and to the university at large. We may recoil at the idea that our service work and our teaching matter very little or not at all when promotion and salary decisions are made. We may even detest the thought that "doing" theory—no matter what kind of theory we do—is an overtly political act and not just an intellectual one within our institutions. However, we ignore these circumstances at our own peril. Those of us who are veterans of the tenure wars understand the power inequities within the university, but newcomers may not. New faculty need to understand that the practice of theory—that is, theory as an institutionally approved endeavor—provides them with one way of acquiring a modicum of power and prestige within the university and that the possibility for the acquisition of this power represents a crucial consequence of theory as a practice.

A second related consequence of theory concerns its perceived place within composition studies. Within composition studies, the practice of theory is regarded often as an ideological and sometimes highly polemical enterprise. Again, I must emphasize here what I mean by "the practice of theory": as a practice, theory represents a kind of institutionally sanctioned discipline—an academic area of interest—and not any one particular mode of inquiry, philosophic point of view, or conceptual scheme. As a kind of politicized institutional practice within composition studies, theory has been regarded by people such as Maxine Hairston as a thoroughly partisan, and, for that reason, dangerous activity. She disapprovingly tells us that

> out of a need to belong to and be approved by the power structure, [composition theorists] immerse themselves in currently fashionable critical theories, read the authors that are chic—Foucault, Bahktin [sic], Giroux, Eagleton, and Cixous, for example—then look for ways those theories can be incorporated into their own specialty, teaching writing. (184)

I believe that Hairston is largely correct in her assessment of the political nature of theory. In the area of composition studies, all of us "need to belong to and be approved by the power structure," but I do not share Hairston's fears about the consequences of this fact.

As a practice, theory functions as a kind of hermeneutics of suspicion (see Ricoeur). The practice of theory in composition studies or elsewhere requires us to view suspiciously any individual theory that attempts to bring the practice of theory to a close. In fact, the practice of theory protects and perpetuates itself by rejecting any one hegemonic theory; no *particular* theory can ever dominate the practice of theory because the mission of theory as a practice is to interrogate continually all theories. Gary Olson makes this same point, I believe, when he distinguishes between "theory, the noun" and "theorize, the verb":

> Theory, the noun, is dangerous from a postmodern perspective because it entices us into believing we somehow have captured a truth, grasped the essence of something; theorizing, the verb, can be productive (so long as a "theory" is not the objective) because it is a way to explore, challenge, question, reassess, speculate. Theorizing can lead us into lines of inquiry that challenge received notions of entrenched understanding that may no longer be productive; it can create new vocabularies for talking about a subject and thus new ways of perceiving it. (54)

As Olson suggests, the practice of theory always appears as an irritation to established schools or points of view, for it continually questions and badgers complacency. Because the practice of theory—the act of *doing* theory no matter what kind of theory we do—requires us to view suspiciously our individual theories, we find ourselves continually critiquing and revamping our beliefs, and it is this need for ongoing revision that, in part, troubles Hairston. For Hairston, this demand for continual critique appears unproductive and even irrational; she wants the nagging theorists to stop questioning our beliefs and to refrain from revealing our unstated ideological assumptions. But the practice of theory cannot grant this desire, for the practice of theory exists to uncover just such desires. To participate in the practice of theory requires us to view suspiciously every theoretical point of view and every ideological position, including our own, and this often uncomfortable and irritating requirement constitutes a second important consequence of the practice of theory.

If theory possesses, as an institutional practice, serious and important consequences for composition studies (although it may possess no consequences for the actual practice of writing), graduate students and newcomers to the profession might do well to understand the nature of these consequences, especially the political consequences. Because these political and institutional consequences impinge upon every facet of our professional lives, one of our curricular concerns should be the development of courses that help students to explore the consequences of theory, for certainly newcomers to composition studies would be better served if we discussed more widely and openly the ramifications of theory both for the practice of writing and for the profession itself.

Publication in the Field of Composition Theory
When we practice theory—that is, when we attempt to disseminate what may be called for lack of a better term *theoretical scholarship*—no strictures exist that can ensure in advance the publication of a specific manuscript, for, obviously, no rules can account for the variables and the vagaries of the publication act in general. Although no "theory" about publishing theory exists or could exist that guarantees the publication of a particular manuscript, rules-of-thumb clearly do exist. For example, an author certainly should develop an interesting point; the point should be relevant to a specific audience; the author's argument should be clear; the manuscript should conform to specified style requirements; and so on. However, these commonsense tips in no way constitute a theory that, when followed, ensures publication. In fact, an author might follow all of these rules-of-thumb and still not get a manuscript published. Just as theory possesses no consequences for the practice of writing, theory (although it sounds strange to say so) also possesses no consequences for the practice of theory.

Although no theory determines, controls, or guides the practice of theory, two general guidelines (in addition to the rules-of-thumb mentioned above) may help to increase the chances of successful publication in the area of composition theory. First, an author should be thoroughly familiar with the discourse that constitutes the institutional practice of composition theory (what Gary Olson in another chapter of this book calls "the scholarly conversation"). This advice may seem so self-evident that it requires no emphasis or even elaboration, but, judging from my experience as a journal editor, I believe that authors frequently repeat arguments that have been made already in an area or they fail to ground and to contextualize their arguments within the relevant and prevailing scholarship (the "conversation") that constitutes the area and thereby fail to demonstrate the significance of their arguments. Clearly, these difficulties may be overcome quite easily by taking graduate courses in composition theory or by reading widely in the many journals that publish scholarship in the field, but no matter how authors become familiar with the professional discourse that marks off composition theory from other institutional practices, they must be able to speak the idiom of theory in order to participate fully as scholars in the area.

Although we may decry this proliferation of specialization, we cannot avoid the plain fact that composition studies now constitutes a mature discipline with several sub-disciplines, and success nowadays as a scholar in this discipline generally requires specialized training in the idiom of one or more sub-disciplines. Of course, when we consider other disciplines, specialized training (or knowing the idiom) seems entirely appropriate. For example, a student in anthropology would not immediately begin the study of a particular culture without first knowing the idiom that anthropologists employ in order to understand one another. Similar to anthropology or any other institutional practice, composition theory also possesses (for better or worse) its own idiom, and those who understand and employ this idiom increase the likelihood of seeing their work published.

A second general guideline that may help authors increase their chances of successful publication in the area of composition theory concerns the relevance and the importance of their arguments. Although authors may communicate fluently in the idiom of composition theory, their manuscripts may add nothing relevant or important to the conversation in the field. In order to acquire feedback about the relevancy and the importance of their writings, authors, particularly scholars new to composition studies, should make every effort to solicit help and advice from established scholars in the field. By working with a mentor (or, better yet, mentors) from either inside or outside their home institutions, authors can acquire realistic appraisals of the relevancy and importance of their arguments, and, even more important, they can acquire feedback that will help them revise and improve their manuscripts before they submit them for possible publication.

These two commonsense guidelines emphasize the importance of viewing composition theory as an institutional and, therefore, thoroughly social practice. When we treat composition theory as an institutional practice—a practice that includes, of course, the publication of research—we avoid the futile attempt to govern the writing act by appealing to an account of the writing act in general. We understand writing in all its varieties (including scholarly writing) to be uncodifiable practices that help us make sense of the world's wild dance. At least since Plato, we have searched without success for a theory that might choreograph this dance, and we have discovered only that no theory tells the world what to do. For composition theory, then, the most grand theory of all is no theory at all.

Works Cited

Berkenkotter, Carol, and Thomas N. Huckin. "Rethinking Genre From a Sociocognitive Perspective." *Written Communication* 10 (1993): 475-509.

Berlin, James A. "Contemporary Composition: The Major Pedagogical Theories." *College English* 44 (1982): 765-77.

Bizzell, Patricia A. "Cognition, Context, and Certainty." *Pre/Text* 3 (1982): 213-24.

Brandt, Deborah. "The Cognitive as the Social: An Ethnomethodological Approach to Writing Process Research." *Written Communication* 9 (1992): 315-55.

Brodkey, Linda. *Academic Writing as Social Practice*. Philadelphia: Temple UP, 1987.

Bruffee, Kenneth A. "Social Construction, Language, and the Authority of Knowledge." *College English* 48 (1986): 773-90.

Elbow, Peter. *Embracing Contraries: Explorations in Learning and Teaching*. New York: Oxford UP, 1986.

Emig, Janet. *The Composing Processes of Twelfth Graders*. Urbana: NCTE, 1971.

Faigley, Lester. "Competing Theories of Process." *College English* 48 (1986): 527-42.

Fish, Stanley. *Doing What Comes Naturally: Change, Rhetoric, and the Practice of Theory in Literary and Legal Studies*. Durham, NC: Duke UP, 1989.

Flower, Linda. *The Construction of Negotiated Meaning: A Social Cognitive Theory of Writing*. Carbondale: Southern Illinois UP, 1994.

Flower, Linda, and John R. Hayes. "A Cognitive Process Theory of Writing." *College Composition and Communication* 32 (1981): 365-87.

Freedman, Sarah Warshauer. "Crossing the Bridge to Practice: Rethinking the Theories of Vygotsky and Bakhtin." *Written Communication* 12 (1995): 74-92.

Giroux, Henry A. *Border Crossings: Cultural Workers and the Politics of Education*. New York: Routledge, 1992.

Goleman, Judith. *Working Theory: Critical Composition Studies for Students and Teachers*. Westport, CT: Bergin, 1995.

Hairston, Maxine. "Diversity, Ideology, and Teaching Writing." *College Composition and Communication* 43 (1992): 179-93.

Knapp, Steven, and Walter Benn Michaels. "Against Theory." *Critical Inquiry* 8 (1982): 723-42.

Knoblauch, C.H. "Rhetorical Constructions: Dialogue and Commitment." *College English* 50 (1988): 125-40.

Lay, Mary M. "Feminist Theory and the Redefinition of Technical Communication." *Journal of Business and Technical Communication* 5 (1991): 348-70.

Macrorie, Ken. *Uptaught.* Rochelle Park, NJ: Hayden, 1970.

Moffett, John. *Teaching the Universe of Discourse.* Boston: Houghton, 1968.

Murray, Donald. *A Writer Teaches Writing: A Practical Method of Teaching Composition.* 2nd ed. Boston: Houghton, 1985.

Nystrand, Martin, Stuart Greene, and Jeffrey Wiemelt. "Where Did Composition Studies Come From? An Intellectual History." *Written Communication* 10 (1993): 267-333.

Olson, Gary A. "Theory and the Rhetoric of Assertion." *Composition Forum* 6 (1995): 53-61.

Roy, Alice. "The Grammar and Rhetoric of Inclusion." *College English* 57 (1995): 182-93.

Toulmin, Stephen. "Literary Theory, Philosophy of Science, and Persuasive Discourse: Thoughts from a Neo-premodernist." Interview with Gary A. Olson. *Philosophy, Rhetoric, Literary Criticism: (Inter)views.* Ed. Gary A. Olson. Carbondale: Southern Illinois UP, 1994. 194-219.

Trimbur, John R. "Consensus and Difference in Collaborative Learning." *College English* 51 (1989): 602-16.

Vitanza, Victor J. "Three Countertheses: Or, A Critical In(ter)vention into Composition Theories and Pedagogies." *Contending with Words: Composition and Rhetoric in a Postmodern Age.* Ed. Patricia Harkin and John Schilb. New York: MLA, 1991. 139-72.

Welch, Nancy. "One Student's Many Voices: Reading, Writing, and Responding with Bakhtin." *Journal of Advanced Composition* 13 (1993): 493-502.

Observation-Based Theory Building

LINDA FLOWER

Research in rhetoric and composition begins in a problem—maybe it's a mystery, a perplexing event, a missing piece; maybe it's a conflict between assumptions and observations; or maybe it's the discovery of contradictions in our own beliefs or practices. It begins in a problem (which we refuse to dismiss by invoking an a priori theory) that leads to inquiry and ends in an explanatory account. Publishing in rhetoric and composition is an extension of this inquiry—not just a report of its results. Publication requires an argument for interpretation, one that is built on justifications that persuaded us and, we hope, will convince others. This chapter describes how observation-based theory building helps those writing about research to build such a case for interpreting and responding to genuine problems.

Problem Posing in Rhetoric and Composition
Consider, for example, the kind of problem which the following question raises: *What does it take to link literacy, education, and social action?* Can reading and writing support action for social justice, and if so how? And what about competing approaches, such as introducing multicultural perspectives in reading assignments, versus leading students to engage in cultural critique, versus teaching strategies for collaborative, intercultural rhetorical action? Does it matter which alternative we choose?

This problem of linking literacy and action does not, of course, exist in the abstract. For Elenore Long, whose recent study provides my example, this problem was embedded in a concrete rhetorical situation that helped her pose the problem as a researchable question. In her study, college students moved from reading about literacy and intercultural discourse to working for eight weeks at Pittsburgh's inner-city Community Literacy Center as mentors for urban teenagers. It was a relationship that turned some social patterns upside down, as college student mentors, "illiterate" in the discourse of the inner city, tried to support the expertise of the teenagers as these teenagers created a document and conducted a community conversation on issues of risk, violence, and stress in the lives of urban youth. During this experience, the mentors developed their own inquiry and, returning to the university, wrote papers on community literacy and intercultural collaboration.

In this context, Long's theoretical concerns took shape as a more precise, situated, researchable question: *What are students in this situation in fact learning? How do they come to understand the link between literacy and social action in their own experience?* To be specific, if they see mentoring as an opportunity to transfer their literate expertise, do they see it as an effort that may also work to reproduce the status quo? If mentoring might tend to reinforce a liberal illusion of social uplift, does it also significantly challenge the assumptions or practices that support racism; does it disturb the normally unquestioned authority of elite discourses (those that the college students are themselves working to control)? More importantly, as students become aware of the conflicts within this rhetorical situation (which include some of their own assumptions, goals, and values), how do they transform those conflicts and negotiations into understanding?

Consider, for instance, a college student named Keith. How does he handle the friction among his own goals? These instances of friction start with a desire to minimize his power position in his relationship with Chanda, an African-American teenager, even as she is often surprised and amused at his politicized reading of her day-to-day life. All the while, Keith also wants to push Chanda to rigorous thinking about her writing, longs to entice her to interrogate her own assumptions as he does, and at the same time wants her to produce a publishable text for the project on time. As these images of literate action come into play, what does Keith make it mean? The researcher's circle is completed when Long places her situated inquiry—into the ways students construct their experience and interpret its meaning—in the context of other claims: *How does this insight into the meanings students construct speak back to a disciplinary, theoretical debate about the links between literacy and action—about how these links are forged in practice and how forging such links might constitute rigorous rhetorical action.*

I sketched this series of questions because it exemplifies the kind of problem—really, the particular mix of problems—that is emerging in published scholarship in rhetoric and composition and that distinguishes its research from standard work in literary criticism, cultural theory and critique, or educational research. Let me note four hallmarks of these "good" problems and the kind of rhetorical knowledge they help us construct.

First, such problems raise a significant theoretical *and* action-oriented question. They are not limited merely to critiquing other positions, but are committed to finding a better place to stand. Such questions call for a conditionalized theoretical account that examines some of our own valued assumptions and educational practices and asks our answer to be accountable to the complexities of the world in which it operates.

Second, the problems we pose for ourselves in this hyphenated discipline of rhetoric and composition call for situated inquiry and for an interactive social and cognitive explanation. To elaborate, the problems of rhetoric are not located simply in texts, nor in the world of competing readings and academic debate that surrounds texts. The place for inquiry in rhetoric and composition—the place we go for study—is located in the literate practices of real people and the dilemmas they pose, which will inevitably involve their thoughts, feelings, and actions as well as words. Such a place will ask us to see abstract concepts—such as the nature of literate practice, the influence of discourse communities, the struggle of learning, or the process of social cognitive construction and the transformation of knowledge—as situated actions. Building a *situated* rhetorical theory means being accountable to the complicating presence of actual writers, diverse literate practices, and social and cultural contexts. Building an *interactive* theory means recognizing that writing is at once an individually purposed and culturally shaped act, a private and public event, and a social and cognitive process. It can be difficult to capture this complex interaction in a single study, but our theories must be alive to this array of generative forces.

Third, the answers we seek, the situated theories we seek to build, cannot rest their arguments on appeals to scientific method or abstract validity, or to the elegance and internal coherence of our interpretation, or, for that matter, to the politically correct work of other theorists. Standing in the real world of literate practice, acknowledging the educational tradition of rhetoric and the social role of composition, we need to look at our work in the spirit of Deweyan pragmatism. The meaning of our account will be defined in its consequences; its truth value will be judged through the understandings it allows and the actions it enables.

The great challenge in rhetoric and composition is to construct theories of rhetorical interaction that can themselves support literate action. As educators, the action we can foster does not take place within a social abstraction or a collective, but in the minds of individual students. Therefore, we need a vision that locates the thinking, acting, self-aware writer within our larger constructs. We need a vision that can recognize the reality of a writer's bounded intentionality and socially constructed knowledge—and within the center of that understanding illuminate the space for possibility, options, and action by individual writers.

Finally, problems such as those posed in published scholarship in rhetoric and composition call for what I have called *negotiated meanings*, provisional resolutions forged out of the awareness of conflict (*Construction*). The accounts we build will arise from the negotiation of multiple strong arguments, alternative truths, competing perspectives, perplexing observations. And in the same spirit, the actions we envision will have to be answerable to competing truths and realities, to support a complex and qualified understanding.

The particular challenges posed by problems like these are deeply rooted in the simultaneously theoretical-and-situated agenda of rhetoric and composition. They call for observation-based theory building, which in turn raises important questions about the nature of observational inquiry itself, particularly the problem of objectivity. Because some of the recent feminist debates over the "science question" have opened this issue up in an articulate way, I want to begin with some feminist approaches to objectivity as Sandra Harding and Donna Haraway discuss them. I will then look in more detail at how observational research contributes to theory building in rhetoric and composition.

Research and Objectivity

Some feminist approaches to objectivity begin with the unequivocal assertion that "science has always been a social product—that its projects and claims to knowledge bear the fingerprints of its human producers"—and that as a fully social activity it will "inevitably reflect the conscious and unconscious social commitments of inquirers" (Harding, *Science Question* 137, 201). Feminists have based this recognition on historical analyses that reveal the effects of gender bias and show how cultural projects work themselves out in research as they do in any cultural institution. Such analyses undercut naive claims that the rigorous adherence to supposedly value-neutral methods of science can ensure objectivity. Feminists have also mounted a critique of the conceptual dichotomizing that characterizes many theories in science: culture versus nature; objectivity versus subjectivity; public versus private; the rational mind versus the prerational body, irrational emotions and values. Because these dualities are often linked to a valued masculinity and devalued femininity, such dualities not only use science to promote social "gender agendas," but they also create a reductive vision of nature; they are themselves a failure of objectivity (136). Finally, feminists have argued that the problems of bias in science are located in two key places. The first is in the way standard methodologies, especially in social sciences, can reduce data in ways that eliminate significant information through a "focus on quantitative measures, variable analysis, impersonal and excessively abstract conceptual schemes"—a focus that tends to see differences in terms of hierarchical structures rather than "reciprocal, interactive relations of complexes" (105-06). The depersonalizing moves done in the name of attaining more objectivity—creating a subject/object relationship between the observer and the observed—import a distance and distortion that undercut their very goals. The second source of bias, feminists have shown, is in the way our political motivations for inquiry define the problems we think important enough to study, how they select the methods that "constitute rigorous procedure, and how they shape the context of discovery, [the place] where problems are identified as appropriate for scientific investigation, hypotheses are formulated, key concepts are defined" (Harding, *Whose* 144).

These critiques have laid important groundwork for rethinking the authority claims of science. However, feminists like Harding and Haraway—although they disagree on the path to take—insist that it is time to go beyond textual analysis and mere critique and to develop more adequate images of objectivity. As Harding remarks, we cannot have it both ways and insist that feminist (or any other kind of) inquiry can offer "alternative explanations of the natural and social world that are 'less false' or 'closer to the truth,' and at the same time question [in the sense of discard] the grounds for taking scientific facts and their explanations to be the reasonable end of justificatory arguments" (Harding, *Science Question* 138). Just because objectivity is not an absolute, we can't dismiss its role in building convincing arguments that justify our claims and still insist that our claims are better than those we see as biased. These feminists—who see research as dedicated to important social agendas—are also impatient with the easy solutions of relativism. The more difficult alternative they propose is a rhetorical one which depends on case building. It is marked by an initial premise that does not assume that objectivity can attempt to rest its authority on a claim that it is "value neutral." This feminist objectivity makes no claim to conduct "value-free, impartial, dispassionate research" that promises to identify and eliminate social values from research (*Whose* 143). It functions instead like other valued, vital but limited tools in the rhetorical process of case building.

The question, then, is what do new approaches to objectivity look like which are concerned with the "origins and or consequences of their problematics and practices, or with the social values and interests that these problematics and practices support?" (*Whose* 147). Harding speaks for standpoint theorists who find a solution in starting with the viewpoints and the experience of women, especially women speaking from the positions of subjugation who can challenge our mainstream social perspectives and assumptions. But in contrast to some versions of standpoint theory, she makes it clear that such positions yield only standpoints that generate good projects, not claims. Such perspectives have no greater claim to *objectivity* than any other position, nor do they offer any "reliable grounds for deciding just which claims to knowledge are preferable" (*Whose* 123).

Harding's analysis of this debate in 1987 and again in 1991 makes it clear that feminism has not created the "successor science" it aims for, but she sees the ferment of critique and problematic proposals as a necessary step in the search for that goal: "A maximally objective science, natural or social," she says, "will be one that includes a self-conscious and critical examination of the relationship between the social experience of its creators and the kinds of cognitive structures favored in its inquiry" (*Science* 250).

Donna Haraway is even more forceful about the high stakes that surround the challenge to face the objectivity problem, to go beyond critique and develop what she calls a "feminist objectivity":

> Feminists have to insist on a better account of the world; it is not enough to show radical historical contingency and modes of construction for everything. . . . Feminists have stakes in a successor science project that offers a more adequate, richer, better account of a world, in order to live in it well and in critical, reflexive relation to our own as well as others' practices of domination and the unequal parts of privilege and oppression that make up all positions. (*Simians* 187)

The problem is: how do you construct a usable, not an innocent, doctrine of objectivity that allows "the possibility of sustained, rational, objective enquiry" without pulling the "god-trick" of promising a totalizing vision and claiming it has the disinterested power to produce one? This feminist objectivity demands of us, as she says, *"simultaneously* an account of the radical historical contingency of all knowledge claims and knowing subjects, *and* a no-nonsense commitment to faithful accounts of a 'real world'" (187). Haraway insists on three points. First, an objective or faithful description of the "real world" is "responsible" in the sense that it can be called into account. Its claims rest not on speculation or a priori values, but on embodied knowledges and on locatable knowledge claims (191). Second, by insisting on the embodied nature of all vision, this objectivity does not promise to deliver a totalizing, universal, or reductive account of the world. Instead, it offers an account of situated and embodied knowledges; the knowledge claims it makes are not about Knowledge or Truth, but about particular and specific embodiments of knowledge seen from the particular perspective of the present observer. "The moral," Haraway says, "is simple: only partial perspective promises objective vision" (190). Finally, although this vision of research outlaws the "god-trick" of asserting its grasp on universal principles, it resists retreat to an ineffectual stance of relativism and simple pluralism. In place of a singular truth, it argues that the partial, locatable, and critical knowledges it describes are in fact linked to one another by the webs of connection and shared conversation.

As Haraway reminds us, in the controversy over a concept like "objectivity" we must not fall into easy polarities and lose our grasp of some fundamental goals for doing research. Here, for instance, Gregory Cizek criticizes a polarizing proponent of qualitative research who hails it as

> an *alternative* [emphasis added] to traditional research methods that are theory driven, hypothesis testing, or generalization producing (see Peshkin, 1993). . . . This is nuts. If research doesn't relate to anything we currently know (i.e., theory driven), if it doesn't address a question of interest posed by the researcher (i.e., hypothesis testing) or produce knowledge that others can use and is *bound* to a particular setting (i.e., not generalizable), then how can it even be called research? (27)

The question here is not whether we need objectivity, rigor, or principles, but what these terms mean in practice. Both Haraway and Harding are emphatic that researchers draw inferences and make connections (generalize and theorize). The open, hard-to-answer question is: how far can that inferential leap go; how broadly can we generalize, on what basis, and in whose interest? Neither of these writers answers that question because there is no answer in the abstract. It's a question that each researcher has to answer, a case he or she has to build in the context of the work at hand. And the feminist vision makes that responsibility an even more clearly rhetorical problem.

In a lucid review of feminist inquiry applied to composition, Gesa Kirsch and Joy Ritchie make the rhetorical problem even more explicit. They attempt to grapple with some of the dilemmas researchers can face in trying to enact in their work a "politics of location" in which reflection and self-analysis of the observer become an enterprise nearly equal in significance to the observations in question. In Kirsch and Ritchie's account of the feminist agenda, research is a political act to the extent that for them the overriding ethic of empowering women can even, it seems, call for suppression or distortion of one's data. Moreover, research (at least the ethnography on which they focus) is also expected to be an act of personal, reciprocal, self-discovery for both researcher and subject.

What is troubling about this ethnographic version of feminist inquiry, however, is that it seems to lack the strong demand for rigor, for scrupulous care with data, and for the *search for* objectivity which give such balance to the accounts of Harding and Haraway.[1] In Haraway's "no-nonsense commitment to faithful accounts of a 'real world'" (187), it is clear that the politics of "doing research" in a valued way can become an end in itself—an end that appears to dominate and at times even replace the grounding focus we see in Haraway on a problem to be plumbed, on a mystery to be understood, or on a belief or hypothesis to be tested before it poses as a guide to action. The problem posed by Kirsch and Ritchie's version of feminist inquiry is in part a rhetorical problem for readers. It is no longer clear how the practice of such research differs from the writing of critical theory, philosophical *pensées*, or personal essays. If research matters, if we are trying to build situated knowledge that can guide action by building cases and testing one another's claims, then we must be able to assume that when other researchers are building a case they are guided by Harding's "simultaneous" commitment to self-reflexivity *and* to the world we would understand—to an uncompromised, vigorous effort for a *conditionalized* objectivity. Research (unlike other literate practices) explores the interpretive biases and limitations of the writer's own observations, not for the sake of self-exploration (as worthwhile as that is), but to build a better case—to hint at more of the local truths making up a "real world" that exists beyond our interpretative bias and perspective.

The kind of research supported by the feminist "objectivity" of Haraway and Harding has parallels to the contested, negotiated meaning that, as I argued earlier, emerges from rhetorical dilemmas. As Haraway puts it, speaking for herself and other feminists, the "doctrine and practice" of objectivity for which they argue "privileges contestation, deconstruction, passionate construct, webbed connections, and hope for transformation of systems of knowledge and ways of seeing" (192). It is a view of objectivity that seems particularly suited to the kind of problems published scholarship in rhetoric and composition faces.

Research and Observation-Based Theory Building

The problems at the heart of rhetoric and composition—the problems of situated, social and cognitive literate action—call for a kind of theory-building which is not afraid of research and for a kind of research that is willing to grapple with its own limitations in order to go beyond isolated "results" to theory-building. The goal of a situated, social cognitive theory is intimately bound up with the problem of how to build one and with the role research plays in this process. Since some members of the community broadly defined as "English" see research itself as a threat to the humanities, especially research that uses empirical methods, perhaps we should start with this concern. Let me be concrete. A few years ago at Purdue's summer Rhetoric Seminar, I talked to a young woman who was working on her degree in literature at another institution. That night, as we were sitting around drinking wine, she told me that she "didn't believe in doing research." I was a little taken aback that an aspiring scholar would reject any method of inquiry out of hand, almost as an article of faith. It soon became apparent that her vision of empirical research was itself so reductive that she never saw beyond the methods, the numbers, and the tables she couldn't read to the common sense on which research and its rules of evidence are built or to goals we both cared about. My remarks here are in a sense addressed to that young woman and to our need for a broader vision of research as a tool for building contextualized and integrated theories of writing.[2]

Any theory, if it is to offer a broadly explanatory account of a significant human action or body of knowledge, will have to meet many criteria, including logical consistency, clarity, scope and parsimony. A situated rhetorical theory must do more. First, like other "grounded theories," it must *fit* the situation being studied (that is, it can be applied without force; its categories are clearly reflected in the data), and it must *work* (that is, it must offer an explanation of the process that is meaningful to us as both theorists and educators) (Glaser and Strauss). Also, to be an accountable interpretation of social cognitive action, it must be built on a fine-grained, richly specified vision of the process in question. Grand, speculative theories are well designed to capture the imagination, but they are also associated with the rhetoric of conflict among competing theories, one position striving to preempt the other in a zero/sum game. Fine-grained, observational theories can encourage the rhetoric of exploration and construction. They direct attention to the process under study and open the door to continued modification of themselves. They also allow (even invite) us to recognize significant variations in the way this theory plays itself out in different settings, from a storefront school to a college classroom, from one writer to another.

There are many valued paths that lead to theory. Theory can be based on historical scholarship or on extrapolations from prior theories, in much the same way we adapt classical rhetoric to modern problems or adapt Burke's dramatistic analysis of literature to composing. Theory can also grow out of what Janice Lauer and J. William Asher call rhetorical inquiry: a deductive process in which the theory-builder both examines and argues for a set of premises and conclusions, a mode that can combine the strengths of a speculative leap with reasoned support. Theory can also grow out of research: a process in which one's orienting premises enter into dialogue with a set of close, systematic observations of writers at work. Observation-based theory building is carried out in rhetoric with an expanding repertoire of empirical methods, ranging from the controlled methods of experimental research to the descriptive methods of ethnography, case studies, and process tracing using cued recall and protocol analysis.

Any basis for theory-building (whether it is historical scholarship, systematic observation, or personal experience) is merely a springboard, a means to an end. We must remember that theory-building is ultimately a constructive, rhetorical act: to create a structured, explanatory account of an interactive process like writing will inevitably force us beyond available evidence and into the probabilistic reasoning that is at the heart of rhetoric (Perelman and Olbrechts-Tyteca). The path we take will differ from other paths in the kind of argument and evidence it can generate. Let me quote Janice Lauer and William Asher's definition of "rhetorical inquiry" as one approach to theory building:

> Rhetorical inquiry, then, entails several acts: (1) identifying a motivating concern, (2) posing questions, (3) engaging in heuristic search [based on analogy] (which in composition studies has often occurred by probing other fields), (4) creating a new theory or hypothesis, and (5) justifying the theory. (5)

The approach I am calling observation-based theory building will lead to yet a different sort of argument with its own distinguishing features. First, unlike an empirical study using data primarily to test or confirm a carefully delimited assertion, the goal of this process is theory. In trying to construct a more comprehensive, more explanatory account, observation-based theory building draws on research for its heuristic power as well—going a step beyond the data in an attempt to honor the data. Second, it differs from the process Lauer and Asher describe in that it is driven to a greater degree by the generative power of close or systematic observation. Observation is used not merely to justify or test a theory but to help pose questions, structure the search, and frame hypotheses. We can see observation-based approaches at work in emerging theories across the field: Hull's deepening account of workplace literacies and the patterns of inequity they systematize; Dyson's developmental picture of early writing as a child's negotiation of visual, verbal, and social meanings; Bazerman's cumulative analysis of how rhetorical intentions, available schemas, and necessary conventions interact in the history of scientific discourse; Bereiter and Scardamalia's writing-based model of learning as a social cognitive process of knowledge transformation;

Witte's semiotic account of text, context, and intertext at work in the writing of grocery lists and professional documents; Heath's picture of how different literate practices function, fit, and misfit in different social settings; and my own portraits of how outer voices become inner voices whose conflict leads to the construction of new negotiated meanings. These, and other bodies of work I might have mentioned, reflect a cumulative attempt to build a theoretical picture grounded in observation.

I want to focus my discussion on this observation-based route to theory building, not to compare it to others or argue for its advantages, which like any method's are mixed, but to describe some of its goals and limitations, as well as some of the problems of research itself, so that those interested in publishing such research will have a clearer idea of its strengths and weaknesses. I would like to organize my comments around what I see as three features of this particular process of inquiry.

Two Sources of Evidence

(1) *Observation-based theory is built from the union of two sources of evidence: it springs in part from an intuition or an argument and in part from the complementary evidence of close, systematic observation and data.*

Let me illustrate this joint process with an example and a theoretical dilemma from a Reading-to-Write study in which first-year students prepared think aloud protocols in their dorm rooms as they composed a short paper and then used their texts and transcripts of the protocols to identify some of their own composing strategies (Flower et al.). We observed students making important strategic decisions about the task at hand, and about how to manage it, that had a significant impact on how teachers perceived their work. While some, for instance, gave themselves the goal of merely summarizing the source text and its "authorities," others represented the task as synthesizing and creating new organizing ideas. This study revealed the enormous importance of task representation, and how widely students differ on what they think is required. But it also left us with an important question: does the strategic knowledge we observed in this situation play a critical role in students' attempt to enter academic discourse; does it really matter for most students? Or would strategic awareness—about how they are representing a task to themselves—be merely a luxury, useful only *after* one has learned the "basics" and the conventions of a new discourse?

My own intuition about this strategic process could be framed as argument from analogy. Far from being a luxury, valuable only to well-educated college students, this strategic knowledge, I would argue, is closely related to the critical consciousness that provides the starting point in Paulo Freire's literacy programs. Those adults enter literacy, not by first trudging through and *banking* knowledge of the basics, but by using sounds and letters they already recognize to "make up" words that express their own experience and goals. They become makers and users of literacy from their first evening session. As Freire and others like Ann Berthoff argue, knowing your own knowledge, whatever it is, and discovering your own power to make meaning stands at the heart of these astoundingly successful literacy programs. To that I would add, if such knowledge can catapult an unlettered Brazilian farmer into literacy, what might such self-awareness offer to a college student who stands merely on the threshold of a new form of discourse?

I like the spirit of this argument. It captures my own intuitions; it is based on a premise I know is shared by other educators; and it builds on an analogy to a clearly successful case showing the power of strategic consciousness in learning new ways to use language. And yet this argument alone is not enough. One wonders, does the analogy really *fit*? And even if it does apply at some level of generality, does it *work* as a genuinely useful explanation; will it describe the experiential reality of students learning a particular kind of discourse? An argument alone will not tell us what may in fact be happening with our students. For instance, what is the strategic repertoire your students bring to college? Does context or the background of your particular students lead to important differences in their goals or strategies that we could/should anticipate? Does the theory outlined in the Reading-to-Write study even fit the data of your experience and your students at all?

It is in response to questions like this that observation-based theory building turns to a second source of evidence: the data of experience. Close observation is demanding; systematic observation even more so. I think of Shirley Heath's detailed descriptions of children's speech spanning a nine-year period and how, from these patterns, consistent, deep-running disjunctions between the culture of home and the culture of school began to emerge. I think of Anne Dyson's systematic study of children's early writing and drawing, a study which eventually contradicted the assumption that narrative is the first and natural mode for all children and, which in doing so, showed that certain children (marked as developmentally delayed by their teachers!) were in fact becoming writers by a different but equally "natural" path. I think of the Reading-to-Write data which tracked the unpredictable twists and turns of writers' minds at work; how this record captured the interplay between reading, writing, and thinking that the students' text did not register, and in doing so revealed some of the dilemmas and decisions a teacher never sees. In all of these studies and others like them, the goal is a more explanatory theory, but the starting point is the data of close observation.

We must not forget that "data" is itself a selected piece of experience—the speech the observer chose to write down, the classroom exchanges the ethnographer was there to capture, the thoughts which occupied the conscious attention of writers as they thought aloud. But compared to more ad hoc forms of personal observation and the fragile records of unprompted memory, these formal records of experience provide a large, detailed, and stubbornly independent picture the observer must then account for. In being *collected* according to a broad and systematic sampling plan, the data one must be accountable to is itself less likely to be covertly patterned, pat, or biased in an unacknowledged way. Such data actively resists the observer's desire to "discover" that single example which will "prove" a preordained point. Good data is assertive and intractable. In the dialogue that goes on between intuition or emerging theory on the one hand and the data on the other, these records of experience have the habit of contradicting one's cherished assumptions and pet theories. The data always contains more possibilities than we can grasp. It may even ask us to negotiate multiple representations of meaning, multiple symbol systems as when an ethnographer must translate non-verbal actions into words or when we move from a rich intuitive perception to a coding scheme we can explain to someone else (Flower and Hayes). This very richness is the source of a central dilemma for research. And that is my second point.

Data and Meaning
(2) *Data is only data; a theory is a construction based on data.*
    All data can do is provide the foundation for interpretation. And in observation-based theory building, as in much research in rhetoric, we have to take genuine leaps. We have to go beyond the data to probabilities, because our goal is not merely to describe but to understand, to infer and to explain something we want to know. Data is the grist for an interpretive act. Moreover, theory making is never disinterested. We do research because, as a part of an educational community, we have constructed the burning questions we want to answer; we have already named the mysteries we want to plumb. We use data both to initiate and to constrain our interpretive leaps.
    To say that data is only data is also to make a statement about epistemology. In taking an observation-based approach to theory building, one cannot treat data as if it were a source of immutable, objective facts or transparent proofs, even when that data comes from personal experience. When data is used to build an interpretive theory, it cannot be "read" directly without reference to the rules of evidence that constitute the discourse of research. To say that the "data shows" something can only mean, at bottom, that our interpretation of that data has tried to live up to the evidentiary rules of research.
    To understand the role of data in theory building, we should not ask "what the data means" but "how it is used to make meaning" within the researcher's interpretive act. It is clear that to do so one must reject the positivistic assumptions associated with nineteenth-century science and behaviorism. What may be less clear is that to understand the role of data we must also be critical of the naive readings of empirical research within our own community. We need to be as sensitive to unsophisticated or reductive readings of the language of research as we are to reductive readings of literature. A newcomer to this discourse must learn how to read and to use its conventions because a number of these moves reflect some important

assumptions about what data can and can't mean. For instance, in using others' research one cannot treat the findings of a single study as an unconditional, generalizable assertion of the "research has shown..." variety. This overextension by a reader usually occurs when someone is overly eager to appropriate a result. Equally problematic are the naive readings driven by the goal of critique which attribute such overextensions to the research itself or assume that researchers who value empirical observation hold a variety of positivistic assumptions or see their results as unmediated statements of natural fact.

To use the discourse conventions of research with sophistication, you must treat your discussion of data as a process of case building. Two of the most common features of unsophisticated writing (and reading of) research appear when (1) people assume that the act of mounting "evidence," especially statistical evidence, constitutes a broad claim about the validity or truth of a conclusion in some ultimate sense (see Knoblauch's clear statement of this issue), or (2) when people read a correlational claim as no different from a claim of causality. Within the conventions of research, the "results" of a given study, especially those which merely show a correlation, are just one more piece of evidence in a cumulative, communally constructed argument. The special virtue of a claim that has earned the name "result" is that it has been subjected to a given research community's more stringent rules of inference (Hayes et al.). Terms such as "evidence," "results," and "validity" can be loaded concepts to someone just entering this discourse. They contribute to misunderstandings in part because their meaning must be grasped in *the context of specific research methods*. Seen *in situ*, they do not refer to ultimates or absolutes but to *tools* that help build more persuasive arguments. For instance, one could read statements about "significance" and "validity" (expected in a research paper) as if they were general assertions of value, reflecting the common usage of those terms. Whether the reader accepted this reading or assumed the researcher intended it, the misreading would be the same. In context, these terms of art refer in fact to methods one can use to test the strength of one's evidence. For example, the notion of "construct validity" does not refer to a construct's approximation to Truth, but to the use of procedures for testing its coherence with existing theory or practice. The meaning of "validity" lies in its operational definition: it refers to a set of procedures designed to measure consensus with the rest of a discourse community (see Lauer and Asher) or to preclude certain rival hypotheses which other researchers could be expected to pose (Huck and Sandler). To achieve construct validity means to pass such tests.

In trying to understand how data is in fact used in the discourse, we must also look skeptically at the practice of decontextualized or anachronistic readings of research, often conducted in the name of discovering hidden assumptions. As humanists we are well prepared to write eloquent critiques of Locke's theory of knowledge, to construct abstract or theoretical dichotomies, and to tease out the manifold implications of key words (such as, *validity, significance, data*). But to understand the discourse of modern research we cannot simply extrapolate from history or the *OED*. A sophisticated reading of research depends on understanding the context of doing research, on knowing how key terms and concepts function-as-method within the practice of the discourse. Acontextual readings, which do not see the methods behind the words, often overgeneralize about what researchers mean. Or they lead to the peculiarly ahistorical assumption that someone doing empirical analysis does so from a set of nineteenth-century, unqualified, simplistic, or positivistic premises. These premises are not only unnecessary to doing empirical observation, they have been largely long abandoned in even the hard sciences (see O'Keefe). For example, compare the following two ways of talking about research:

> [Experimental, Clinical, and Formal research in composition share] the *positivist tradition's fundamental faith* in the describable *orderliness of the universe:* that is, the belief that things-in-the-world, including in this case people, operate according to determinable or *"lawful"* patterns, general tendencies, which *exist quite apart from our experience of them.* (North 137; emphasis added)

It is unlikely that many practicing researchers would agree with this account of their premises. By contrast, Stephen Jay Gould's comments on the relation of knowledge and culture offer an alternative view of research in which social construction and observation both play a part. The following comments come from an article which traces the contribution of three culturally "determined" theories of vertebrate evolution. Although Gould sees each theory as building on an historically shaped and ultimately flawed interpretative framework, his view of research allows data and interpretation to enter a constructive dialogue:

> Popular misunderstanding of science and its history centers upon the vexatious notion of scientific progress.... The enemy of resolution, here as nearly always, is that old devil Dichotomy. We take a subtle and interesting issue, with a real resolution embracing aspects of all basic positions, and we divide ourselves into two holy armies, each with a brightly colored cardboard mythology as its flag of struggle....
> These extreme positions, of course, are embraced by very few thinkers.... Science is, and must be, culturally embedded; what else could the product of human passion be? Science is also progressive because it discovers and masters more and more (yet ever so little in toto) of a complex external reality.... Science is not a linear march to truth but a tortuous road with blind alleys and a rubbernecking delay every mile or two. Our road map is not objective reality but the patterns of human thought and theories....
> But this history [of three views on the development of vertebrates] is not only a tale of social fashion.... Each world view was a cultural product, but evolution is true and separate creation is not. (16-24)

Gould takes a strong stance on the interaction of data and ideology, a stance which I think marks observation-based theory building as well. Although empirical methods grew up in the context of logical positivism and eighteenth- and nineteenth-century science, the most rigorous sort of empirical inquiry can be carried out with very different assumptions about what those "results" might mean. Ironically, the process which practicing researchers actually argue about is both more interesting and more problematic than these "cardboard mythologies" are.

In practice, research is a process of case building in which data is a privileged form of evidence. Because the conclusions to which we aspire in the humanities and social sciences are not susceptible to logical demonstration or proof, we depend on argument and justification. We are operating in what Perelman and others have described as the province of rhetoric: the truths we arrive at are judgments about what is probable. And, as Stephen Toulmin has argued, our judgment about what is probable is intimately related to our purpose in doing research or in making a deliberation. Imagine two groups of researchers wanting to understand the place of Black English Vernacular in education. Linguists intent on recognizing/justifying linguistic diversity are likely to draw on different methods of analysis and justification—and to reach different conclusions about the phenomenon—than would educators focused on the effect Black English Vernacular has on social and economic equality (see Donmoyer).

Given that discoveries are contingent on the goals of investigation, the critical question becomes: what constitutes a good argument? (see Phillips). This question arises repeatedly in the exciting debate over quantitative versus qualitative inquiry that has raged for the past decade in the pages of *Educational Researcher*, the journal of the American Educational Research Association. This research community lives in a post-positivistic world which acknowledges both the relative nature of knowledge and the social and cognitive process of interpretation in educational research (see Garrison; Howe; Phillips). The problem is how to evaluate the validity, reliability, and meaningfulness of claims made *within* this world (see Fetterman; Firestone; Mathison; Peshkin). In this debate, research methods operate as rhetorical methods in Perelman's sense: they are ways to evaluate the evidence for an idea. For example, researchers use the technique of "significance testing," not to certify Truth or Significance, but to build a case for themselves and others about the relative strength of their evidence, about the likelihood (probability) that the pattern they saw could be seen by others, or that it might appear again, or elsewhere. However, an even more important way to build a case within the research community is to make one's own process of interpretation—one's methodology—transparent. Matthew Miles and Michael Huberman describe this process with exceptional clarity as they talk about the problem of consensus building in qualitative research:

> It seems that we are in a double bind: The status of conclusions from qualitative studies is uncertain because researchers don't report on their methodology, and researchers don't report on their methodology because there are not established conventions for doing that. Yet the studies are conducted, and researchers do fill up hundreds of pages

of field notes, then somehow aggregate, partition, reduce, analyze, and interpret those data. In publishing the results, they must assume theirs is not a solipsistic vision. . . . [They] do have a set of assumptions, criteria, decision rules, and operations for working with data to decide when a given finding is established and meaningful. The problem is that these crucial underpinnings of analysis remain mostly implicit, explained only allusively. . . . We need to make explicit the procedures and thought processes that qualitative researchers actually use in their work. (22)

To say that data is only data, then, is to assert that research is a process of case building and justification to one's self and others. Consider the problem with which I began this discussion: trying to understand how literacy supports social action in the learning—in the conflicts and negotiated understandings—of college mentors. The goal of an observation-based theory would be to create a finely-grained explanatory theory, to construct a more fully-specified vision of this process, based on the data of experience. But because we cannot *finally know* if the patterns we see are there, the methods of observational research should be read as *attempts* to test and verify one's claims, as *attempts* to create more precise operational definitions, and/or as *attempts* to rest claims upon multiple, independent observations based on multiple methods (see Schriver). In this process, empirical observation plays a central and positive role. However, this method of inquiry is not without unavoidable difficulties of its own. In the rest of this paper, I want to concentrate on some of the inherent problems of observation and on the limits of evidence from any source. A theory based on observation, like any argument, is still nothing more than a probabilistic statement. The problem is how to respond to the necessary uncertainty of our own interpretations.

My mind goes back to that young woman working on her literary dissertation, developing her own new reading of a text. It was the *specter of empirical methods* that made her reject research. Why should one do a detailed, even at times quantifiable, analysis of writers in action? Why should theorists do more than assert, describe, and present persuasive examples of the evocative patterns they see? One answer is that *as theorists and researchers we inevitably, constantly, and energetically impose meaning and pattern on the data of experience.* We begin a study, we leap to an argument, and yet all too often, when we return to that larger world of our data, when we analyze it more, asking if it fits our hypothesis, we see we were "wrong." Our interpretive act created a lovely, theoretically appealing, logically consistent pattern. It would have made a great journal article. But as a theory aspiring to explanatory breadth it was wrong. Our theory may, for instance, have described the striking performance of Jeannelle and Jason to a "T," but on closer analysis we see that it violated the experience of every other student in the study.

There is a double bind in this profession. We know as theorists that our interpretative acts cannot be "right" in any final sense, but, unfortunately, they can be wrong in some important ways: they can fail to fit or account for the experience at hand; they can fail to do justice to the data, to the process, or to the people we are trying to understand. The process of rhetorical inquiry Lauer and Asher described has always been alive to this problem, insisting on the tests of internal coherence and consistency. And, in fact, many tentative perceptions are discarded by those means long before we turn to other, more elaborate filters. But the complexity and data-rich detail that both cognitive and contextual studies generate can create additional problems.

The Contribution of Empirical Methods

(3) *Observation-based theory turns to empirical methods because it is sensitive to its own limitations.*

Given enough time, people—including teachers, researchers, and literary critics—will always perceive patterns, of some sort, in anything. In the face of this human tendency, observational research relies on two acts of common sense. The first is to subject these observations and interpretations to the test of reliability. As my colleague John Hayes once said, looking at protocols is a little like looking at clouds: if you look long enough you can always see a pattern. The question is: would anyone else see it too? Does this pattern in the data exist only in the eye of the beholder or the mind of the theorist? A formal test of reliability among different observers is a response to this dilemma.

In practice this simply means that the researcher must articulate the pattern he or she perceives into a coding scheme that tells another observer how to read the data (for example, how to recognize a goal, an act of resistance, or a commonplace of academic discourse when one of these postulated events appears in the data). By convention, researchers expect at least eighty percent agreement as a basis for asserting reliability. Sometimes reliability is simply checked at the end of a study and the agreement score reported as another piece of evidence. However, this process of developing a shareable reading of the data can be even more valuable when it is used in the early stages of analysis to create a more sensitive and finely-grained theory. In this process the researcher asks a co-coder to analyze a sample of the data using the tentative theoretical statement (expressed as a coding scheme) that the researcher has developed from his or her own close analysis. The (inevitable) points of disagreement between coder and co-coder become sparks to insight as they challenge a researcher to articulate intuitions, recognize disconfirming evidence, and see the diversity of meaning his or her own categories may embrace. Reliability comparisons, used as a generative technique, can lead to substantial changes in interpretation as a researcher progressively reshapes his or her claims to better reflect the data. What began as a method of confirmations becomes a step in an epistemic process. The exuberance of our pattern-making powers, fueled by an initial piece of evidence, is only problematic, then, if we disregard conflicting messages from the data itself. The test of reliability is one way these "messages" are spoken.

Observational theory building tries to deal with its own limitations at a second critical point by turning to another method that systematizes common sense. It sends the theorist to the resistant, uncompressed body of the data as a whole, with *the injunction to listen to that data—to construct meaning—in a systematic way*. The metaphor of "listening" to the data is used in research not because people literally assume data can speak for itself without our constructive effort, but to dramatize the need to avoid selective observation and the willful imposition of one's own assumptions. The art of listening to the whole involves not only an openness to contradictory and disconfirming evidence, but a perverse zest for rival hypotheses and an active search for unpredicted patterns that might be more fully supported by the data than those predicted. Imagine, for example, that you are at a critical point in theory building. You have discovered a meaningful pattern:

- You have found some striking examples of students creating—and then dismissing—their own personal elaborations as they read and write

- Or you have just done a brilliant explication of a protocol or a student text, or completed a revealing case study

- Or you have noticed that your advanced writers seem willing/able to establish their personal authority early in a text, in ways your basic writers fail to do

You have the beginnings of a theoretical statement about some of the cognitive/contextual dynamics of authority.

As a meaning maker, you have imposed a new order on the data of experience. And the question you must now answer for yourself is: is this new order an interesting but isolated pattern? Would this local explanation account for the other texts in the folder, would it fit the other protocols, would it describe what those forty students actually do and how the two classes really differ? *In essence, does your pattern fit the data at hand?* No theory will be a complete or perfect fit. Indeed, the object of theory building as opposed to case studies is to isolate certain critical features from the "noise" that constitutes the rest of the experience. And we must remember that we are constructing meaning based on our own definitions of "meaningful." Given those premises, there are still some hard questions we want to ask about the fit of our interpretations.

One of the first commonsense methods of empirical research is to test the fit by asking: is there a rival hypothesis that offers a better explanation? Many theories of discourse will seem true at some level of generality—for example, advanced students of anything have more authority than beginners. However, rival interpretations that challenge the "authority" hypothesis might include these: Does my operational definition of "personal authority" really capture a writer's personal attitude, or can I only claim to have seen certain textual conventions (such as the use of "I") that seem "authoritative?" Or perhaps the assignment is really producing this effect: maybe the advanced writers are working on a familiar genre for which they know the conventions for asserting and supporting a claim, regardless of their personal investment or confidence. Or perhaps the real variable here is topic knowledge: the advanced writers are doing research papers which immerse them in rich bodies of information and evidence, and so their authority is logos; the basic writers, however, were assigned an expressive/descriptive paper which leaves them swimming against the current, forced to use the subtle conventions for establishing ethos and personal authority in an artful genre. Experimental research methodology has formalized some of the most common sources of rival hypotheses into a set of standard threats to validity (see Huck and Sandler). Before making a claim about causality, researchers should be able to eliminate rival hypotheses, such as the effect of "mortality" in which only the students who liked the class or shared the observer's bias remained in the sample at the time of evaluation. Perhaps the most devastating rival hypothesis to an experimental study is that what appears to be causation is only correlation. For example, imagine that children's writing ability was shown to increase with cultural literacy, with shoe size, or with some other variable. One might claim causality, but in fact all of these supposed causes may simply reflect the critical variable of age.

In experimental research one tries to control for outside influences in order to exclude such rival claims in advance. In the more exploratory enterprise of observation-based theory building, it is difficult to deal with rival hypotheses through control. However, this concern still enters the process as an effort to capture observations that escape the mold, to actively explore alternative interpretations of the data. Studies of reasoning and inference-making have clearly documented our tendency to look only for positive instances which confirm a hypothesis and to happily ignore counter evidence (see Wason and Johnson-Laird). Data-based observation encourages an expectant stance toward new data that can leave the theorist open to revision. But more than that, by asking the researcher to make a theory operational—explicit enough to be reliably used by another observer—it allows the data to speak back on its own resistant terms and may encourage rival, complementary, or more explanatory patterns to emerge.

At times, research methodology allows us to ask how well a theory *fits* and how well it *works* in yet another way by asking if the pattern or frequency of our observation is strong enough to be surprising: have we uncovered a broadly descriptive pattern or only another interesting but idiosyncratic event? For instance, the particular ways of negotiating or avoiding authority that we observed in a few of our basic writers may, on a more careful look at the data as a whole, be a phenomenon that is in fact normally distributed across all sorts of students, maybe even across all sorts of adult writers. Developing a voice, taking a rhetorical stance may be a problem we all share. If that were the case, our theory asserting that the texts of basic writers can be distinguished by the absence of personal authority and/or our educational innovation based on the differences we thought we observed would be resting on a very shaky premise. Although we might be able to build a convincing argument about a general relationship between personal authority and writing, when it comes to grounding our theory in the data of experience and testing its explanatory power, the data in observation-based theory building has a chance to reply and tell us that we have not yet captured the "truth" of this experience. Our theory does not yet *fit* or *work* for the situation we hoped to explain.

Here is one place where an estimate of probability, in the form of elementary statistics, can play a useful role in exploratory research. Assume that we have observed a number of cases in which basic writers fit our imagined pattern and fewer cases of advanced writers who do so; or assume we see in our protocol data a growing number of elaborations made during reading and discarded during writing. Is this pattern a meaningful description of the fate of elaborations? Does our pattern of authority-taking actually distinguish one group of students from another? A simple test for statistical significance lets us compare the frequency or distribution of the events we see with what might occur by chance, at random in a normal population of students or in a data set the size of ours. If our pattern is much more frequent than chance would dictate, it begins to look surprising, and the probability that we have found a meaningful category increases. The conventions for claiming statistical significance are rigorous: for a pattern to appear surprising it must have the probability of appearing by chance less than five times in one hundred or, in some cases, less than one time in one hundred—a result that is expressed as a probability (p) that is equal to or less than a given level of occurrence (for example, $p = .05$ or $p < .05$). Notice too what "significance" means here; it is a conservative and probabilistic statement which only asserts that the pattern we claim to have seen is unlikely to have occurred by chance. Under some circumstances, we might choose a statistical tool that is less rigorous than a "significance test" and more sensitive to partial or weak but interesting patterns (Glaser and Strauss)—that is, we could choose to be a little more easily impressed.

The point of all this is not to prove a claim but to understand more about the strength and predictive power of the patterns we have created. Statistics, by their very nature as tests of probability, are not designed to prove that a point is true; rather, that it isn't probable. Once we decide to move beyond a single case study and talk about the pattern of the whole, when multiple and complex patterns are interwoven throughout a text or throughout the performance of readers or writers, it is often impossible to grasp the patterns of frequency or distribution without turning to a test of probability or a statistical test of correlation. Simple counts and even averages are often deceptive. More importantly, statistical tests are often the only way to acknowledge the negative evidence and the counter examples in our data in a rigorous and systematic way. They allow us to fit our theorized pattern, like an imaginary transparency laid over the data as a whole, and to see where the pictures match—and where they don't.

Creating and Testing Interpretation

To return to that young woman again, what I hope she came to see in our conversation was that the attempt to *systematically test the fit* between your vision and your data is not an attempt to eliminate recognition of variety but actively to attend to it. Nor is it an attempt to certify validity, to assert you have found truth, or to replace the richness of experience with numbers. In a way it is just the opposite: it is a way to listen to more of that experience. It is also a response to the limitations of our own ways of knowing and to our extraordinary ability to see patterns in anything. It is a response to our theory-guided tendency to seek out what we can currently imagine and to see what we already believe. All methods are ultimately *weak* methods, just as all our theories are only partial. In observation-based theory building, these two attempts to test claims—that is, to test for reliability and for a fit to the data with or without statistics—are often powerful not because they are an instrument of proof, but because they are a hedge against our own fallibility. But more than that, these instruments of caution can also be turned into generative tools for building more finely grained theories that are more likely to work and fit.

Let me conclude with a final issue we face in building broadly significant, but firmly situated, observation-based rhetorical theories. My own work offers an example of the problem. The Reading-to-Write study used a rich body of data to build a tentative *theory* of strategic knowledge and its role in learning to manage academic discourse. This theory emerged from a value-laden interpretative framework concerned with how individual students can take authority over their own writing by gaining awareness of their own interpretive process. At the same time, I believe this theory is a sensible and careful description of the students we observed. And its focus on goals, strategies, and awareness offers at least one way to describe how cognition and context work together as reader/writers construct meaning. But will my description of how cognition and context interact fit the data of *your* students? Will my more general argument for the role of strategic consciousness itself hold when we examine other contexts? I can't say. A genuine observation-based theory of strategic knowledge in writing, if we as a field develop one, will not be the product of any one study or any one writer or theorist. Observation-based theory building is a cumulative effort. It is shaped by a community of observers working from different points of view, with different methods, and in different contexts of observation. More importantly, such a theory will be shaped by the tension between its own two goals, which are to create, on the one hand, a meaningful *interpretation* of the world and, on the other, to *test that constructed reality* in clear and careful ways against the rich and contrary data of experience.[3]

Notes

[1]My concern here is focused on implications this line of argument and its priorities could have for the hope of learning more from data than what we bring to it. However, their article, like the present one, is trying to foreground the deliberate balancing act reflective research requires, and our goals are, I believe, close in spirit when they argue that "the researcher may have to offer multiple accounts, and multiple conclusions, may have to let the dialogues and problems in the data emerge when there are conflicts" (Ritchie, personal communication, 2/18/96). The abiding problem is negotiating the balance of goals.

[2]An earlier version of the following discussion appeared in my "Cognition, Context, and Theory-Building."

[3]I especially want to thank Elenore Long, Marlia Banning, Beverly Sauer, John Ackerman, Janice Lauer, David Kaufer, Stuart Greene, John R. Hayes—and the young woman visiting Purdue—for their stimulating and supportive discussions of these issues.

Works Cited

Bazerman, Charles. "Physicists Reading Physics: Schema-laden Purposes and Purpose-laden Schemas." *Written Communication* 2 (1985): 3-23.

Bereiter, Carl, and Marlene Scardamalia. *The Psychology of Written Composition*. Hillsdale, NJ: Erlbaum, 1987.

Berthoff, Ann. "Reading the World . . . Reading the Word: Paulo Freire's Pedagogy of Knowing." *Only Connect: Uniting Reading and Writing*. Ed. Thomas Newkirk. Upper Montclair, NJ: Boynton, 1986. 119-30.

Cizek, Gregory J. "Crunchy Granola and the Hegemony of the Narrative." *Educational Researcher* 24 (1995): 26-28.

Donmoyer, Robert. "The Rescue from Relativism: Two Failed Attempts and an Alternative Strategy." *Educational Researcher* 14 (1985): 13-20.

Dyson, Anne Haas. "Individual Differences in Beginning Composing: An Orchestral Vision of Learning to Compose." *Written Communication* 9 (1987): 411-42.

Fetterman, David M. "Qualitative Approaches to Evaluating Education." *Educational Researcher* 17 (1988): 17-23.

Firestone, William A. "Meaning in Method: The Rhetoric of Quantitative and Qualitative Research." *Educational Researcher* 16 (1987): 16-21.

Flower, Linda. "Cognition, Context and Theory Building," *College Composition and Communication* 40 (1989): 282-311.

——. *The Construction of Negotiated Meaning: A Social Cognitive Theory of Writing*. Carbondale: Southern Illinois UP, 1994.

Flower, Linda, and John R. Hayes. "Images, Plans and Prose: The Representation of Meaning in Writing. *Written Communication* 1 (1984): 120-60.

Flower, Linda, et al. *Reading-to-Write: Exploring Cognition in Context*. New York: Oxford UP, 1990.

Freire, Paulo. *Pedagogy of the Oppressed*. Trans. Myra Ramos. New York: Continuum, 1986.

Garrison, James W. "Some Principles of Postpositivistic Philosophy of Science." *Educational Researcher* 15 (1986): 12-18.

Glaser, Barney, and Anselm Strauss. *The Discovery of Grounded Theory: Strategies for Qualitative Research*. Chicago: Aldine, 1967.

Gould, Stephen Jay. "Pretty Pebbles." *Natural History* 97 (1988): 14-26.

Haraway, Donna. *Simians, Cyborgs, and Women: The Reinvention of Nature*. New York: Routledge, 1991.

Harding, Sandra. *Whose Science? Whose Knowledge?: Thinking from Women's Lives*. Ithaca, NY: Cornell UP, 1991.

Harding, Sandra. *The Science Question in Feminism*. Ithaca, NY: Cornell UP, 1986.

Hayes, John R., et al., eds. *Reading Empirical Research Studies: The Rhetoric of Research*. Hillsdale, NJ: Erlbaum, 1992.

Heath, Shirley B. *Ways with Words: Language, Life and Work in Communities*. Cambridge, Eng.: Cambridge UP, 1983.

Howe, Kenneth R. "Against the Quantitative-Qualitative Incompatibility Thesis, or Dogmas Die Hard." *Educational Researcher* 17 (1988): 10-16.

Huck, Schuyler W., and Howard M. Sandler. *Rival Hypotheses: Alternative Interpretations of Data-Based Conclusions*. New York: Harper, 1979.

Hull, Glynda. "Hearing Other Voices: A Critical Assessment of Popular Views on Literacy and Work." *Harvard Educational Review* 63 (1993): 20-49.

Kirsch, Gesa E., and Joy S. Ritchie. "Beyond the Personal: Theorizing a Politics of Location in Research in Composition." *College Composition and Communication* 46 (1995): 7-29

Knoblauch, C.H. "Rhetorical Constructions: Dialogue and Commitment." *College English* 50 (1988): 125-40.

Lauer, Janice M., and J. William Asher. *Composition Research: Empirical Designs*. New York: Oxford UP, 1988.

Long, Elenore. "The Rhetoric of Literate Social Action: Mentors Negotiating Intercultural Images of Literacy." Diss. Carnegie Mellon U, 1994.

Mathison, Sandra. "Why Triangulate?" *Educational Researcher* 17 (1988): 13-17.

Miles, Matthew B., and A. Michael Huberman. "Drawing Valid Meaning from Qualitative Data: Toward a Shared Craft." *Educational Researcher* 13 (1984): 20-30.

North, Stephen M. *The Making of Knowledge in Composition: Portrait of an Emerging Field*. Upper Montclair, NJ: Boynton, 1987.

O'Keefe, Daniel J. "Logical Empiricism and the Study of Human Communication." *Speech Monographs* 42 (1975): 169-83.

Perelman, Chaim, and L. Olbrechts-Tyteca. *The New Rhetoric: A Treatise on Argumentation*. Trans. J. Wilkinson and Purcell Weaver. Notre Dame: U of Notre Dame, 1969.

Peshkin, Alan. "In Search of Subjectivity—One's Own." *Educational Researcher* 17 (1988): 17-22.

Phillips, D. "After the Wake: Postpositivistic Educational Thought." *Educational Researcher* 12 (1983): 4-12.

Schriver, Karen A. "What Are We Doing as a Research Community? Theory Building in Rhetoric and Composition: The Role of Empirical Scholarship." *Rhetoric Review* 7 (1989): 272-88.

Toulmin, Stephen. *Foresight and Understanding*. New York: Harper, 1961.

Wason, Peter C., and Philip N. Johnson-Laird. *Psychology of Reasoning: Structure and Content*. Cambridge: Harvard UP, 1972.

Witte, Stephen "Pre-text and Composing." *College Composition and Communication* 38 (1987): 397-425.

Conducting Research in the History of Rhetoric: An Open Letter to a Future Historian of Rhetoric

JAMES J. MURPHY

History, it has been remarked, is the reconstruction of important human questions from the recorded answers of the past. We know as a fact, for example, that a Greek text called *Phaedrus* has survived from the fourth century before Christ. We know that the attributive author is Plato. Almost everything else associated with these facts is a matter of dispute. Why was it written? What are its sources? What does it mean? Is it ironic or literal? What has been its influence? How does it relate to its author's world view, to his other works, to the culture of the time, to our own contemporary concerns?

In other words, the existence of a book about rhetoric tells us only that someone at some time for some reason wished to express some ideas about the subject. The "fact" of the book's existence is in that sense an "answer" to what Lloyd Bitzer has called the "exigency" of a given "rhetorical situation." But one can say about rhetoric what Jacques Maritain says about philosophy: "The history of philosophy is not the history of its books"; that is, just knowing about its books is not sufficient ground for a history of a subject. Much more is needed. No book is an island. Or, as Aristotle puts it, "A man does not think he understands a thing until he knows the 'why' of it" (*Metaphysics* I.1).

How, then, does one write a history of rhetoric? Perhaps it might be better to ask this question in another, more practical way: how does one become a historian of rhetoric? The first requisite is curiosity. This may seem an obvious statement, but human experience tells us that people do their best when they are doing what they like to do. If you enjoy reading and talking about rhetoric, if you sometimes wonder whether you are missing anything, if you would like to know more (and you don't know how much time and effort it would take to know more), then you are a good candidate for becoming a good historian of rhetoric. And, on a practical level, tenure comes to those who do well, consistently over time, in a clearly-defined area of research.

Curiosity, of course, is interest in the unknown. That means that you have to spend half a lifetime discovering what is already known so that you can see where the edges and the frontiers are. But how can you be enthusiastically curious about a subject unless it is an important one? This means that you not only need to know what rhetoric is, but you also need to know why you think it is valuable (and have answers for those who say it is merely a pernicious form of human deception). Ultimately, this will involve you in some philosophical as well as definitional questions, but since you will not be equipped to approach such matters until you have mastered vast ranges of historical data anyway, you can safely postpone your final answers until you are satisfied that you have a good grasp of the whole history of the subject. (One of the scourges of contemporary rhetorical scholarship, by the way, is that some journal editors allow people with a narrow range of knowledge to publish sweeping surveys or syntheses unhampered by either data or experience.) In other words, you don't have to delay your studies until you know every possible detail.

But you will need a working definition of the subject if you intend to try to find "rhetoric" in history. Let me suggest one I have found useful: *rhetoric is the study of means for future discourse*. What distinguishes rhetoric from grammar, then, is that grammar analyzes the language itself, not its future uses. What distinguishes rhetoric from logic is that logic analyzes the validity or invalidity of argumentative forms, not the uses of those forms in the future.

In this respect it is important to remember that everyone who has ever lived has lived in "modern times." Everyone lives in a present, has a past, and has a future to prepare for. Every writer and speaker faced/faces this situation. For example, there was a time in the life of Abraham Lincoln—say, 1859—when the *Gettysburg Address* was not even thought about, was still a piece of future discourse. Yet, history shows that in 1863 he was able to produce a superlative example of language use. Apparently, he had a lifetime of preparation for the exigency of that day at the cemetery. The analysis of his personal abilities to prepare for that future discourse—to reconstruct his personal "rhetoric"—is an appropriate if difficult task for the historian. This kind of analysis of an individual's personal rhetoric is one type of useful activity for the rhetorical historian.

Yet, Lincoln never wrote down for us in his present a set of principles or advice about language use that we might follow in our own futures. However, hundreds and hundreds of others over the centuries have done just that, presenting in written form their advice to others about future language use. These are the "books of rhetoric" which are usually seen as the backbone of the history of rhetoric. It is remarkable that today we do not have a comprehensive list of such books, let alone a history which places all of them in context. By contrast, virtually every other field of human endeavor—law, philosophy, literature—has a wealth of information available through bibliographies, encyclopedias, biographies, histories. The intellectual territory of almost every human discipline has been mapped out, except for rhetoric.

To be sure, there are some resources available (see the appendix at the end of this chapter), but even their authors will admit that their coverage is limited. And even taking all the major studies together, there are significant gaps in our knowledge of the history of rhetoric—for example, the period from the death of Aristotle to the advent of Cicero; nineteenth-century England; non-Western rhetorics (for example, those from Asia and Africa); the fifteenth-century change from manuscript to print; the rhetorics of South America; the continuous relation between rhetoric and education; and any number of others. There is much work to do. And if it is worth doing, it is worth doing well.

With some sense of what "history" means, then, it may be useful to turn to the everyday pragmatics of writing and publishing about the history of rhetoric.

Pragmatics for the Historian of Rhetoric

Several strategies and rules of thumb will help you become a productive, publishing scholar in this area.

Learn what is already known. This may be the most difficult task of all. There is no single book in any language which provides a complete history of rhetoric. On the other hand, there are some places to start. Three books in English which cover a long range of time are George A. Kennedy's *Classical Rhetoric and Its Christian and Secular Traditions*, Thomas Conley's *Rhetoric in the European Tradition*, and the anthology of translations edited by Patricia Bizzell and Bruce Herzberg, *The Rhetorical Tradition*. (Details of these and other key works may be found in the appendix to this chapter.) Ancient Greek and Roman rhetorics have been studied heavily, medieval rhetoric fairly completely, while Renaissance rhetoric is just now coming under comprehensive examination. Three annual bibliographies are worth noting for these periods: *L'Année philologique* (classical), *Medioevo latino* (medieval), and *Bibliographie internationale de l'humanisme et de la Renaissance* (Renaissance). Research in the period after about 1700 is characterized by studies of individual authors or books rather than syntheses. A careful program of reading can provide at least an outline of what is already known. One useful guide to such reading is a book edited by Winifred Bryan Horner, *The Present State of Scholarship in Historical and Contemporary Rhetoric*; this book is divided chronologically into eight chapters, each written by an expert in that period.

Study the history of education. Rhetoric and education have been linked since the beginning. After all, both rhetoric and education prepare for the future. In Roman times, rhetoric was the core of the standardized curriculum which the Empire systematically spread throughout the world, and this Roman influence lasted in Europe and America well into early modern times. There are numerous histories of education.

Work on a gap. Pick an area that you discover has not been covered, or not covered well. It is better to strike out into new territory than to seem merely to be quarrelling with what others have written. For example, in 1982 Nan Johnson pointed out the importance of Franz Theremin, an apparently small addition to our knowledge of the nineteenth century, yet in 1991 she was able to relate this data-bit to the larger picture she sets out in her *Nineteenth-Century Rhetoric in North America*. It is helpful to make even the smallest contribution of knowledge where none had existed before because you or someone else may be able to build on it.

Establish a long-range plan. Set long-range goals even while starting small. A study of Nietzsche's lectures on rhetoric, for example, can lead to research on other aspects of the European nineteenth century, on the relation of philosophy and rhetoric, or on education. Where do you want to go from the first study? When you start down a research road, ask yourself about your ultimate destination. (On a practical level, a clearly articulated long-range plan is invaluable not only for the understanding of colleagues but for tenure committees and granting agencies as well.) And language skills must also be a part of your planning: if you intend to learn how revolutionary educators like Johann Sturm and Philip Melanchthon approached the teaching of writing, now is the time to enroll in Latin and German reading classes. (And it is an interesting question whether editors should permit the publication of an interpretive article about, say, *Phaedrus*, written by someone who knows no Greek.)

Think about methods. You can teach yourself historical methodologies. As you read historical studies for their knowledge, look also at their forms and approaches. You will find that many approaches are possible—which should not be surprising considering that historiography (like any kind of writing) is a rhetorical process subject to multiple modes of invention, arrangement, and expression. Note how Wilbur S. Howell matches logic and rhetoric in his two books on English rhetoric. How Debora Shuger uses a concept—the Christian Grand Style—to track trends in her *Sacred Rhetoric*. How Thomas Conley and George A. Kennedy use chronology. How Winifred Bryan Horner uses both biography and institutional history in her *Nineteenth-Century Scottish Rhetoric: The American Connection*. How James A. Berlin traces varying epistemologies. You may find it useful to keep a log of the methods you find that are used in what you deem to be the best scholarship. (Indeed, you can also find intriguing historiographic ideas in recent publications—mostly articles rather than books—advocating revisionist, Marxist, feminist, hermeneutic, or anti-Western approaches; some of these are listed in James L. Kinneavy's chapter, "Contemporary Rhetoric," in Horner's *Present State of Scholarship*.)

Avoid publishing on only one topic. There is a natural temptation to re-do what is easiest. But once you have done a study you should in all justice apply to yourself the same criterion you used in the first place—that is, where are there gaps in our knowledge? Move onward; move to the edge at least. One habit that helped kill classical studies in America was lifetime concentration on a single subject (for example, a former colleague of mine, after years of work, published a whole book dealing with just three lines from a speech of Demosthenes).

Depend on primary sources. Whatever the time period or the precise subject matter, use secondary sources only as a means to identify the primary sources that you need in order to make your own judgments. For instance, read Alexander Bain's *English Composition and Rhetoric* (1866) for yourself after someone has told you it's an important book. If you don't, how can you place it in American history? Or how can you compare Bain to John Franklin Genung or Henry Day? (Unfortunately, many journal articles should not say "by John Smith" but "compiled by John Smith" to indicate that the composition was one of mere opinion-collection.) Of course, the language skills of the researcher may place limits on the scope of primary sources available to her or him: should a researcher in all conscience lay out a long-range plan which includes works available only in translation? Perhaps, if the primary sources are used only as rough survey data—but not if the argument depends on crucial textual passages. This may seem an overly rigorous standard, but its value can be tested readily by laying side-by-side any three translations of the opening section of Book One of Aristotle's *Rhetoric* (or almost any other key text).

Follow the Ten-Year Rule. You will always know more than you can write. Consequently, you will have to make choices about what to publish. Just as a foundation makes a wall possible, and a wall makes a roof possible, so what you write about the history of rhetoric makes it possible for others to build on it. Let me suggest a criterion which I have tried to follow for many years as an editor and publisher: "The Ten-Year Rule." That is, what is worth publishing is that which will still be valuable to others ten years from now. This involves judgments about what is worthwhile to a serious historian of rhetoric—for example, identifying (and describing) a hitherto unknown book will be valuable because it allows for building on new knowledge; providing a new cultural background for another book will be valuable. On the other hand, an article simply attacking another article, or a five-page reply in the "Forum" section of a journal, will become as obsolescent as yesterday's stock market report. Generally, when writing and publishing on the history of rhetoric, it is not useful to spend valuable compositional time in current debates (except possibly as recreation). In technical rhetorical terms, *confirmatio* tends to outlast *refutatio*. Your long-range plan looks to the future, not the present. To borrow a dictum from architecture, the answer to a bad building is not a criticism but the erection of a better building.

Teach and speak about what you think you know. Take every opportunity to address audiences about your knowledge. Not only will the effort toward coherence force you to see your own gaps, but you may well hear yourself saying things you weren't conscious of knowing. If your academic culture permits it, you might consider offering an extra seminar on your favorite subject to get student feedback. (Most administrators welcome free contributions, though sometimes colleagues may resent it.) In the same way that a conference paper forces you to organize, a lecture or a class not only can organize you but can provide audience reaction. Keep notes on reactions. I have found it useful to make a tape recording of talks and lectures so as to capture extemporaneous remarks made in an effort to explain matters to an audience. (This can sometimes be painful but is well worth the effort.)

Analyze what editors and publishers print. Publishing proves to be a rather personalized business. Each journal has its own *ethos*, audience, and set of expectations of authors. So has each commercial and university press. If you wish to submit to a journal like *Rhetoric Review* or *College English* or *Rhetorica*, take the time to scan five years' worth of their issues; you will find not only stylistic differences but differences in emphasis and subject matter. Usually, journal editors prefer to receive a completed manuscript written in their stated format, but sometimes they will respond to inquiries in advance of submission. Remember, though, that editors are usually busy and may not have time for a formal written reply; therefore, you might try writing a letter to the editor with your proposal, stating that you will follow up with a telephone call in two weeks' time. This obviates the need for the editor to take the time to write. Book publishers are more difficult to approach, but keep an eye out for the presses that publish scholarship in your field; visit the conference book exhibits and talk with the editors there about your idea. Don't send a completed manuscript (or even sample chapters) out of the blue. Instead, write a two-page preface (the way it would appear in the book), together with an annotated table of contents. If an editor is interested, then you'll be asked for more.

Use personal resources. I recall overhearing someone at a conference reception exclaim to her companion, "We're in a room full of footnotes!" Indeed, the room was full of authors. Unbeknownst to most aspiring writers, these people, well known though they might be, still struggle with the same problems of research, writing, and publication as others less well known. Like all writers, they know more than they write. So they are a resource. If you hunger for knowledge about a subject, you need to look to all the resources available. But you can't expect one of them to respond to a general demand like "tell me all about *X*." Instead, frame in writing a single specific question and say that you will telephone in two or three weeks; again, as with editors, use the telephone as an easy way to communicate without forcing them to the labor of writing. Understand, however, if they are too busy. But if they do talk with you, you may in a few minutes discover things you might otherwise have spent weeks pursuing.

Arrange your own conferences. Once you have reached a certain level of knowledge about your subject, consider getting other interested people together to discuss the topic. The serendipity that comes from intellectual exchange is uniquely valuable. An easy way to start is to propose a panel or session at an existing annual meeting like those sponsored by the Conference on College Composition and Communication or the Rhetoric Society of America, with yourself as both chair and one of three speakers. With that experience you can later propose a set of several coordinated panels on various aspects of the same subject. Then try a small conference on your own campus; see if you can get a stipend for a keynote speaker from the outside as a way to lure people from your immediate area. But do it anyway if that is not possible. Finally, if you find these occasions valuable, organize a major conference whose contents are planned as a book; in other words, make the book the ultimate objective of the gathering. This means that you match speakers to the subjects which need to be covered, not the other way around. Granting agencies look for conference experience as well as subject matter knowledge, so it is possible that a panel proposal for the CCCC meeting could be the first step toward a major grant later on from the conference division of the National Endowment for the Humanities.

Investigate small research grants. It is a fallacy to say that research always depends on money, but there may be times when you need to travel to a certain library, or to have time away from teaching to finish a project. Again, this is an area where it is best to start small—and early. If your long-range plan envisions travel or a leave, even if it is several years away, then you should begin in advance to look into the possibilities. That way you will be prepared when application deadlines loom up. For example the American Philosophical Society (Philadelphia) provides postdoctoral grants in all fields up to $4,000 or $5,000; the Newberry Library in Chicago offers twelve different residential fellowship programs at the library; and the American Council of Learned Societies offers not only major fellowships but a popular program of $500 travel grants for those reading papers at international meetings. There is a useful list of such grants in the "Fellowships and Grants" section of the *PMLA* Directory issue published each September. Again, this is an area where experience counts: success in obtaining smaller grants is a helpful argument in seeking larger ones.

Set a writing schedule. As Robert Boice discusses in another chapter of this book, writing is an exercise involving discipline, and like other forms of exercise it strengthens the exerciser. So it needs to be done regularly. Set yourself production deadlines, even if you know that sometimes you will not achieve them. File-management is a critical element here: as you study a subject, start a file (in a folder or on a disk) and then keep adding material to it as you find it; you may find that a file for "miscellaneous" will keep splitting into separate files as related materials show up. Keep a separate bibliography file. Coherence in your writing depends on being able to find the data you have collected, but even more important is file-management that enables you to find documentation to support your arguments as you write. Historiography is, of course, a form of argumentation, with propositions and assertions requiring support. Your efforts to write about, say, the teaching of writing in Mechanics Institutes in nineteenth-century England will quickly tell you whether you know enough yet to prove what you say. (Just as speaking or lecturing about it will.) The gaps you find will then become research subjects, and the whole process will continue to move forward.

An Inference

In sum, then, writing about the history of rhetoric is a long-range project, incremental both for the writer and the reader. It depends on the expanding knowledge base of the writer to identify the known and to go beyond that to the as-yet unknown. It demands self-discipline in research and in writing. It requires practical ingenuity in marshalling resources. Above all, it aims at expanding our knowledge of a major human activity.

If history is indeed the reconstruction of past issues, one may wonder whether those issues will be the same ones we concern ourselves with today. In respect to language use, only the historian of rhetoric can answer that question. Some have argued that the rhetorical impulse—the desire to make ideas and express them—is the same among all people in all times; others argue that each time and place is so different that each must be seen individually. Also, some argue that human beings are essentially the same in all times and places, while others point to essential cultural and individual differences. Whatever the historian of language use can discover, then, may help us to resolve some modern issues as well. In that sense, all history is modern history.

Works Cited

Aristotle. *Metaphysics*. Trans. W.D. Ross. *The Basic Works of Aristotle*. Ed. Richard McKeon. New York: Random, 1941.

Bain, Alexander. *English Composition and Rhetoric: A Manual*. London: Longmans, 1866.

Johnson, Nan. "Three Nineteenth-Century Rhetoricians: The Humanist Alternative to Rhetoric as Skills Management." *The Rhetorical Tradition and Modern Writing*. Ed. James J. Murphy. New York: MLA, 1982. 105-17.

Kinneavy, James L. "Contemporary Rhetoric." *The Present State of Scholarship in Historical and Contemporary Rhetoric*. Rev. ed. Ed. Winifred Bryan Horner. Columbia: U of Missouri P, 1990. 186-246.

Appendix: A Basic Library for Studying the History of Rhetoric

The items listed here are starting points. Each will lead to other sources as well as provide essential historical data.

General Works

Bizzell, Patricia, and Bruce Herzberg, eds. *The Rhetorical Tradition: Readings from Classical Times to the Present*. Boston: Bedford, 1990.

Conley, Thomas M. *Rhetoric in the European Tradition*. Chicago: U of Chicago P, 1994.

Horner, Winifred Bryan, ed. *The Present State of Scholarship in Historical and Contemporary Rhetoric*. Rev. ed. Columbia: U of Missouri P, 1990.

Kennedy, George A., *Classical Rhetoric and Its Christian and Secular Tradition from Ancient to Modern Times*. Chapel Hill: U of North Carolina P, 1980.

Murphy, James J., ed. *A Short History of Writing Instruction from Ancient Greece to Twentieth-Century America*. Davis, CA: Hermagoras, 1990.

Vickers, Brian. *In Defence of Rhetoric*. New York: Oxford UP, 1987.

Period Studies

Berlin, James A. *Rhetoric and Reality: Writing Instruction in American Colleges, 1900-1985*. Carbondale: Southern Illinois UP, 1987.

Clark, Donald Lemen. *Rhetoric in Greco-Roman Education*. New York: Columbia UP, 1957.

Golden, James L., and Edward P.J. Corbett, eds. *The Rhetoric of Blair, Campbell, and Whately*. Carbondale: Southern Illinois UP, 1990.

Horner, Winifred Bryan. *Nineteenth-Century Scottish Rhetoric: The American Connection*. Carbondale: Southern Illinois UP, 1993.

Howell, Wilbur Samuel. *Eighteenth-Century British Logic and Rhetoric*. Princeton, NJ: Princeton UP, 1971.

——. *Logic and Rhetoric in England, 1500-1700*. Princeton, NJ: Princeton UP, 1956.

Johnson, Nan. *Nineteenth-Century Rhetoric in North America*. Carbondale: Southern Illinois UP, 1991.

Kennedy, George A. *A New History of Classical Rhetoric*. Princeton, NJ: Princeton UP, 1994.

Monfasani, John. "Humanism and Rhetoric." *Humanism and the Disciplines*. Philadelphia: U of Pennsylvania P, 1988. Vol. 3 of *Renaissance Humanism: Foundations, Forms, and Legacy*. Éd. Albert Rabil, Jr. 3 vols. 171-235.

Murphy, James J., ed. *Renaissance Eloquence: Studies in the Theory and Practice of Renaissance Rhetoric*. Berkeley: U of California P, 1983.

——. *Rhetoric in the Middle Ages: A History of Rhetorical Theory from St. Augustine to the Renaissance*. Berkeley: U of California P, 1974.

Murphy James J., and Richard A. Katula, eds. *A Synoptic History of Classical Rhetoric*. 2nd ed. Davis, CA: Hermagoras, 1995.

Shuger, Debora K. *Sacred Rhetorics: The Christian Grand Style in the English Renaissance*. Princeton, NJ: Princeton UP, 1988

The Politics of Electronic Scholarship in Rhetoric and Composition

Todd Taylor

In "Technology, Utility, and Amnesia" published in *College English* in 1995, Deborah Holdstein claims that English departments are not too far behind the times in terms of appreciating and adjusting to technology-driven changes. She suggests that scholars—mainly from within the field of computers and composition—who continue to emphasize the political gulf between the electronic and print worlds suffer from a suspicious form of amnesia that has caused them to forget or deny all of the progress that has been made, a convenient brand of forgetfulness that allows these scholars to draw attention to themselves. But, as Fred Kemp points out in a heated online debate concerning the Holdstein essay, conceding that computers are here to stay in terms of their clerical utility as compared to acknowledging the ways that technology redefines our roles as teachers and scholars are two vastly different things.

To explore the degree to which Kemp is correct and Holdstein misses the mark, I propose a not-so-necessarily hypothetical question that will require the balance of this chapter to answer fully:

> *Given the present-day academic reward system, which of the following options would be more valuable: participating in an online discussion of a serious scholarly issue, or investing the same amount of time toward the development and presentation of a conference paper?*

Questions such as these are becoming increasingly important for the tenured and untenured alike. Despite the desire to be open-minded about innovation, what should a senior scholar recommend to a junior scholar regarding these issues, given our current standards of evaluation? And to what degree should an untenured faculty member or graduate student heed such advice?

I will return to these questions later in this chapter, but for now it will probably be useful to provide some background. First, I will describe the print versus electronic camps in their exaggerated, polarized positions, especially according to Jay Bolter's concept of the Late Age of Print. Then, I will examine a more down-to-earth view of this debate, a tenuous compromise position or "middle ground" in the politics of electronic scholarship.

Finally, I will analyze the grammar of the *curriculum vitae* as a way to illustrate my central point, which is that participating in and contributing to electronic forums is an extremely valuable but currently under-appreciated scholarly activity; however, until at least the end of this century, these activities will be mostly valuable not as ends in and of themselves but as a means to an end, and that end currently is the traditional print-based publication or the print-oriented conference paper. In other words, investing time in online scholarship may be worthwhile for a number of reasons, but unless this investment results in a conventional publication, it will not be endorsed or rewarded by the current systems that determine hiring, tenure, and promotion.

The print world is in fact so dominant that we are currently unable to point to very few examples of electronic scholarship as indicative of an alternative to conventional published scholarship. As of the writing of this chapter, the field of rhetoric and composition has only one established, purely online outlet for the publication of original scholarship (an electronic journal called RhetNet), and it is only a fledgling publication at best. Thus, on the one hand, it will be difficult for me to discuss electronic scholarship in very concrete terms. On the other hand, proponents of online writing would argue that online scholarship is valuable precisely *because* it escapes description in any traditional sense, that if electronic scholarship truly represents a type of revolution then, by definition, its grammars, shapes, and styles challenge traditional forms and elude definition. Consequently, you will not find in this chapter a focus on online journals or electronic publishers but rather an examination of prototypical forums such as Internet discussion groups and real-time conferences because these media, unlike mere digital versions of the printed page, signal a significant break with the print world and with the profession's current reward system. I argue that the current reward system is unfortunate, not because electronic scholarship is somehow essentially better than print, but because the traditional system so heavily commodifies scholarship as a product instead of validating the intellectual processes of experimentation and dialogic interchange. And it is no accident that in the previous sentence I used the clichéd p-words, *product* and *process*, for the field of rhetoric and composition has the added onus of needing to reexamine the way it values electronic scholarship in light of the pedagogies it supports and the theories of literacy for which it argues. For if we examine carefully the politics and practices of scholarship in our field, it should be clear that the current-traditional paradigm—with its accompanying modernist, romantic, and essentialist perspectives that we so strongly denounce—has as its primary artifact the printed book.

"Us Versus Them" in the Late Age of Print

While Holdstein may be wrong when she claims that the battle between the technophobic and the technophilic is over within departments of English, she does make the compelling argument that "us versus them" mentalities are not a particularly constructive way for us to negotiate technology-driven changes in our notions of literacy. And she correctly blames online proponents for often perpetuating such antagonistic perspectives. For example, in *Writing Space,* Bolter describes the current era as "The Late Age of Print," claiming that we live in a transitional time in which the essentially antithetical worlds of print-based and electronic-based literacies struggle for domination. He writes, "As we look up from our computer keyboard to the books on our shelves, we must ask ourselves whether 'this will destroy that'" (2). His concept of the Late Age of Print obviously harkens to the Marxist notion of the late age of capitalism, implying that the fundamental structures, norms, and currencies of post-industrial culture are being redefined as the means of production are transformed. I support the assertion that we currently reside in a transitional period, but the degree to which the print and electronic worlds are fundamentally antithetical is questionable: are we well-served by thinking "this will destroy that"?

If we are not well-served by such dichotomous thinking, then how *should* we approach the changes that technology brings? What sort of framework should we use? In *Technologies of Power*, Majid Tehran outlines four such approaches: technophobia, technophilia, techno-neutralism, and techno-structuralism. Technophobia and technophilia are obvious enough: both suggest an uncritical, knee-jerk response to technology. The techno-neutral position views technology as value neutral; that is, because machines are inanimate tools, they do not have the ability to substantially change the world themselves. For example, the techno-neutralist would object to the convention of personifying technology in statements such as "the printing press forever altered the world" or "computers enable students to write more fluently" because such statements mislead us into assigning agency to technology. Finally, a techno-structuralist would examine the rhetorical convention of assigning agency to technology according to the ways such rhetoric creates and maintains particular ideologies. Cynthia Selfe and Richard Selfe's essay "The Politics of the Interface" is a good example of a techno-structuralist approach: the Selfes do not presume that advanced technologies are either inherently good, evil, or neutral. Instead, they focus on critically examining the ways technologies and debates about technology play a role in ideological control.

My point is that we need to establish a critical framework through which we can examine and discuss the politics of electronic scholarly publishing; we need a perspective from which we can sort out the hyperbolic claims both for and against technology so that we can make informed decisions about our profession. And I believe a techno-structuralist approach is more constructive than others. Perhaps such a framework can get us beyond "us versus them" dichotomies so that we can consider important issues in scholarly publishing without getting trapped in arguments about the "nature" of either print or electronic literacies.

This does not mean, however, that everyone will agree with a techno-structuralist approach. In fact, phobias and philias will certainly continue to thrive, especially within writing programs and departments of English. For example, in talking to many colleagues, I consistently find one of two diametrically opposed opinions about the scholarly value of Internet discussion groups: these groups tend to be characterized as either exceptionally pedestrian or extraordinarily useful, and these antagonistic characterizations create problems for those who are trying to decide whether or not to invest their time in such activities. Such either/or perspectives demonstrate that, while a techno-structural approach may seem appropriate, other ideological frameworks that hold sway in many departments today continue to construct technologies as either essentially beneficial or detrimental. Since it is apparent that we must continue to negotiate the tensions between deeply-embedded traditions and new perspectives, we should take a close look at the arguments that both the technophobes and the technophiles make concerning electronic scholarship. Instead of simply presenting a list of the tenets of each of these polarized camps, a dialogue between two imaginary scholars, Gates and Ludd, might more clearly reflect the attitudes we are likely to encounter in the hallways of our departments.

Gates: Print is dead, books are dead, and anyone who continues to publish scholarship and teach classes in a non-electronic environment is living in the past. Either climb aboard or get left behind.

Ludd: Absurd! You're not thinking intelligently about the future, much less the present. In one form or another, books have been around for millennia and will continue to flourish. They are part of the core of civilization, both culturally and epistemologically. Look around you! The printed page still rules the world. For example, cite one great work by one prominent scholar in our field that exists online.

Gates: See, that's just the point: you still think in terms of antiquated notions of textuality; you're still obsessed with the idea of classic authors and classic texts. What we're witnessing with online scholarship is the emergence of completely new conceptions of textuality, conceptions that demonstrate the vacuity of the image of the great autonomous author and the text that supposedly *belongs* to him or her. Because the hypertextual structures of much online writing more closely mesh with the cognitive processes of readers, online readers now become more like readers/writers—even more so than reader-response critics suggested in the days of print culture. It simply no longer makes sense to talk in terms of "classic texts."

Ludd: Well, I've seen some of these so-called *hyper*-texts, and to me they're just fancy books. In fact, as David Dobrin describes in "Hype and Hypertext," we're really not witnessing the emergence of a new textuality: hypertext is just a new gimmick—like newspapers were a new gimmick, or magazines, or even the novel. Most of these hypertexts have tables of contents like printed books; they read front-to-back and left-to-right like all other books in English. Who cares if you don't have to read chapter one first? I usually don't read any book in perfectly linear order anyway, unless it's a work of fiction that I've never read before. And the hypertexts that don't follow conventional, book-like formats are so far out and confusing that I can safely say they don't "mesh" with the cognitive processes of any person that I know.

Gates: Well, regardless of whether or not you believe that hypertext represents a revolution in writing, the democratic nature of computer networks, in particular the Internet, brings about profound changes in the way we approach writing, reading, and scholarship. For example, one of the primary means of evaluating the quality of an educational institution has been to examine its library holdings. Suddenly, with the Internet, even a respectable university library can't compare with the amount of information that we can now put on a desktop with a simple phone-line connection.

Ludd: Sure, but the information in libraries is *valuable* as compared to the trash on the Internet: it's researched, reviewed, edited, time-worn. Because of the economics of the publishing industry, books that eventually find their way onto library shelves are of the highest quality because they had to compete in the market place. Any joker can "publish" a bucket of nonsense on the Internet.

Gates: You're again thinking like an old-fashioned, elitist scholar. First, the publishing industry is anything but an unbiased place in which good works survive and the trash, as you call it, gets weeded out. Books don't "find their way" onto library shelves; somebody puts them there, and the mechanisms through which one manuscript gets published and another doesn't are as political as any other arena of competition. Second, you really hit the nail on the head when you said books were "time-worn": by the time a manuscript rests on a library shelf its scholarly usefulness has already been dramatically diminished. Fiction writers make a living by creating stories that they must sell as commodities; so they obviously need to control the manufacturing and distribution of their products. However, as scholars, our profession is (or should be) about the creation and dissemination—not the commodification—of knowledge, and the world of print creates tremendous obstacles in this regard. Journal articles, after being submitted for review, often take one to two years to reach print, and scholarly monographs generally take two to five years. That's serious lag-time.

Ludd: Sure, waiting for something to reach print is a problem. But it's the price we pay to guarantee that what eventually counts as knowledge or scholarship is authentic, original, intelligent, and well presented. The review process simply takes time, and it's worth it.

Gates: Yes, review is essential. But you're still wanting to live in the Stone Age. Just because something is published electronically doesn't mean that it hasn't been reviewed. The review process is also being used in online scholarly publishing, and the fact that an author can more quickly and easily receive feedback from readers who are miles away means that online writers are even *more* likely to make use of the review process than print writers. A manuscript can be composed, delivered, reviewed, revised, and published electronically, all in a fraction of the time it takes to do so in print. And, as Lester Faigley pointed out in a recent interview, the economics of publishing are such that the publishers of scholarly journals, which are almost exclusively non-profit, will eventually discover that publishing online is their only option in the face of shrinking library budgets and rising printing costs (Taylor 60).

Ludd: So far you've been touting the liberating and democratic free flow of information that online publishing promises, but you fail to paint a complete picture when it comes to access. Computers, telephone lines, and information autobahns all cost money. In fact, the PC itself is in many ways a $2000 obstacle to the free flow of information. And those who are probably most seriously in need of access to information and to publishing opportunities are those who can least afford the tolls on the information superhighway.

Gates: This is precisely why it becomes the obligation of educational and municipal libraries to reconstitute themselves according to the changes that online technology brings: they need to become places where anyone can access online resources. It's obvious that our culture at large denies many people access to avenues of power. However, within that culture, public libraries and educational institutions—while far from being completely egalitarian—can, in some ways, counter these inequities.

Ludd: Still, I'm not convinced that everyone will feel comfortable curling up with a computer screen for an evening of writing or reading; technology simply alienates people. The PC that my department provided is really nothing more than a fancy typewriter, a writing tool that isn't nearly as comfortable, convenient, or friendly as pen and paper. And I find the intimacy of holding a book in my hands, turning the pages, and even smelling the paper an important (although emotional and visceral) part of studying and thinking. I'm not willing to sacrifice that, and I don't know anyone who prefers reading a screen to reading the printed page. Furthermore, there are so many great books out there that, even within rhetoric and composition, I know I'll never have the time to read them all. I don't need additional online texts whose quality is certainly questionable.

Gates: Well, eventually all those "great books" will be most easily and cost-effectively available online anyway; thus, readers in the future will obviously need to get beyond your romantic smoking-jacket-and-cozy-den approach. In fact, through online philanthropies such as Project Gutenberg, many so-called classic texts are now available free of charge.

Ludd: Say what you want, but when it comes time to submit your work to a review committee that will determine whether or not you get hired, promoted, or tenured, you're going to be sorry if you hand in a computer disk for a dossier. You know as well as I do that the printed page is still what matters; everything else is just a distraction. In fact, it's time for me to end this distraction by going back to my office for some real research.

Gates: Me too, except that I'm going out into the 'Net to read the most current research and to talk live with colleagues all over the world instead of having to wait five years later until their thoughts "find their way" into print.

The Political "Middle Ground" and The Grammar of the CV

In response to the question I posed earlier about the advisability of investing one's time in electronic scholarship, Ludd would recommend that scholars avoid electronic publishing and research, while Gates would argue that online scholarship is where all the action is. Ludd and Gates are obviously caricatures, but one still wonders what the middle ground between their two positions might look like. Of course, you might continue to argue, as Bolter's concept of the Late Age of Print suggests, that the poles are fundamentally irreconcilable; that is, either print or electronic publishing will eventually dominate to the necessary exclusion of its opposing form. Knoblauch and Brannon claim that certain opposing philosophical approaches to pedagogy are fundamentally antithetical and contradictory and that, in terms of pedagogy, sometimes there can be no middle ground (1). Does a similar principle apply in the struggle between print and electronic scholarship? Regardless of whether such principles really do apply, we can assume that many scholars will continue to operate as if the online and print worlds *are* mutually exclusive.

Yet, something that Ludd said may provide a clue as to what a middle ground might look like. Ludd mentioned a departmentally provided PC, and I think we can all agree that desktop computers are fairly common in faculty offices. However, as Ludd points out, many users approach these technologies as nothing more than souped-up typewriters. And those who go one step beyond such limited approaches probably make use of other electronic technologies only in the most clerical ways, such as using e-mail only for memos and informal correspondence. Consequently, when Holdstein claims that departments of English are not opposed to the dramatic changes that online writing presents, she is in effect working to establish a middle ground between the print and electronic poles. Yet, we need to question whether this middle ground politely glosses over what may be a tremendous gulf between those who value online scholarship and those who do not. In other words, we must ask whether compromise positions such as Holdstein's actually constitute a fabricated middle-ground that allows the profession to appear technologically correct, despite our actual practices. Whenever faced with what appears to be a potential revolution, scholars often find themselves in tenuous and contradictory positions. As those whose occupation is the creation, dissemination, maintenance, and revision of knowledge, scholars often argue that one body of knowledge is more or less accurate—is more or less what we consider the truth—while simultaneously finding themselves charged with the constant pursuit of new ideas. Thus, it can be very difficult for us to admit that we are opposed to something new, although our practices suggest that sometimes we are. It seems that Holdstein provides a good example of this phenomenon. By claiming that we truly appreciate online writing, Holdstein takes what amounts to be a political middle ground that allows scholars to act as if they are not opposed to online writing when, in fact, our practices suggest otherwise. As an example of what I mean by "practices," it might be useful to examine one of the most revealing "texts" in our profession: the *curriculum vitae*.

Earlier I mentioned that my colleagues tend to be of one of two minds about Internet discussion groups: they tend to believe that these resources are either low-brow or extremely beneficial. Discussion groups go by various names such as bulletin boards, listservs, lists, and so on; and if you have never experienced one of these groups, it might be helpful to think of them as elaborate, continuous dialogues that are mediated though the Internet. For instance, say you are interested in writing program administration. You might want to join a discussion group called WPA-L in which the dialogue focuses on related issues. Once you "subscribe" to WPA-L, a message that any of the two hundred or so other subscribers sends to a central location will appear within minutes in your e-mail account as well as the accounts of the other subscribers. Any of the subscribers can then reply to those messages, also known as "posts," so that the list begins to develop an ongoing conversation that takes place across regional and national boundaries. Obviously, this sort of exchange can, but will not necessarily, provide an important resource for scholars in any field. The problem is that because these resources are so new, we have yet to figure out exactly how they should work and how we should evaluate their professional usefulness. And the grammar of the vita demonstrates this fact.

Imagine that you spend a solid hour or two a week participating in or simply reading the conversations that come through WPA-L. Where should you list this experience on your vita—if at all? The most likely place would be to include your membership to WPA-L in the same place that you list other professional affiliations, such as a membership in NCTE or MLA. But this is a tricky business. Imagine if Ludd were the chair of the committee deciding whether to hire you or give you a promotion; putting WPA-L in the same category as the hallowed MLA might suggest, in Ludd's thinking, that your professional values are askew. Ludd aside, how important is a membership in either WPA-L or MLA? Neither membership necessarily requires any effort whatsoever; you could "join" either and simply ignore the conversations going on in WPA-L or *PMLA*—no one will know if you haven't read a word. If, on the other hand, you actually contribute to the online conversation in a discussion group, you have almost certainly gone far beyond the amount of commitment and engagement that a membership in MLA requires. For example, after Holdstein published "Technology, Utility, and Amnesia," an in-depth, two-week-long discussion ensued in the ACW-L discussion group that surpassed anything that a conventional reader-response section in a print journal could have supported. In fact, Holdstein herself submitted a number of responses to the discussion and, by doing so, extended the "text" of her original article, thereby making the original print version somewhat obsolete. The post-Amnesia discussion is archived on the Internet so that it is as easily available as the original *College English* article (see Kemp). Furthermore, many scholars had the opportunity to participate fully in the debate, not just those selected by the editor, and not just those whose comments could be crammed into the reader-response section of a journal. Not only do such exchanges allow for genuine dialogue and rebuttal (unlike print journals), they are also much more current because they engage, settle, and unearth issues before print journal editors can even begin to address what has happened.

Imagine that you had participated in the post-Amnesia debate. You would have spent a good two to three hours studying the original article and the online discussion. Eventually you might have felt compelled to spend an hour or so composing and submitting to ACW-L your original thoughts on the subject, even though it would have required you to temporarily shelve the conference paper on which you were working. Perhaps others would have responded favorably to your comments, or perhaps your insights might have altered the course of the conversation. Where do you list this experience on a vita? Should you include copies of your comments in your dossier or tenure application? At this point, just before the turn of the century, we have no clear standards concerning this type of scholarship. However, if your comments were published in the reader-response section of *College English*, you certainly would have placed copies of *that* text in your dossier, or at least cited it in your vita. The fact that the post-Amnesia conversation—which was more substantive, current, far-reaching, and dialogic than a print response could ever be—does not seem to have a clear place in our profession suggests that we need to reexamine our standards of evaluation.

Furthermore, senior scholars have been slow to participate in the development of online scholarly activities. Table 1 lists the major online resources in the field of rhetoric and composition as of January 1, 1996; and you will notice that graduate students and junior faculty members are currently almost completely responsible for developing these resources.

Table 1
Major Online Scholarly Resources
in Rhetoric and Composition as of January 1996

Resource	Founder's Original Status
ACW-L	new asst. professor
CREWRT-L	graduate student
H-RHETOR	asst. professor
JAC-Online (e-journal)	graduate student
Kairos (e-journal)	graduate student
MBU-L	new asst. professor
NCTE-TALK	graduate student
Netoric Cafe (a MOO)	graduate student(s)
Pre/Text	tenured professor
RhetNet (e-journal)	graduate student(s)
WAC-L	asst. professor
WPA-L	tenured professor

The table includes three primary types of online scholarship: discussion lists, MOOs, and e-journals. I have already described discussion groups. MOOs are like text-based conference calls in which any number of scholars can participate in a real-time conversation that takes place across the Internet. Netoric Cafe currently provides the field's only consistent MOO, and it is often more social, informational, and pedagogical than scholarly. E-journals (electronic journals) consist of refereed scholarly articles and conversations, much like those found in a print journal. All three of the current e-journals in the field were initiated by graduate students. One of them, *JAC Online*, merely reproduces articles that have already appeared in the print version of *JAC*. And of the other two, only *RhetNet* has so far established a reputation of any significance. Thus, rhetoric and composition currently has only one serious, truly online forum for publishing original scholarship, *RhetNet*, and it is presently managed by graduate students. While the landscape of electronic publishing is certain to change in the years to come, it is apparent that such changes are likely to be very slow if senior scholars continue to fail to play an active role in developing these new forums.

Other evidence further demonstrates that our departments are trying to take the possibilities of online writing seriously but are still not comfortable making a firm commitment to these new media. For example, in her paper at the 1995 CCCC convention, Denise Weeks described a project in which she studied the 1994 *MLA Job Information List* and discovered widespread disagreement over the technological literacies that schools were looking for in the *curriculum vitae* of new hires; as a whole, these institutions demonstrated an increased interest in hiring people with backgrounds in technology, yet Weeks showed that their criteria were highly inconsistent and ambiguous. And even though NCTE and MLA have published position statements that clearly acknowledge the scholarly value of innovative pedagogical material and textbooks, in-depth reports on the development of software for the writing classroom indicate that faculty who have undertaken such tasks consistently receive no recognition for the scholarly contributions of such work (see LeBlanc). Again, departments are taking the political middle ground by claiming that they value innovation and expanding possibilities for scholarship, but when it comes to rewarding such efforts, this middle ground turns out to be shaky at best.

Electronic Scholarship as a Means to an End
How then should we answer the hypothetical question posed earlier in this chapter: what should we recommend to ourselves and our colleagues regarding the investment of time in electronic scholarly publishing? On the one hand, slight changes in the conventions of the *curriculum vitae* and the *MLA Job Information List* suggest that a time may arrive when electronic scholarly publishing is valued and rewarded, but this does not seem likely until at least after the turn of the century. On the other hand, those conventions need not dictate all of our actions and decisions; we are not forced to answer these questions solely in terms of no-risk, careerist choices. In some ways, scholarship is about taking risks: "to boldly go where no one has gone before." Publishing your work online or working to develop an electronic scholarly forum may turn out to be a worthwhile risk if the world really *does* change in the ways that people like Bolter believe it will. For the time being, however, we should avoid deceiving ourselves or those to whom we give advice about the current politics of electronic scholarly publishing. For the time being, Ludd is almost certain to be correct: you will be sorry if your list of publications is not comprised almost exclusively of traditional, print-oriented scholarship.

Yet, the situation is not that bleak. I believe the best answer to my central question is that the two options of investing in either online or print scholarship are not mutually exclusive. It is possible to spend time in both worlds and succeed, so long as one is aware that, presently, scholarship must be published in print form if it is to receive full recognition. In other words, online writing can currently serve as means to an end, and the end valued most highly in academia is the conventional publication. For instance, spending a number of hours participating in the post-Amnesia debate could serve as intriguing research that eventually supports an article or a conference paper; that debate certainly played an important role in the chapter you are currently reading. And if scholars find value in reading print journals and attending conferences, it is partially because through such forums they gain exposure to the most current thinking. Participating in a solid Internet discussion group can keep the scholar in constant touch with the newest ideas much more effectively than a once-a-year conference can. Furthermore, discussion groups often provide an important social function whereby we are able to stay in contact with our colleagues whom we do not manage to see very often. And once your work has been accepted for publication, e-mail is typically the most efficient means of communicating with editors during the revision and production process.

In short, we should encourage each other to be creative about using electronic resources to help develop our research, but, at present, it is probably not wise to pursue online publishing actively unless you are an established scholar. We should not expect that investing time in electronic exchanges will be *directly* recognized as a valuable scholarly activity, but savvy scholars know that spending at least some time engaged in online conversations can have tremendous *indirect* benefits both in terms of quality and efficiency.

Before I end my discussion on the politics of electronic scholarly publishing, I feel compelled to address three important ethical issues. First, the advice I have tried to provide in this chapter is based upon the desire to be candid about what I see as the realities of the current political situation in our field; thus, my foremost ethical concern has been to avoid being misleading about these new types of scholarship, especially since they appear on the surface to be very exciting yet underneath are rife with pitfalls for a scholar struggling to advance.

My concern for those who will inevitably shape the future of our profession leads to a second issue: what ethics should define the proper role of the scholar? I am forced to admit that I find my perspective on the politics of electronic scholarship somewhat distastefully careerist. That is, my first ethic necessitates that I address the "facts of scholarly life," regardless of how unpleasant those facts can sometimes be. My ultimate recommendation, that electronic scholarship is mostly valuable as a means to an end, continues to support the commodification of scholarship in terms of the products that the researcher manufactures and markets. As I said earlier, I believe that ethically the scholar should be dedicated to the expansion and dissemination, not the commodification, of knowledge. And while there are many moments when this more ideal ethic is fortunately in effect, it is naive to pretend that other forces—especially economic and political forces—are not also in play. Thus, the ethic of wanting to provide honest advice conflicts somewhat with the ethic of not wanting to commodify scholarship.

Third, as scholars in rhetoric and composition we have the added ethical responsibility of trying to realize within our own scholarly communities the values we promote in our writing programs and within our students' discourse communities—we should practice what we preach. When we encourage students to experiment with and acknowledge the validity of multiple literacies and dialects, we should be prepared to do the same ourselves, including experimenting with electronic literacies. When we argue against product-oriented approaches to writing, we should similarly condemn product-oriented approaches to our own scholarship. When we seek to encourage genuine dialogic exchange in our classrooms, we should admit that Internet discussion groups are the best versions of such exchanges that we have within our own scholarly communities. When we ask students to conceive of writing as a socially constructed, public act, we should question whether the reading of a conference paper in a tiny, isolated conference room compares favorably to the publication of that work on the Internet. If we claim to want to foster resistant discourses that lead to critical consciousness, then we should distrust anyone who casually dismisses electronic publication as necessarily unscholarly. It comes down to this: if we ask students to open their minds, learn new ideas, and intimately integrate some of those ideas into their lived experiences, then we must admit that we as scholars have a long way to go toward enacting this same ethic in our publishing practices and reward systems, especially regarding the possibilities that online writing presents.

Works Cited

Bolter, Jay David. *Writing Space: The Computer, Hypertext, and the History of Writing.* Hillsdale, NJ: Erlbaum, 1990.

Dobrin, David. "Hype and Hypertext." *Literacy and Computers: The Complications of Teaching and Learning with Technology.* New York: MLA, 1994. 305-15.

Faigley, Lester. *Fragments of Rationality: Postmodernity and the Subject of Composition.* Pittsburgh: U of Pittsburgh P, 1992.

Holdstein, Deborah H. "Technology, Utility, and Amnesia." *College English* 57 (1995): 587-98.

Kemp, Fred. http://english.ttu.edu/hypermail/acw-l. Internet. 10 Oct. 1995.

Knoblauch, C.H., and Lil Brannon. *Rhetorical Traditions and the Teaching of Writing.* Upper Montclair, NJ: Boynton, 1984.

LeBlanc, Paul. *Writing Teachers, Writing Software.* Urbana: NCTE, 1993.

Modern Language Association. *MLA Job Information List.* October, 1995.

Selfe, Cynthia L., and Richard Selfe, Jr. "The Politics of the Interface: Power and its Exercise in Electronic Contact Zones." *College Composition and Communication* 45 (1994): 480-504.

Taylor, Todd. "CCCC, Difference, and Electronic Literacies: An Interview with Lester Faigley." *Composition Studies* 22.2 (1994): 47-64.

Tehran, Majid. *Technologies of Power: Information Machines and Democratic Prospects.* Norwood, NJ: Ablex, 1990.

Weeks, Denise. "Techno-Reverberations: Changing Institutional Values." Conference on College Composition and Communication. Washington, D.C. 24 Mar. 1995.

Work Habits of Productive Scholarly Writers: Insights from Research in Psychology

ROBERT BOICE

Early in my career as a researcher in psychology, while I was still haunting prairie dogs and mapping the social relationships of toads, I discovered a second, unbidden calling. Colleagues were coming to me for help with writing because I seemed to write with ease and enjoyment. I soon realized that I not only enjoyed working with writers but that the interaction benefitted me at least as much as them in that I felt compelled to take my own advice about ways of working efficiently and was getting more writing done and published. Thereafter, I began conducting serious research and treatment programs for colleagues. Still, not all of my colleagues wanted help with their habits and working conditions as writers; some of them coached students as writers but rarely applied the same kinds of care or advice to themselves. Their own writing, it seemed, had to be put off until every other responsibility had been taken care of; then, as a rule, they would try to write while hurried and fatigued. No wonder some of them had learned to dislike writing and to doubt their own competence.

In this chapter I relate how I have learned to help colleagues, even the reluctant ones, write with more comfort and fluency. I sample the kinds of studies I have conducted, and I draw out the findings that might interest teachers and scholars in rhetoric and composition. I end with a discussion of the strategies proven most effective for helping faculty acquire more productive work habits. Some of the pointers might even prove useful to those who teach writing more than they write.

Early Developments

After my unplanned commitment to become a writing therapist for academics, things changed rapidly for me. My casual programs for writers grew into psychological experiments where I varied my approaches and then measured writers' progress. I had more to learn than I realized. There were few leads on how to help writers overcome blocking and other inhibitions. There was still less about coaching writers in ways of working more efficiently and successfully, especially at the professional level. There *were* precedents in psychoanalysis, notably Bergler's interpretation of writing blocks as the symbolic rejection of mother's milk in the form of refusing to write. But even if I had found his view credible, I couldn't have imitated his therapies; he provided no clear hints about how to help writers undo their blocks. And there were folkloric directives about how to unblock: put your work away until you feel more inspired. I tried that approach with some writers and found that more often than not the day of inspiration was long in coming. Clearly, professorial writers needed something more immediately effective, especially those who faced deadlines including tenure decisions. The only other precedent available seemed to hold the most promise: a behavioristic approach that employed strategies to force writers to write whether they felt like it or not.

First, I began conducting systematic programs by modelling after a few, single-subject studies by behavioral psychologists. I enlisted six colleagues who had longstanding writing blocks ("Increasing"). During months when the forcing "contingency" was in effect (that is, the writers had to write for a brief period every day to earn things like access to morning showers or daily newspapers), these writers averaged several pages of prose per day. But during alternating months when the contingency was removed, writing productivity dropped off markedly, below the levels that met reasonable needs for scholarly output. My inclination was to suppose that this merely meant ordinarily blocked writers would have to work in the permanent presence of external contingencies that forced them to write, but the main problem was that most of these professorial writers disliked being forced, and some refused to continue with the contingencies.

In sequels, I tried ways of making the forcing more tolerable. One such method demonstrated that working on a forced schedule of brief, daily sessions not only produced more output than writing spontaneously but that the regular regimen generated more creative ideas ("Contingency"). In a follow-up study ("Experimental"), I gave half my subjects close personal attention in weekly psychotherapy sessions, compared to half who worked in a home study program, mostly on their own. Both methods worked reasonably well, but in both methods the writers disliked being forced. With it they wrote; without it they usually did not.

So I knew that I needed to find broader, less aversive strategies. I looked next to the cognitive therapies just beginning to supplant behavioral types. First, I needed to know something about how writers' thoughts helped or hindered their fluency. In a large and tedious study, I enlisted blocked academic writers to record their "self-talk" while they were writing; their thinking at these and other occasions when they felt pressured to write was predictably negative. Still, no one had previously documented it, and some of its aspects proved surprising. Here are the most common problems reported by writers when preparing to write (the numbers in parentheses indicate the percentages of *blockers* versus *nonblockers* who reported the cognition as salient):

- work apprehension and laziness (95% vs. 100%)
- procrastination, wanting to do something other than writing (90% vs. 55%)
- dysphoria, feeling too sad or anxious to write (77% vs. 25%)
- impatience about wanting to get caught up at once (77% vs. 35%)
- perfectionism (69% vs. 40%)
- evaluation anxiety (32% vs. 15%)
- rigid rules about writing (12% vs. 10%)

Two things surprised me. One was the dominance of work aversion and impatience as blocking agents; prior to these results, experts had supposed that perfection and anxiety would head the list. Another was the relatively high levels of negative cognitions about writing reported by fluent writers. These negative cognitions even matched the dislike of blockers for the difficulty and distastefulness of academic writing (see the first item in the list above). But a closer look at these data provided a clue about why nonblockers managed to write despite negativity. Of all their self-talk recorded while writing, nonblockers spent less of it in maladaptive thinking (that is, thoughts that discouraged writing) than did blockers (42% versus 72%). Significantly, nonblockers were more likely to experience self-talk that encouraged writing (49% versus 7%). In other words, nonblockers were not immune to discouraging thoughts about writing (it is, after all, often tedious), but they were better able to balance it with positive cognitions and to get on with their work.

I used that set of findings to help devise a series of strategies for blocked writers. Early attempts were successful in lessening the complaints about forcing; the writers were fairly comfortable in spotting their maladaptive thought patterns and replacing them. The same cognitions that had bothered blockers most in the survey study proved most crucial; the biggest gains in measurable productivity and in self-rated satisfaction were made when these thoughts were replaced. In sum, this is what I learned: the usual negativities in blockers' thinking do matter but they are rather easily replaced with optimistic thoughts. Their diminution even proved helpful to already fluent writers who wanted to write with more comfort. Still, cognitive therapies left me feeling that something was missing. These strategies worked reasonably well, almost as reliably as forcing, but only so long as the writers continued to meet with me. In a way, then, I hadn't gotten past the forcing, even if the prospect of writing in order to please me was less loathsome than having to write to be able to shower for the day.

I continued to experiment with various strategies, such as automatic writing, freewriting, and so on (even Transactional and Gestalt strategies), but the number of colleagues who needed to survive the tenure process took me back to more systematic searches for better methods. Meanwhile, it was becoming apparent that the best strategies for fluency and comfort are probably *combinations* of traditional therapies. In order to see how traditional therapies compared and combined, I needed to conduct comparisons under conditions as closely similar as I could make them (at least that is our belief in the religion called psychology). Then, with the conditions made comparable and the singular potentials of therapies established under optimal conditions, I could integrate them in ways that would indicate if combined therapies are more efficacious.

A Combined and Comparative Study of Therapies

In my main study about the efficacy of combined interventions, there were five groups of ten academics, all of them blocked according to an assessment test I had devised (*Professors*). They volunteered to remain with the experiment for at least nine months of constant record-keeping and meetings. The experiment took almost a decade to "run" (as we say in psychology) and is the most extensive test of writing block therapies I know of. Let me briefly describe the five treatment groups.

Freewriting. These ten participants, like all the others, met with me individually each week for sessions of ten to thirty minutes. Like all other participants, they spent their first month with me establishing a baseline measure of how much they would write without an obvious therapeutic intervention. After the baseline period, this group worked mainly at practicing freewriting. In short, these writers began each daily session for the second month with ten minutes of freewriting. I coached them intensively until they used the ten minutes to write, without editing, to produce material with some relevance to the prose they would write after the freewriting exercise. In the next month, the third, our meetings continued but the formal treatment was suspended. In the month after that, the intervention was reinstated—and so on, alternately, until the nine months were completed.

Contingency Management. These ten writers, once into their second month, agreed to employ contingencies that would force them to write every weekday for sessions of an hour. They too experienced alternate months when the intervention (the contingency) was suspended.

Cognitive-Behavioral Therapy. These ten writers practiced ten minutes of self-therapy (coached by me at first) in a cognitive mode that included noticing maladaptive self-talk, stopping the negative cognition by disputing its irrationality and wastefulness, and starting a new and more positive line of thought (for details see Boice, "Combined" and *How Writers*). During alternate months, faculty in this group suspended formal noting of negative self-talk (and its curatives), so they did not share them with me in weekly meetings (but they, like other groups, were not prohibited from carrying out the exercises on their own).

Social Skills Training. This strategy had no clear precedent, except in my own research. I had long sensed that writers needed to become practiced at soliciting social support and at handling editorial criticism if they were to persist as fluent scriveners. Here, I hoped, might be an intervention that would help maintain the momentum induced by other interventions (see McCaul, Glasgow, and O'Neill for a more general discussion of this problem). The ten members of this group spent the first ten minutes of their scheduled, hour-long sessions practicing a series of exercises and plans, some of them to be carried out elsewhere. In one of these exercises, for instance, I coached them in simple but effective methods of responding to criticism, even unfair and uninformed sorts, by first finding something in the critic's comments with which to agree honestly.

Combined Treatments. These ten subjects experienced the four interventions mentioned above in a sequential fashion that eventually combined them all. They too had alternate months off from formal interventions for more spontaneous work on their projects. In addition, a larger group of writers underwent the combined procedure: the twenty-seven subjects who returned to participate for a second academic year.

Results of Comparative and Combined Stages. All of the singular treatments worked but none nearly as impressively as the combined format. Clearly, combined treatments are the approach of choice (despite the tradition favoring singular interventions). A comparison of the singular treatments in month eight, the last period with the intervention in effect for the academic year, provides a reasonable picture of how well each of them worked in the long run (the percentages of sessions in which writers met their preset goals of productivity, usually a page of prose per day, appear in parentheses):

- freewriting alone (13%)
- contingency management alone (68%)
- cognitive therapy (25%)
- social skills training (22%)
- combined, year 1 (72%)
- combined, year 2 (50%)

Not only did the combined approaches produce more stable, persistent levels of productivity over time, they also encouraged moderation (notice the modest but stable and sufficient level of compliance shown by writers who experienced the combined strategies in year two; they reported none of the pressure that contingency groups members had). Combined group members also fared better in the editorial process (one hundred percent completed and submitted manuscripts in that year; fifty percent gained acceptance in a refereed outlet; seventy percent of those rejected moved quickly to revision and resubmission). Still, each singular method had its advantages. Freewriters had more sessions with immediate starts than other groups. Contingency writers produced more pages per week on average (almost five pages) than did other groups. The social skills group reported more well-being as writers than any but the combined group. But overall the combined group excelled in dimensions including sessions with relaxed, slow-paced, reflective writing that promoted discovery and enjoyment.

Well before this lengthy study was finished, I had begun other programs for writers based on a combined approach. The emerging data of the long project were too convincing to ignore. With the help of some trial and error, I settled into an arrangement of steps that essentially paralleled those just described. That is, stymied writers began by establishing momentum (and its motivation), imagination (by way of systematic collecting and prewriting), confidence and productivity (with the use, initially, of contingency management), patience and self-control, and a sense of audience that includes resilience in the face of criticism.

After nearly two decades of observing and helping colleagues (mostly new faculty) thrive in professorial careers, I suddenly noticed that of all new hires, perhaps ten to twelve percent at the large public campuses I have studied make impressively fast starts, as do about an equal number of new graduate students. These individuals stood out as exemplar teachers and writers. I studied them systematically to try to specify what made their work habits most efficient. Their patterns of behavior and cognition were similar to the patterns I had been teaching in combined therapies. But there was an advantage in seeing how exemplars taught themselves to find fluency and comfort: at last I had a better sense of the natural sequencing and specific skills involved in optimal performance, and I could see an even greater value of combining interventions than before. This information on naturally acquired comfort and fluency, it seemed to me, could be integrated with my combined therapies approach to produce an even more effective basis for facilitating faculty writing. The result of mingling exemplary practices with proven interventions has been by far the best method I have found yet.

"Deft novices" in the professoriate offer a useful example because they acquire efficiency in strikingly similar ways. In contrast to other writers, they are most likely to engage in the following behaviors: they work patiently (for example, while waiting and putting off decisions about what to write, they playfully prepare to write) and as a result feel more motivated and imaginative; they work regularly at writing but far less, overall, than they had imagined necessary; their output increases and stabilizes; they suffer far less pain and uncertainty at writing; they learn to loosen up and to allow others, even critics, to do some of the work; and they often maintain low profiles, at least initially. Most do not rush to excel as stylists; instead they begin by figuring out *how to work.*

In what lies ahead, I summarize the acts of exemplars through simple strategies that have proven most effective for both normal and blocked writers who seek more fluency and comfort. Although I don't discuss all the derivations of those guidelines, I do provide the essential details of how they are practiced in my programs. Each guideline describes the practices that over one hundred faculty have judged most essential to progress. I assume, incidentally, that all faculty writers can learn better ways to work. Academics of all stripes have benefitted in both subjective and measurable ways in this program, and, in fact, experienced writers actually make better participants than do rookies.

Guideline 1: Wait Actively

In my experience, academic writers already know how to wait *passively*. They await Muses and hope for brilliant ideas that will impel writing without hard work. They want clarity to come spontaneously, without planning or deliberativeness. This kind of waiting often produces little more than suffering and silence. Passive waiting works unreliably because it depends on mysterious, unpredictable forces instead of building motivation gradually, surely. Passivity misleads with its initial feelings of freedom because it eventually leaves writers feeling hopelessly behind, guilty, and incompetent. In the end, passive waiting exposes writers to a cruel oppression: the pressure of deadlines and expressions of contrition. In other words, passive waiting risks procrastination and blocking.

At first glance, *active* waiting seems no different. It too means waiting; it too means not rushing to begin (just as good sleepers do not *try* to sleep; they let it creep up on them); and it too means setting the stage for the motivation that will produce a sense of ease with writing. But active waiting is different. It requires both the patience of delaying closure and the tolerance of preparing informally at the same time. Active waiting means listening and thinking while resisting the temptation to formalize plans and to plunge ahead with them. It means putting imperfect, incomplete ideas on paper or screen and living with their ambiguity for awhile. Active waiting helps writers because it induces movement away from inaction. Less obviously, it helps temper impatience by putting off the pressure to be a perfectionist and to expect quick results. With patience, writers begin playfully, tentatively. By waiting until they have a sense of something interesting to say, writers help motivate themselves. Motivation borne of patient preparation works far more reliably than shame, looming deadlines, or sorcery.

Writers who do *not* wait properly, who impatiently rush, face the daunting task of trying to do several complex activities simultaneously: devise a significant plan, find motivation, and write fluidly. The result, called cognitive overload, is the most common reason why writers block (Boice, "Writing"). Writing inhibitions owe more to impatience, to not waiting properly, than anything else. Much the same thing happens in stage fright: anxious speakers delay preparations and then, pressed for time, formulate something hurriedly. As they grow apprehensive, they build increasingly impatient expectations. On the one hand, they doubt their competence. On the other, they demand far more from themselves than they would expect of other speakers. The result, once on stage, is predictable. They have to determine what to say while saying it. They overload and confuse themselves. As they struggle, they become more self-conscious and more anxious. At best, they excitedly hasten their presentations without sensitivity to audience needs. At the least, they practice a maladaptive way to work that leads to more passivity and avoidance.

Despite the pitfalls of passive waiting, many esteemed writers advocate it with conviction. Some hint that they put off writing until an ideal mood sets in. But what if it doesn't appear; what if it is time to write and you are not ready? Indeed, we can far more readily find advocates for passive waiting than for active waiting ("if you don't feel like beginning or continuing a manuscript, put it away until you do"). Even when they describe what might be active waiting, prominent writers say little about what they do to nurture ideas and momentum. How do they know that waiting will produce results? We can only guess. It is easier, I have found, to locate information about the penalties for not waiting actively.

Active waiting in writing is rarely taught, and it is more difficult than it looks; it is the single most demanding task that writers face in learning to work. Patience and its short-term discomfort cause more writers to quit writing than any other factor. Without this patience, writers cannot reliably tolerate the preliminaries that make writing less painful, more efficient, more motivated. Without it, writers reflexively assume they are too busy to wait: "I'm way behind and don't have time to play around. I need something to make me write now, with some dramatic results." Paradoxically, the same faculty who complain about busyness are most likely to end up waiting *passively*. While they acquiescently wait to write, they busy themselves with other, often trivial, activities. Passive waiting pushes aside goal-oriented action while it spurs the perfectionism that makes starting even harder: "I'm very busy right now so I'll wait for a big block of completely undisturbed time in which I can do a lot of writing. Maybe I'll set aside a whole weekend. You don't do your best writing in little snippets, and I'm not going to settle for second-rate writing."

One problem with waiting for ideal conditions is that they may be a long time coming. Another is that when big blocks of free time do appear, writers may use them to escape or rest. (And after that, understandably, they grow more certain that they have too little time to write.) A third problem is that once they are finally writing, procrastinators feel obliged to hurry. Deadlines and rushing discourage the playfulness, revisions, and successes that lend enjoyment and efficiency to writing.

Impatience builds insidiously, in circular fashion. The anxiety, fatigue, and poor reception that accompany rushed work make writing an increasingly painful, avoidable task. Then, when crucial work is put off, self-esteem declines. Left unchecked, impatience makes writers irritable and intolerant. Another thing confounds writers who try to temper impatience: active waiting is sometimes harder and more painful (at least at first) than passive waiting. Patience begins as an alien act in writing because it requires calm and tolerance in a task we customarily execute with all possible intensity and self-absorption. Many of us learned to write as fast as possible during essay tests, or we procrastinated and then rushed to meet term paper and dissertation deadlines.

Patience can be found in simple practices of relaxation and pacing. It grows when we put off closure while playfully trying new ideas and connections. It comes automatically with the reinforcements of noticing that different, seemingly irrelevant or incorrect things can inform and enliven already favored ideas. It hinges on rehearsing, beforehand, ways of combatting temptations to be impulsive. All these acts of patience in writing can be translated into easy exercises. Ironically, these exercises need a bit of patience if they are to work.

An easy way to begin practicing waiting actively is to pause while remaining active in unusual ways. Here is a strategy I use. First, *before writing, pause to reflect* on the problem to be solved and to jot down ideas and plans. That is, pause before starting as a way of slowing down. When you begin with a pause, you instil a less fatiguing pace of work. At first, keep it simple: try waiting for just five seconds beyond the time when you would have started writing. What should you do while waiting? *Talk to yourself about what you will write* and generate momentum by talking *playfully*. When thoughts about starting are flexible and undemanding, beginnings are less strenuous (for example, "Let's see if I can't think of anything else to write. I can begin by admitting that I'm unsure how to begin"). Curiously, this reflective pause works even better when you are sure what you want to say and are impatient to get it on screen or paper. With a few seconds to hear yourself saying and resaying it, you may think of other, better things to write. You might write what you want to say more simply. Even if you stick to your plans, you will have slowed and relaxed yourself. Then, *pause occasionally during writing*, especially once you are on a roll. Here, too, start slowly in changing old habits (with perhaps no more than a single five-second pause to refresh and renew). Finally, *use pauses to relax and contemplate*, but do not use them to worry. The more you learn to make writing pleasant and educational, the easier pausing and waiting become. Initial acts of relaxing can be as simple as focusing on breathing, on a few successive inhalations and exhalations passing pleasantly through your nose. Contemplation needs be nothing more than a reminder of what you have been saying, of what makes it interesting, of where it may lead.

Pauses and patience prove especially valuable in fostering *flexibility in pacing*. With patience, writers learn to change speeds at will, to speed up for spurts of euphoria and spontaneity, to slow down for clarity and perspective. Many writers report their first real breakthrough in finding a sense of freedom as they practice flexibility in pacing; oddly, they find magic in discipline. With that newfound freedom, writers sense the powerful forces behind impatience: it comes from constantly pressing and hurrying in order to feel in control. Impatience stems from the fear that momentum will not return after a break. It builds with worries that an idea already in mind will fade and disappear during an interruption of intense concentration (or that a pause might turn into an escape from writing to something more enjoyable). Effective writers see that pauses need not interfere with adaptive kinds of control. Done correctly, pausing *nurtures control*. Writers slowing to break learn the value of making a note or two about thoughts currently in mind. Externalizing what was only implicit (and possibly fleeting) does more than preserve the thought; it evidently makes ideas even clearer than if the breaks and notes had not happened. And making notes during pauses encourages even more reflection and connection than might otherwise have happened. Thus, patience *nurtures better quality work*.

Pacing has many benefits. A generally slowed pace fosters reflectiveness, restfulness, flexibility, and control. Pacing adds insurance against the extremes of momentum that push aside pauses and patience, and it reins in a uniquely troublesome part of impatience and rushing: the near-mania known as hypomania. Manias are attractive for their euphoria, lack of struggle, seeming fluency, confidence, and quick results. For busy writers behind in their schedules, hypomania offers great binges of rushed work and concomitant excitement and quick completions. But manias are inefficient and unhealthy in the long run. They impel impulsivity and exhaustion; they are followed by a disinclination to resume writing, even depression. Worst of all, they perpetuate the erroneous belief that the best writing demands the suffering of a Dickens or an E.B. White.

In short, before beginning to write, decide how you will pause and how you will pace yourself (that is, how you will wait). When you mentally rehearse acts of waiting beforehand, you will be more successful in finding patience and tolerance. Remind yourself of when you would like to pause and of what pace you would like to follow. Imagine where you may be tempted to stray from your plans and how you can cue yourself to get back on track ("It's the very time that I tell myself that I don't need a pause that I have to be most on guard; that's precisely the moment when I will get up out of my chair and stretch for a minute"). Prewriting as waiting brings more reflection, rest, patience, flexibility, and control; and more than any other strategy writers can engage in (at least according to my studies), it most clearly portends success.

Guideline 2: Begin Early (Before Feeling Ready)
The most reliable motivation comes in the wake of regular involvement in writing, not in advance of it. Efficient writers often begin working before feeling ready. They start with informal things that ready them for writing, while they wait and patiently put off temptations to rush or force themselves

(Guideline 1). When writers begin early, they move out of the passivity that forestalls motivation and discourages imagination. Paradoxically, beginning before feeling inspired requires patience and tolerance; it demands a leap of faith. When writers begin early, they must trust the generative properties of work. They need enough patience to let preliminaries like talking, reading, noting, and collecting produce ideas and momentum. Above all, they require tolerance. Without it, they cannot survive the ambiguity of not knowing what, exactly, they will say for awhile. Without it, they cannot abide the tentativeness, imperfection, and slow pace of preliminary work. A well-known fact from studies of student writers makes an important point about beginning early: expert writers are most likely to take time to plan before writing; that is, they combine an early start with waiting; they use patience and trust to delay closure about what to write (Hayes and Flower). Beginning early, before being ready to write, affords time to plan, encourages the writer to notice new material and connections, distributes the load of trying to plan and write at the same time, and rewards patience. Beginning early, then, depends on the kinds of slowing and relaxing discussed in Guideline 1. A casual beginning eases the pain of writing. When writers begin early with approximations and plans, there is no abrupt onset for writing, less occasion for anxiety and blocking. Beginning early *helps reduce the usual aversiveness of writing*—its pressures, worries, and fatigue.

Early starts require practice at beginning well before having thought much about a paper. Exemplary academic writers, while working at getting ready for writing, deliberately commit themselves to a reasonable *minimum of time* that can be spent on preliminaries. How much of waiting and of preliminaries is enough? For writers accustomed to immediate starts (or to passive waiting until feeling fully ready), five minutes of patient preliminaries suffices at first. However, as composition research demonstrates, expert writers invest surprising amounts of time in waiting and preliminaries; they often spend as much time waiting and preparing as writing (and, more surprising, they get far more writing done than writers who wait passively for readiness). Other unexpected things happen when writers become skilled at patience and at beginning before they feel ready. First, they *do more revising and editing*, even when they have to force themselves to do the extended work before feeling like doing it. Second, motivation builds up subtly, effortlessly. Writers who learn the value of starting without having to force themselves or to spend time warming up find themselves working *regularly* at writing. What had been an occasional, chancy activity becomes a regular habit.

Guideline 3: Work in Brief Daily Sessions
Durable motivation is a matter of habit. What distinguished geniuses like Einstein, T.S. Eliot, and Freud is that they worked at their craft daily. What helps writers feel like writers and feel like writing is the discipline of regular work. In fact, successful writers often brag about their habits (Hemingway is

reported to have claimed that he wrote every morning at the crack of dawn). Another factor that distinguishes geniuses is that they simply produce more than do other people—some of it good, some of it not (Simonton). Their regular work and their ever-accumulating productivity may be the key to their success (see Ericsson and Charness). Thus, ease and enjoyment in writing require lots of practice.

How can academics, who have many other responsibilities, manage to write more? Two factors are essential: working daily and keeping sessions brief. The fact is that *brief, daily sessions end up taking less time and producing more output* than sporadic outbursts of writing. It is no coincidence that most successful writers (including many newswriters) work in brief daily sessions. When writers work daily on a project or two, the ideas and habits stay fresh in mind, so less time is needed for warm-up. When we manage even a page per day, the accumulation more than suffices to make us far more productive writers than we were. When we limit writing to regular brief sessions, the result is better quality writing and less fatigue. And when we learn to work daily, we struggle less over motivation and imagination. When we look forward to writing, we think more of ideas and connections we can use, less about how we might fail.

In itself, though, daily work is not enough to ensure ease and enjoyment in writing. Many fluent writers, E.B. White and Dickens among them, have made writing regular but miserable and unhealthy. We know what needs to be added: working before feeling ready (and distributing the cognitive load of planning and writing over time), and working at a moderate pace. One way to practice establishing brief daily sessions is to begin before feeling ready (to write every day, usually briefly); wait (that is, be patient about not finishing everything at once); find a regular time and place for writing and make writing-related activities routine and automatic; chart and post your progress; and employ contingency management in the short run until productive habits are instilled. Establishing brief daily sessions builds motivation, imagination, and automaticity; distributes cognitive loads (not just in prewriting but also in keeping material fresh in mind); increases confidence borne of discipline; and builds confidence from the rewards of completing lots of writing.

Guideline 4: Stop

Stopping in timely fashion can be as difficult and important as starting. Without the skill of stopping on time, writers cannot become regular workers who enjoy writing. When writing sessions grow into marathons (or "binges"), writers are unlikely to work again for awhile. When we have trouble stopping, we tend to tire ourselves. Writing done under fatigue tends to be confusing and overdone for readers. Certainly, when writers have momentum, they dislike interrupting it: they want to add that extra passage or two. And when writing grows strongly euphoric, stopping becomes unthinkable.

When writers binge, they not only run overtime (into time needed for other activities), they also work with a self-focus and rushed intensity that discourage rest or revision. With timely stopping, writers develop an important kind of tolerance: a tolerance for ambiguity.

Guideline 5: Spend as Much Time on Preliminaries as on Writing
Many writers worry about deficiencies in imagination ("I'm afraid I'm not very creative or original"). They wait passively, hoping to manage this bit of genius without much preparation or help. Exemplary writers surprise their peers with their efficient solutions to finding imagination. They not only begin writing early and informally (that is, they prewrite), they also work with an ever-higher level of planfulness: exemplars become active collectors and filers of information that could relate to their writing—news clippings, for example. They carry notepads with them to help them record interesting observations and thoughts. And like efficient, happy writers and teachers, they spend only moderate amounts of time preparing (prewriting or preteaching); indeed, they usually spend no more time at preliminaries than at more formal acts of writing or teaching (see Boice, "Writing").

Teachers help make the point because they (especially when relatively new at teaching) often spend many more hours preparing than necessary—that is, if they work inefficiently. Surprisingly, when teachers balance time spent between preparing and teaching, they fare better. Students rate them more highly in all the positive dimensions of teaching. Students themselves evidence more learning. And, finally, efficient, balanced teachers rate their teaching, their enjoyment in doing it, and their commitment to improving it more highly than do inefficient, unbalanced teachers. Thus, balance not only economizes on time and reduces fatigue, it also helps teachers (and writers) prepare only what needs to be said and displayed (for example, expert teachers tend to present fewer main concepts but more examples of each). Most importantly, balance forces teachers to go to class less than perfectly prepared. While efficient teachers arrive with a clear, manageable organizational scheme in mind or on paper, they also leave some of the details and examples tentative. This means that once in front of the class they must be more imaginative and spontaneous. It leaves them more inclined to involve students in generating some of the details and examples. Both of these outcomes, the moderate improvisation and the strong involvement of students, help make classes more reflective and efficient.

Perhaps the parallels to writing are apparent. When we balance prewriting with composing, several familiar tendencies are enhanced. Writers prepare with more imagination and motivation (because they spend more time than usual at preliminaries). They remain more open to noticing creative ways of solving the problems they pose. They approximate prose in ways that make transitions from planning to formal writing far easier. And, with all that time available for preliminaries, writers grow more likely to let other people do some of the work (such as having editors and teachers comment, on the basis of conceptual outlines, about whether they are on the right track, if their organization is clear and compelling, and what they may have overlooked). And, of course, they grow increasingly more ready to write, often without quite realizing it.

Efficient writers emphasize two ways of getting past feeling skeptical that balance is crucial to productive writing. One consists of reminders that the evidence says otherwise. (The most productive, successful authors not only work in moderation, they also balance writing with preliminaries including socializing about their work.) The second is regular practice: only when writers experience the efficiency of moderate, balanced work do they at last see the value of Guideline 5. In the meanwhile, what writers need is the patience and tolerance to give it a try. Balance helps writers blend excitement with patience and certainty with tolerance as it teaches writers how to do just enough to manage steady excellence. Here, at last, writers talk about the joy of getting more from less, and here writers begin to appreciate why "flow," something they had sought but had not known how to achieve, depends on balancing preliminaries with the main event of writing. As Mihaly Csikszentmihalyi says, while flow often appears effortless, it requires highly disciplined mental activity: "Jobs are actually easier to enjoy than free time, because like flow activities they have built-in goals, feedback, rules, and challenges, all of which encourage one to become involved in one's work, to concentrate and lose oneself in it" (62).

Other Guidelines

Yes, there are more guidelines deriving from my work—as many as five more (see "Writerly"). I consider the five just outlined to be most fundamental. Once they are mastered, the others come more easily. In sampling a few more of them, I continue the trend you may have noticed: my explanations are growing briefer (some psychologists call this "fading").

Guideline 6 deals with ways of ensuring that negative thinking doesn't dominate and obstruct writing. It is about balancing positive with negative thinking, always moving toward the former. It means noticing the thoughts and attitudes that commonly hinder or block writing. Most of us know these too well: we are perfectionist and so we conclude we cannot write well enough; we are anxious and so we avoid writing rather than face criticism or rejection. Internal censors dominate our thinking and keep us from proceeding beyond narrow, premature attention to surface concerns such as spelling, grammar, and style. We think of writing as unbearably difficult and unrewarding, and so we opt for something easier and quicker. We think we know enough about what we will write to excuse rushing into prose, and so we find ourselves stumbling and lost.

Negative thinking has even broader effects. Its pessimism and helplessness risk depression and inaction. Its anxieties make us inefficient, impatient problem-solvers. Its excessive self-focus keeps us isolated and shy, unable to solicit social support, and overreactive to criticism. Its self-criticism inclines us to despair and to expect failure. And its impulsivity (borne of impatience and anger) makes it difficult for us to carry out those tasks, like writing, that offer only delayed rewards. The more impulsive we are, the more likely we are to opt for activities that offer immediate rewards and relief: the quick, the easy, the superficial. Positive thinking, in contrast, is far more efficient.

Correctives for negative thinking are not difficult. Strategies that work best in my programs for writers are simple. First, *habitually monitor your thinking during writing sessions.* The keywords to becoming a useful observer of negative thinking are the usual pair: patience and tolerance—patience to keep watching and listening even when nothing seems to be there; tolerance to hear the amazingly negative, depressing, irrational things we often say to ourselves. Begin by noticing (and noting) your self-talk at just one critical time, the few minutes that precede a writing session. Are you worrying about needing to do something other than writing (such as, running an errand)? Are you fretting about getting caught up on overdue work or about writing well enough? Do you anticipate failure and embarrassment down the line, and do you dwell on past disappointments? Have you convinced yourself you are not in the mood, that you need more time to clarify thinking or to look up even more references? Are you still ruminating over a social slight or an argument that keeps you from concentrating on writing? The list could go on, but you see the point. These are thoughts well worth noticing and arresting.

Second, *dispute negative thinking.* This too takes regular practice, and it requires noticing and challenging the usual absurdity and deception of negative thinking by consciously listening to how irrational the negative thought is when it is repeated slowly. If, for instance, you find yourself imagining that your writing surely will be criticized or rejected (or that writing is drudgery and should be put off for the time being) consider this: a bit of reflection exposes the irrationality in supposing that *all* our writing will be disparaged or that we will fare better by putting off the task until we must rush it. This kind of awareness of irrational thoughts helps move writing beyond its usually mindless, inefficient beginnings.

Third, *replace negativities with more constructive, optimistic thinking.* Once you have disputed and dismissed an irrational thought, turn your thinking to getting on with the task (for example, "When I'm immersed in the writing, I'll enjoy it—if I let myself—so instead of worrying and making excuses, I might as well get on with it"). The point of this step is to move away from product orientations to process modes of working (Tremmel calls it reflective practice). In product orientations we look too soon to outcomes, long before there are any; doing so induces pressures about working fast enough and with a perfectionism that can only make writing more difficult than it needs to be. Process styles, in contrast, are more practical and efficient. They focus attention on the present, on how to make the process of writing comfortable and fluent. Process modes help us abandon regrets about the past and anxieties about the future; both can distract us from working patiently and reflectively. With regular practice at process modes of noticing and replacing irrational thoughts, writers learn to keep themselves on track with a simple reminder like the well-known, "Just do it."

Guideline 7, like the sixth, is about self-control. Here, awareness shifts to something too rarely considered by writers: moderating emotions while working. Writing without emotion results in dull experiences, weak motivation, and mundane writing. Writing with too much emotion means rushing past planning and revision to states of exhaustion that make work aversive and difficult to resume. Guideline 7 aims to avoid both extremes. It reemphasizes the strategies of prewriting we saw earlier as a way of generating excitement and imagination for writing, and it places special significance on moderating emotion when it threatens to run out of control. The Stop Guideline continues to be crucial. It also continues to be difficult and annoying to implement for many of the same reasons discussed earlier: once we have momentum, we resist giving it up, especially when doing something that is difficult to get underway; once we are bingeing, we suppose we can at last catch up; once we are rushing, especially beyond our planned stopping point, we enjoy the spontaneity, decisiveness, and confidence. So you might ask: Why stop now? Why try to moderate the emotions involved in such a delightful experience? The answer lies in the nature of hypomania (a near-state of mania), a pathological circumstance that comes with intense rushing and emotional escalation. Its short-term benefits are tempting (and often addictive) but its long-term costs far outweigh them. True, bingeing at writing brings an enchanting euphoria, even a seeming creativity. But both are largely illusions. The problem with hypomania goes beyond the superficial and disorganized writing it often produces, even beyond the exhaustion that makes starting again difficult. Hypomania commonly leads to dysphoria (just as mania begets depression) and its sad inaction. With this cycle in place, writers work only sporadically. When they at last break out of their depressiveness, they work up the emotional state that ensures the opposite experience: hypomania. And when they have exhausted themselves in a binge, they are predisposed to another depression. Not only does hypomania make writing unreliable and inefficient, it also produces mood swings that interfere with everyday living. In fact, hypomania produces a measurable wake of depression, it reduces the output and quality of writing in the long run, and it makes writing seem more difficult. It even undermines the health and social relations of writers (Boice, *How Writers*).

Moderation includes flexibility. On the one hand, those who write with the most fluency and happiness generally keep emotions at low to mid-range levels. On the other hand, they grow more and more aware of the value of changing their pace occasionally. Sometimes they use a burst of excitement to work past their internal censors or to convey the appropriate voice in their writing. Sometimes they write dispassionately (just to get ideas down on screen or paper), knowing they can wait to find more imagination when revising it later. At their best, evidently, they work with a rhythm based in mild happiness, one punctuated by occasional swings in mood that do not persist to the point that impedes returning to base level.

A Final Note

Critics of the kind of research I've been discussing are understandably skeptical about some of the unconventional measures of progress I use. While they offered few qualms about indexing writing productivity in terms of verified outputs of pages per week, they were unaccustomed to gauging progress as teachers or as writers in terms of setting and carrying out plans for pacing work.

The kinds of answers that help assuage these reservations are not hard to come by. First, there clearly *is* tangible evidence of progress in the measures already provided. Elsewhere, in laborious tables ("Developing Teaching"), I present data showing substantial increases in setting constructive goals consistent with the advice of experts in teaching and writing improvement (goals such as interacting more with audiences and soliciting more feedback). The data show gradual but real success in meeting those goals of constancy and comfort (for example, slowed pace and more efficiency in presenting crucial ideas; more acceptance of help and criticism). And the results in those tables differ in expected ways from control data. In addition, the sixteen participants in my first major test of my program showed clear progress in four domains: they more often completed at least one scholarly manuscript per year; they more often had manuscripts accepted for publication in a refereed, scholarly medium; compared to controls, they managed more improvement in scores on standardized, end-of-semester evaluations by students in their classes; and full participants were far more likely to have gotten specific approval of their progress as writers and as teachers from colleagues in their retention/tenure committees. These new faculty were thriving and their colleagues noticed it.

My current research is expanding what was already implicit in the studies I have just outlined. The best way to begin learning fluency and comfort as a writer is to master the basics of efficient ways of working. In my experience, when professorial writers try to get underway by first mastering the skills imparted, say, in Strunk and White, or by demonstrating the ability to write long manuscripts quickly, they stumble. If, instead, they learn how to work at writing, they make far less painful beginnings and find success more quickly and surely than if they do not. First things first.

Works Cited

Boice, Robert. "Combining Writing Block Treatments: Theory and Research." *Behaviour Research and Therapy* 30 (1992): 107-16.

———. "Contingency Management in Writing and the Appearance of Creative Ideas: Implications for the Treatment of Writing Blocks." *Behaviour Research and Therapy* 21 (1983): 537-43.

———. "Developing Teaching, Then Writing Amongst New Faculty." *Research in Higher Education* (in press).

———. "Experimental and Clinical Treatments of Writing Blocks." *Journal of Consulting and Clinical Psychology* 51 (1983): 183-91.

———. *How Writers Journey to Comfort and Fluency: A Psychological Adventure.* Westport, CT: Praeger, 1994.

———. "Increasing the Writing Productivity of 'Blocked Academicians.'" *Behaviour Research and Therapy* 20 (1982): 197-207.

———. *The New Faculty Member: Supporting and Fostering Professional Development.* San Francisco: Jossey, 1992.

———. *Professors as Writers: A Self-Help Guide to Productive Writing.* Stillwater, OK: New Forums, 1990.

———. "Procrastination, Busyness, and Bingeing." *Behaviour Research and Therapy* 27 (1989): 605-11.

———. "Writerly Rules for Teachers." *Journal of Higher Education* 66 (1995) 32-60.

———. "Writing Blocks and Tacit Knowledge." *Journal of Higher Education* 64 (1993): 19-54.

Csikszentmihalyi, Mihaly. *Flow: The Psychology of Optimal Experience.* New York: Harper, 1990.

Ericsson, K. Anders, and Neil Charness. "Expert Performance: Its Structure and Acquisition." *American Psychologist* 49 (1994): 725-47.

Hayes, John R., and Linda S. Flower. "Writing Research and the Writer." *American Psychologist* 41 (1986): 1106-113.

McCaul, Kevin D., Russell E. Glasgow, and Katherine H. O'Neill. "The Problem of Creating Habits: Establishing Health-Protective Dental Behaviors." *Health Psychology* 11 (1992): 101-10.

Simonton, Dean Keith. *Greatness: Who Makes History and Why.* New York: Guilford, 1994.

Tremmel, Robert. "Zen and the Art of Reflective Practice in Teacher Education." *Harvard Educational Review* 63 (1993): 434-58.

Graduate Students as Active Members of the Profession: Some Questions for Mentoring

Janice M. Lauer

The question this essay might be expected to answer is: How can we help students become active in the profession—or, more specifically, to publish during their graduate studies? Instead, I prefer to ask more fundamental questions: How active as members of the profession should students be while in graduate school? Should they strive to publish during their doctoral studies? Where does publishing fit in the roster of preparations that graduate school offers, including becoming scholars/researchers, teachers, and program administrators? Where does publishing fit in the list of activities that they could begin in graduate school such as attending conferences, presenting papers, writing grants, and reviewing books, manuscripts, or their peers' teaching? We've been answering these questions as a field for some time. In our doctoral programs, we have been encouraging and facilitating professional activity. As a field, we have welcomed newcomers, giving them platforms and recognition at our conventions. In many programs, as at Purdue, we have urged students to attend conferences and then submit proposals for these conferences. We have suggested local and state meetings as good forums for presenting their papers and for providing them with experience, confidence, and the opportunity to develop local networks. We have helped them prepare proposals for conferences sponsored by such organizations as CCCC, NCTE, ABCA, and MLA. In our courses, we have encouraged or even required students to write papers with publication in mind. We have kept students apprised of opportunities for conference papers and journal articles. In some doctoral programs, students take courses in article preparation and submission. All of these efforts indicate that our doctoral programs have taken professional activity seriously.

Yet, over the last fifteen years of working with doctoral students, I have developed some ambivalence about these efforts. I suspect that it might be wise now to examine the outcomes of our efforts, asking: What impact has this professional activity had on our students' doctoral education? Have their conference papers led to publication? Have their course papers ultimately appeared in journals? How have these activities led to their continued active participation in conferences and publishing after graduating? This essay raises several concerns that complicate our dedication to these important professional experiences during doctoral study.

Professional Development and the Graduate Student
If rhetoric and composition claims to be a postmodern field, with multimodality and blurred genres, its scholars of tomorrow need to develop a sophistication that entails becoming critical readers of rhetoric and composition studies in different modes of inquiry, understanding their assumptions, methods, limitations, issues, and interdisciplinary connections. Unlike doctoral students in literature, for example, who have previously studied primary literary texts and criticism in high school and in their undergraduate and M.A. programs, many students enter rhetoric and composition doctoral programs with no prior study in the field. A few have had a course or two in composition theory at the M.A. level, usually having learned about these theories through secondary accounts. Occasionally, someone has studied rhetorical history. Consequently, during doctoral study students require time to read primary texts in composition theory, rhetorical history and theory, and empirical research, studying their arguments, research designs, kinds of evidence, and warranting processes. Students also need to examine the copious meta-discourse that interprets these texts (see Lauer, "Rhetoric").

Further, in a number of doctoral programs students must also devote time to meeting requirements in literature or other fields. At some institutions, most of their courses and examinations are *not* in rhetoric and composition. In other sites such as Purdue, students satisfy a requirement for a second field in an area such as literary theory, linguistics, cultural studies, literature, women's studies, and so forth. While enriching, this course work often delays the student's progress in defining his or her area of interest.

In addition, graduate students in rhetoric and composition devote energy to teaching, tutoring, and administering programs, considering these responsibilities to be intellectual work, informed by theories of learning, literacy, and pedagogy. Students plan and teach writing courses not just as a means of support, but as an integral part of their graduate education. Already working as professionals in the classroom, they add to their repertoire of teaching experiences work in different kinds of classes: developmental, first-year, advanced, business and technical writing, ESL, WAC, and so forth. They also direct programs as apprentice administrators. This professional work can become a catalyst for a dissertation or provide grist for publications. But students worry whether they should take time to write and polish an essay stemming from their teaching while they are meeting course requirements, or studying for exams, or completing a dissertation in another area?

During this phase of their education, students hesitate to rush into publication because they don't want to reinvent the wheel or expose their limited disciplinary knowledge. They question whether they should wait until they choose a specialization, until they have developed an area of expertise and ideas new to the discipline. I share their concern and wonder increasingly whether it is wise for them to try to publish course papers that may present ideas new to them but not to the field. In a recent exchange of ideas in *PMLA* about scholarly publishing, Wendell Harris calls for debate on a significant quandary that faces students:

> In order that graduate students may survive in a milieu where they must publish as much and as quickly as possible, they are encouraged to restrict their attention to those literary texts and theoretical approaches that can be quickly blended into at least the outward shape of books and articles. (121)

This prospect makes me worry that pushing students to publish early in their doctoral work may promote expedient but not well thought-out decisions about the kind of inquiry they choose to undertake.

Professional Activity and the Path to Specialization
In the face of these concerns, mentoring is crucial to help individuals map their paths through a department's requirements and make decisions about whether, when, and where to publish. Within any program, students ultimately build their own framework of knowledge, construct a particular area of scholarship, and acquire their own expertise in a mode or modes of inquiry. Each path requires long-range planning and guidance. For example, those wishing to undertake historical inquiry need a complex understanding of canonical and marginalized rhetorical texts, a grasp of layers of interpretation that construct these texts and practices, an understanding of historiography, a working knowledge of relevant languages such as Greek or Latin, and a background in the economics, politics, and epistemology of the culture situating these texts and practices. Those targeting empirical research need backgrounds in such areas as qualitative design or statistics. Those interested in hermeneutic inquiry require a strong background in postmodern theory. Those planning to conduct research in ESL writing need to understand applied linguistics. Those desiring to do research in computers in composition or technical writing need theoretical and technological study in these areas. Students benefit from guidance as they plan and pursue their individual research directions. Mentoring, therefore, can assist students in making these long-range plans and in gaining the depth and expertise necessary for research and, ultimately, publication.

Other factors, such as students' academic backgrounds, can have an impact on their readiness for specialization. Some students bring to a doctoral program a developed research interest that they pursue throughout their studies. Others become fascinated by the multiplicity of issues and research possibilities and postpone their area of concentration or change as they go along.

Another form of mentoring involves the nature of doctoral programs. Programs that have core courses emphasizing the broad knowledge and multiple modes of inquiry described above offer students the chance to build a multi-modal background but may also delay their specialization. Other programs that offer a range of elective courses in rhetoric and composition from which students can shape an individualized program may enable students to concentrate earlier but may also limit their background to courses available at a given time. Some programs encourage certain kinds of inquiry such as ethnographic or historical research because of faculty expertise in these areas while inhibiting other kinds of scholarship because no faculty engage in or encourage those types. Thus, the nature of programs can enable and constrain students as they move toward publication.

Those of us involved in mentoring have been encouraging conference presentations and course papers for publication, assuming, I believe, that they are effective routes to professionalization. But has this been the case? No extensive study has been conducted, as far as I know, to investigate this assumption. Here I will share some of my experience over the years as I have followed our students and graduates. Certainly, giving conferences papers has been an important way for students and other professionals to network and to obtain response to their work in progress. But delivering numerous conference papers during graduate work has also generated some unpredictable side effects. Students discover early on that they can get conference proposals accepted without having completed the research or constructed the argument, while their peers' proposals, based on extensive investigation, are sometimes rejected. These puzzling results have given some students the false impression that becoming active in the profession can be done with little preparation, lulling them into assuming that publication can result from similar minimal investment. For others, presenting numerous conference papers has delayed the completion of their degree or after they graduate has become a substitute for publication as a professional activity.

What about course papers as routes to publication? For years, I expected students to write final papers targeting specific journals. In response, I commented on their work from the perspective of a reviewer for a journal. This experience ultimately helped a number of them to publish these papers, but I have gradually realized that such a requirement doesn't fit everyone's background and needs. There are students so new to the field that they stumble badly when trying to write in the field (see Berkenkotter, Huckin, and Ackerman) or to shape an article for publication, forcing themselves into artificial or inappropriate types of discourse. Instead, I have concluded that such students profit more from writing bibliographic articles, informative essays directed to peers, or a prospectus framing a problem for further research. Now in my courses I suggest a list of long-range assignments (to which they can add), only one of which is an essay shaped specifically for publication.

Publishing and Changes in the Field

The above discussion has focused so far on professionalization while doctoral students are taking courses and examinations. What about when they are writing their dissertations? Should they try to publish then? Here again, mentoring is important because the answer varies with individual students. Yet, a few hard realities obtain. On the job market, those with completed dissertations *and* publications have the best advantage, all other things being equal; but students with a publication or two but *without* a finished dissertation are less competitive and may, if hired, jeopardize their progress toward tenure when they struggle to finish their dissertation while working in a full-time job. On the other hand, students starting a new position with a completed dissertation and no publications sometimes are daunted when trying to place an article or a book prospectus without any guidance and find it difficult to generate the number of publications required for promotion and tenure at certain institutions. In all of these scenarios, students profit from having had some instruction about the processes of publication while they are still in graduate school. A number of rhetoric and composition programs as well as workshops at the CCCC convention have been providing information on such matters. At Purdue, for example, we held a session last year in which the rhetoric and composition faculty shared with graduate students samples of their own letters to editors, prospectuses for textbooks and scholarly books, and promotion and tenure documents. We also prepared a packet of these samples for interested graduates. Recently, in an online exchange, members of the Consortium of Doctoral Programs shared other ideas about preparing students as professionals. At the 1995 CCCC convention, faculty from various schools offered an all-day workshop entitled, "Professional Development for Graduate Students and Those Who Mentor Them."

Changes in the field over the last fifteen years have certainly influenced these questions about whether, when, and how much to publish during graduate school, both enhancing and complicating students' efforts. More of our students come to doctoral work with a rhetoric and composition background and a developed research interest, thereby hastening their publication. Many new journals provide more outlets for work in our field; some even cater to graduate students. Doctoral students' research is increasingly more interdisciplinary, providing them with additional publishing outlets. Our bibliographic resources have improved so that graduate students can more easily locate studies that bear on their research. The number and diversity of our doctoral programs have increased, offering more people the opportunity to prepare for scholarly careers in rhetoric and composition. Finally, promotion committees are gradually gaining an understanding and acceptance of the different types of scholarship in our field. All of these factors motivate our graduate students and recent graduates to publish their work. Other changes, however, have not been so benign. Hiring committees have more candidates in rhetoric and composition to select from, including those who have been teaching and publishing for a while. Departments of English, including departments with heavy teaching loads, expect more and more publication for promotion and tenure. The political climate of departments in which our graduate programs and graduates are situated varies widely. Often our graduates must not only strive to publish quality scholarship but also to inform and persuade their colleagues of its value and position in the field. Types of institutions vary in their requirements.

An Ethics of Care
As we prepare our students for these changing conditions, we inevitably socialize them into the field's style of networking—its tone. Elsewhere I have argued for continuing to foster a tone characterized as an ethics of care, marked by features that include a willingness to nurture, to act in concrete situations with emotional involvement, to make responsible moral decisions in particular human relationships rather than on abstract principles, to step out of one's personal frame of reference into the other's, to be present to the one cared-for rather than to identify with one's possessions (scholarly possessions)—an altruism constructive for the moral agent and the one cared-for (see "Feminization"). A graduate program makes a field's tone palpable for students, modeling the ways in which members of the profession relate to each other whether at conferences or in print. At Purdue, for example, we have been trying to foster this tone in our graduate program in concrete ways, such as by encouraging collaborative projects and papers, working together as a faculty, and meeting weekly with groups of students as they work on their dissertations.

Our students value this ethics of care in their graduate program but wonder if it is out of step with the world of publishing. Can they enact such an ethic as the field's most vulnerable members, just establishing themselves? As they go on the market, prepare their work for publication, or struggle for tenure, they ask: Is an ethics of care a practical way to succeed in the profession? Doesn't publication require bashing others? Aren't caricatures and stereotypes of the complex positions of others, especially of earlier scholars or ideologies, tickets to fame, even survival? Isn't ridicule of entire modes of knowing a savvy tactic? Isn't it efficient, even smart, to read only secondary characterizations of others' work in order to cite them, perhaps even to set them up as easy targets, rather than reading primary texts and arguing seriously with them? Further, they wonder whether an ethics of care can prevail in the concrete situations of ideological diversity that characterize our field? They ask, Will such an ethic help us to counteract the silencing and marginalizing of women in on-line discussions?—a reality that is being exposed by feminist critics of technology (see Hawisher and Sullivan; Takayoshi). These questions resonate with the dilemmas women face as they strive to enter the academy. As Gesa Kirsch elaborates, citing the work of

Aisenberg and Harrington: "Not only do women want to join the academy and succeed, but they are also simultaneously questioning and challenging the academic system in which they find themselves" (3). Is an ethics of care possible, probable, practical, especially for our students who strain to position themselves in the field?

I don't have a simple answer, but I suspect that the stakes are high for the future of the discipline and for our students as scholars. If we believe that communities construct themselves discursively, why can't we and our students stipulate our own definitions of the field, including such features as multi-modality, relationships to practice, and an ethics of care? Why can't we transform the term *disciplinarity* to suit us? Should we not educate students to reshape the field rather than just to survive? Should not our graduate programs prepare students who, through their publications and professional activity, will continue to construct our field, whose dynamism cannot be constrained as it changes, influenced by postmodern theorizing, exploding technology, and ideological and ethical transformation?[1]

Notes

[1]I wish to thank Patricia Harkin, Shirley Rose, and Patricia Sullivan for their helpful advice on this essay.

Works Cited

Berkenkotter, Carol, Thomas N. Huckin, and John Ackerman. "Conventions, Conversation, and the Writer: Case Study of a Student in a Rhetoric Ph.D. Program." *Research in the Teaching of English* 22 (1988): 9-44.

Harris, Wendell. "The State of Scholarly Publishing." *PMLA* 110 (1995): 120-21.

Hawisher, Gail, and Patricia Sullivan. "Women on the Networks: Searching for an E-space of Their Own." *Feminism and Composition*. Ed. Susan Jarratt and Lynn Worsham. New York: MLA, forthcoming.

Kirsch, Gesa. *Women Writing the Academy: Audience, Authority, and Transformation*. Carbondale: Southern Illinois UP, 1993.

Lauer, Janice M. "The Feminization of Rhetoric and Composition Studies?" *Rhetoric Review* 13 (1995): 276-86.

——. "Rhetoric and Composition Studies: A Multimodal Discipline." *Defining the New Rhetorics*. Ed. Theresa Enos and Stuart Brown. Newbury Park, CA: Sage, 1993. 44-54.

Takayoshi, Pam. "Building New Networks from the Old: Women's Experiences with Electronic Communications." *Computers and Composition* 11.1 (1994): 21-36.

Contributors

Robert Boice is professor of psychology at State University of New York at Stony Brook. He is a licensed psychotherapist with a practice limited to writers. For fifteen years he directed developmental programs on writing and teaching for colleagues.

Lynn Z. Bloom is professor of English and Aetna Chair of Writing at the University of Connecticut, past president of the Council of Writing Program Administrators, and past chair of the MLA Division of Teaching Writing. In addition to numerous publications about biography, autobiography, American fiction, and composition studies, she edited *The Essay Connection* and *The Lexington Reader,* and she coedited *Bear, Man, and God: Eight Approaches to William Faulkner's "The Bear"* and *Inquiry: A Cross-Curricular Reader* (with Edward White).

Theresa Enos is associate professor of English at the University of Arizona, where she teaches undergraduate and graduate courses in writing and rhetoric. She is founder and editor of *Rhetoric Review,* and currently she is the CCCC representative to the NCTE College English Section, and president of the Council of Writing Program Administrators. She is general editor of the *Encyclopedia of Rhetoric and Composition,* editor of *A Sourcebook for Basic Writing Teachers* and *Learning from Histories of Rhetoric,* coeditor of *Defining New Rhetorics* and *Professing the New Rhetorics,* and author of *Gender Roles and Faculty Lives in Rhetoric and Composition.*

Linda Flower is professor of rhetoric at Carnegie Mellon and a director of the Center for the Study of Writing and Literacy. Her recent book, *The Construction of Negotiated Meaning: A Social Cognitive Theory of Writing,* uses negotiation theory to explore the learning of college students and lays a foundation for her current work on intercultural collaboration and community literacy.

Richard C. Gebhardt is professor and chair of the department of English at Bowling Green State University. He served as editor of *College Composition and Communication* from 1987 to 1994, and his articles have appeared in such journals as *CCC, CE, JAC, RR, TETYC,* and *WPA.* His *CCC* article "Balancing Theory and Practice in the Training of Writing Teachers" won the 1978

Richard Braddock Award. He also edited *Scholarship and Academic Advancement in Composition Studies* (with Barbara Genelle Smith Gebhardt).

Joseph Harris is associate professor of English and director of the composition program at the University of Pittsburgh. He is editor of *College Composition and Communication* and author of *A Teaching Subject: Composition Since 1966* and of *Media Journal: Reading and Writing About Popular Culture* (with Jay Rosen).

Gail E. Hawisher is associate professor of English and director of the Center for Writing Studies at the University of Illinois, and she serves as assistant chair of NCTE's College Section Committee. She has coedited the *CCCC Bibliography of Composition and Rhetoric* and currently coedits *Computers and Composition: An International Journal for Teachers of Writing*. She has coedited several books, and her articles have appeared in *CE, CCCC, RTE*, and *Written Communication*, among others. Her most recent book is *Computers and the Teaching of Writing in Higher Education: A History, 1979-94*.

Maureen Hourigan is assistant professor of English at Kent State University at Trumbull, where she teaches courses in composition, literature, and women's studies. Her publications include *Literacy as Social Exchange: Intersections of Gender, Class, and Culture* and articles and reviews in *JAC, TETYC* and other journals. She is currently coediting a collection of essays on grading in the postmodern classroom.

Michael L. Keene is professor of English at the University of Tennessee, where he directs the program in technical communication and teaches in the graduate program in rhetoric and composition. He is coauthor of *The Heath Guide to College Writing* and of *Effective Professional and Technical Writing*, author of the revised eighth edition of W. Paul Jones' *Writing Scientific Papers and Reports*, coauthor of *A Short Guide to Business Writing* (with Harry Bruce and Russel Hirst) and of *The Easy Access Handbook* (with Kate Adams). His publications include articles in *CE, JAC, TETYC, Technical Communication*, and *CEA Critic*.

Thomas Kent is professor of English at Iowa State University, where he teaches courses in rhetorical and literary theory and edits *JAC: A Journal of Composition Theory*. He has published two books: *Interpretation and Genre* and *Paralogic Rhetoric: A Theory of Communicative Interaction*.

Janice M. Lauer is professor of English at Purdue University, where she directs the graduate program in rhetoric and composition and teaches courses in composition theory and classical rhetoric. For thirteen years she directed a national summer Rhetoric Seminar, and she has served as chair of the College Section of NCTE and as a member of the executive committees of CCCC, the MLA Group on the History and Theory of Rhetoric, and the Rhetoric Society of America. She is editor of the composition entries in the *Encyclopedia of English Studies and Language Arts* and coauthor of *Four Worlds of Writing*, *Composition Research: Empirical Designs*, and the forthcoming *Writing in Social Contexts: Inquiry and Action.*

Christina Murphy is director of the William L. Adams Writing Center and co-director of the university writing program at Texas Christian University. She is editor of three scholarly journals: *Composition Studies*, *Studies in Psychoanalytic Theory*, and *English in Texas.* Her books include *Ann Beattie*, *Critical Thinking Skills Journal*, *The St. Martin's Sourcebook for Writing Tutors*, *Landmark Essays on Writing Centers*, *Writing Center Perspectives*, and *Writing Centers: An Annotated Bibliography.*

James J. Murphy is Professor Emeritus of Rhetoric at the University of California at Davis and is founder of the International Society for the History of Rhetoric, its journal *Rhetorica*, and Hermagoras Press. He has published numerous monographs on the history of rhetoric, most recetly *Peter Ramus's Attack on Cicero: Text and Translation of Petri Rami* and *Medieval Rhetoric: A Selected Bibliography.* He has also edited collections of scholarly essays on the subject, including *A Short History of Writing Instruction from Ancient Greece to Twentieth-Century America* and *Renaissance Eloquence: Studies in Theory and Practice of Renaissance Rhetoric.*

Jasper Neel is professor and chair of the department of English at Vanderbilt University. His two most recent books have won national awards: *Aristotle's Voice: Rhetoric, Theory, and Writing in America* won the 1994 W. Ross Winterowd Award, and *Plato, Derrida, and Writing* received the Mina P. Shaughnessay Award.

Gary A. Olson is professor of English and teaches in the graduate program in rhetoric and composition at the University of South Florida. His two most recent books, *Women Writing Culture* (with Elizabeth Hirsh) and *Composition Theory for the Postmodern Classroom* (with Sidney I. Dobrin), were published by SUNY University Press. In 1993 the Council of Editors of Learned Journals presented him with the International Award for Distinguished Retiring Editor for his decade of work as editor of the *Journal of Advanced Composition.*

Cynthia L. Selfe is professor and head of the humanities department at Michigan Technological University. She has chaired the College Section of NCTE and is the incoming chair of CCCC. She is founder and coeditor of *Computers and Composition: An Internationational Journal for Teachers of*

Writing and recently served as coeditor of *CCCC Bibliography of Composition and Rhetoric.* She has also coedited, authored, or coauthored eight books and has published in numerous journals in composition studies. Her 1994 coauthored article on "The Politics of the Interface" won the Ellen Nold Best Article award.

Todd Taylor teaches undergraduate courses in writing and graduate courses in composition theory at the University of South Florida, where he serves as senior editor as well as online editor of *JAC: A Journal of Composition Theory.* He is guest editor of *Teaching English in the Two-Year College* (a special issue on technology) and coeditor with Irene Ward of a forthcoming collection of scholarly articles about the Internet and literacy entitled *Dialogic Space.* His most recent articles have appeared in *WPA* and the *Journal of Business and Technical Communication.*

Ralph F. Voss is professor of English at the University of Alabama, where he teaches undergraduate writing and graduate courses in rhetoric and composition and American drama. He is coauthor of *The Heath Guide to College Writing* as well as author of *Elements of Practical Writing* and of articles and reviews in *CCC, JAC, TETYC, Dialogue,* and *The Writing Teacher.* He has also written *A Life of William Inge: The Strains of Triumph,* articles in *The Dictionary of Literary Biography* and *Kansas Quarterly,* and reviews of scholarly works on American drama in *South Atlantic Review.*

Index